Prehistoric Human Occupation on Rote and Sawu Islands, Nusa Tenggara Timur, Indonesia

MAHIRTA

BAR International Series 1935
2009

Published in 2019 by
BAR Publishing, Oxford

BAR International Series 1935

Prehistoric Human Occupation on Rote and Sawu Islands, Nusa Tenggara Timur, Indonesia

© MAHIRTA and the Publisher 2009

ISBN 9781407304502 paperback
ISBN 9781407334493 e-book

DOI https://doi.org/10.30861/9781407304502

A catalogue record for this book is available from the British Library

This book is available at www.barpublishing.com

BAR Publishing is the trading name of British Archaeological Reports (Oxford) Ltd.
British Archaeological Reports was first incorporated in 1974 to publish the BAR
Series, International and British. In 1992 Hadrian Books Ltd became part of the BAR
group. This volume was originally published by John and Erica Hedges Ltd. in
conjunction with British Archaeological Reports (Oxford) Ltd / Hadrian Books Ltd,
the Series principal publisher, in 2009. This present volume is published by BAR
Publishing, 2019.

BAR
PUBLISHING

BAR titles are available from:

BAR Publishing
122 Banbury Rd, Oxford, OX2 7BP, UK
EMAIL info@barpublishing.com
PHONE +44 (0)1865 310431
FAX +44 (0)1865 316916
www.barpublishing.com

To Yuni, Mada, and Vivit,
My parents,
My relatives on Rote and Sawu

ACKNOWLEDGEMENTS

First of all I would like to express my great thanks to my supervisors Prof. Peter Bellwood and Prof. Matthew Spriggs of the School of Archaeology and Anthropology, Australian National University, for supervising my thesis writing. Apart from their comments and suggestion on my thesis drafts, they gave continuing encouragement and support throughout my thesis writing. Great thanks are also due to my advisors Dr. Peter Hiscock and Dr. Mary-Jane Mountain for general advice regarding with the analyses presented in my thesis.

Thank you to AusAID for giving me the PhD Award that allowed me to study at The Australian National University, and to my own university - Universitas Gadjah Mada in Yogyakarta, Indonesia - for permission to study in Australia.

I must express my great thanks To Lynn Toohey, AusAID liasion officer at Australian National University, for making all arrangements for me while I was studying at the Australian National University.

The field work on Rote and Sawu Islands, Indonesia, was made possible by a grant from the Australian National University PhD research fund for overseas fieldwork. The assistance of Kathy Callen, Graduate Secretary in the School of Anthropology and Archaeology, and of staff in the Research and Scholarships Office, Australian National University, is also ackowledged.

I must also thank the Head of the Indonesian Archaeological Research Centre in Jakarta (Pusat Penelitian Arkeologi Nasional) and Direktor Ditlinbinjarah in Jakarta for permission to undertake this archaeological research on Rote and Sawu Islands.

A special thank you goes to Mohammad Tavip and Yogi Piskonata for helping me in the field, and especially for always engaging in smart problem-solving. Also to the communities of Desa Mokdale and Tuanatuk, on Rote Island, and to the communities of Desa Daieko and Raedewa for their hospitability and friendship during my fieldwork on Sawu. My stays on Rote and Sawu would not have been so much fun and full of good memories without the friendships of Adibu Mbolik, Fola Pane, Reni Zacharias and Makoo in the field. Thank you to Reni Zacharias, Martha Tassie and Soleman Betakore for being my hosts on Rote and Sawu.

Thank you very much to Rote and Sawu Regent, Benjamin Messakh, B.A. and other local government staff on Rote and Sawu Islands, especially Soleman Betakore, who arranged and accompanied us during our surveys and excavations.

I am especially indebted to Dr. Glenn Summerhayes, of the Archaeology and Natural History Department in the Research School of Pacific Studies, Australian National University, now at University of Otago, New Zealand, for invaluable help and supervising me in the process of pottery analyses for the Rote, Sawu and Timor pottery samples and of being a statistical consultant for me.

I express my thanks to Dr. Doreen Bowdery for training me phytolith sample preparation, although I did not have time to apply it to my sites and to Mr. Bob Forrester of the Statistical Consultation Unit, The Australian National University for processing multivariate analysis for the pottery samples.

I also would like to express my gratitude to all staff in the Electron Microscopy Unit, Research School of Biological Science, Australian National University, especially to Dr. Sally Stowe, Frank Brink, David Vowles and Dr. Roger Heady for training me to use the Scanning Electron Microscope for pottery analysis.

I'd also like to thank all my colleages at Universitas Gadjah Mada, especially Djaliati Sri Nugrahani and Daud Tanudirdjo, for always backing me with mental support in the difficult stages of my thesis writing. My thanks are also due to Didik Suhartono for sanning all of the figures and layouting my PhD thesis for publication , and to Agus Trihascaryo for drawing some 'cores' and maps presented in this thesis.

Last but not least, thanks my two daughters Rahmadani Sasongko and Kurniavita Sasongko, and my husband Yuni Sasongko, for all their understandings and many things that I cannot express. For her spiritual support, I thank my mother, Soetarti Roospinudji.

CONTENTS

LIST OF TABLES

Chapter VI

Chapter VII

LIST OF FIGURES

THE RESEARCH CONTEXT

Between the Sunda and Sahul shelves lie the Wallacean islands, never attached to larger land masses during Pleistocene times. This is the most geologically complex and active region within Indonesia (Bemmelen 1949; Audley-Charles 1981), due to its position at the meeting point of four geological plates: the Indo-Australian Plate, the Pacific Plate, the Eurasian Plate and the Philippine Sea Plate.

The Wallacean islands belong to two main groups - the northern consisting of Sulawesi and Maluku, and the southern consisting of the Nusa Tenggara chain (Figure1.1). These chains of islands must have been used as bridges by early human populations crossing from Sunda to Sahul, and vice versa, during the time-span of human occupation of the

region. The capacity of humans to cross water gaps in Wallacea during the Pleistocene is an attractive topic for archaeologists since it implies a presence of sea craft and allied technology.

Birdsell (1977) was the first to theorise about the human migration routes followed to cross the water gaps from Sunda to Sahul. He favoured two possible routes (see Figure1.2), starting from Sundaland. The first (northern) route crossed from Borneo to Sulawesi and then to the Sula Islands. From Sula, one route went via Halmahera to the Bird's Head of western New Guinea, and another went to the southern Moluccan island of Seram, from where people could cross to New Guinea directly, or travel via Aru to

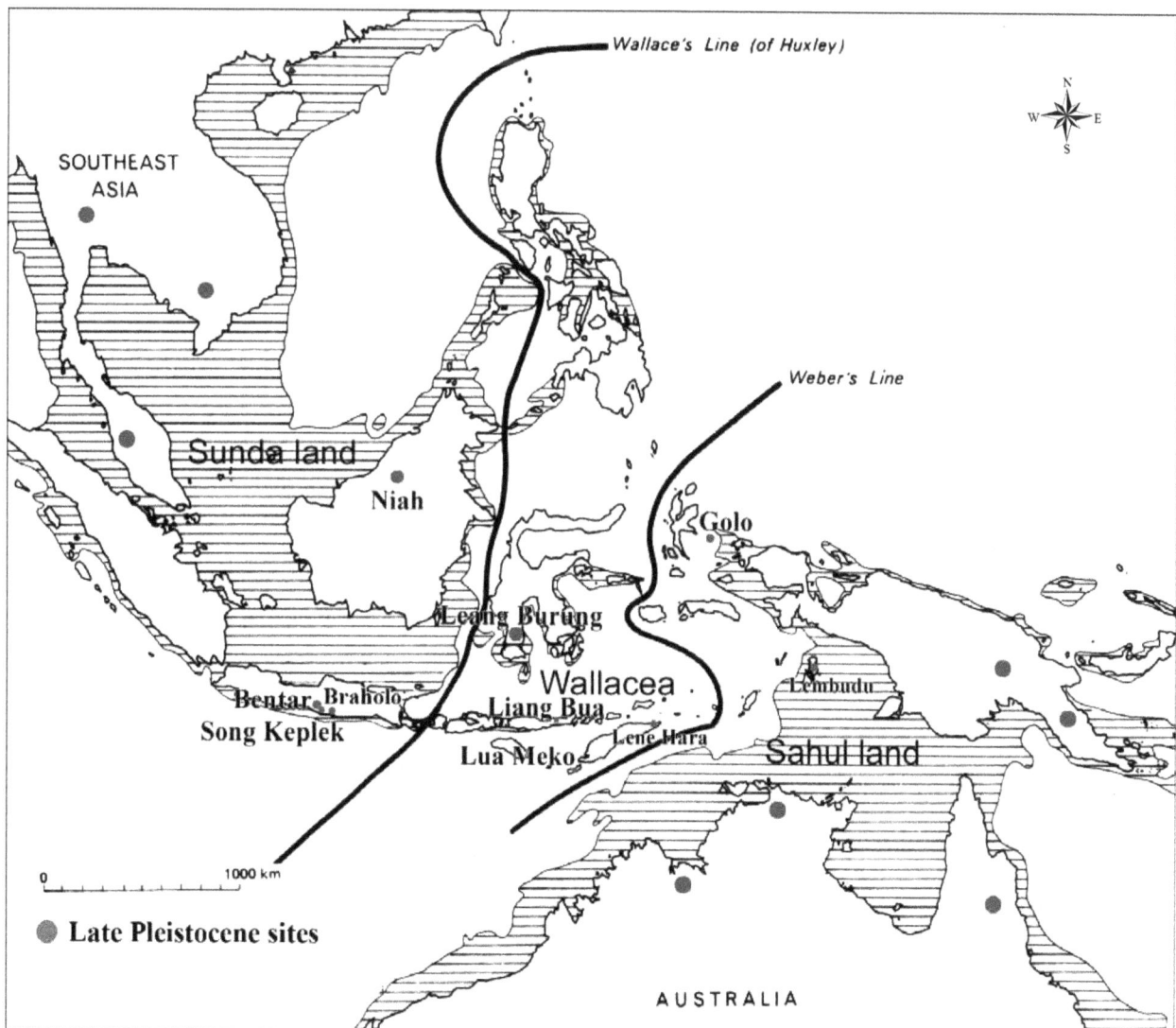

Figure 1.1: Locations of Late Pleistocene sites in Island Southeast Asia compiled from several sources (Glover, 1986; Bellwood, 1997, 1998; O'Connor et al., 2002, 2005; Morwood, 2002; Mahirta, 2004; Simanjuntak, 2002)

1

southern New Guinea. The second, (southern), route crossed Lombok Strait from Bali and continued through the Nusa Tenggara 'stepping stone islands' to Timor, from where one could travel through small islands to reach the Kai Islands and then the Sahul shelf in southern New Guinea, or cross the Timor sea southwards to reach Northern Australia.

The question of when humans first crossed from Sunda to Sahul is still a most intriguing issue in archaeology. Recently, there are some new insights of this issue correlate with development of dating techniques applied in archaeology and more extensive archaeological research in islands Southeast Asia.

Another intriguing issue is the crossing route from Sunda to Sahul that was chosen by human. Based on considerations of distances and island target angles, mediated by other factors such as intervisibility, patterns of winds and currents and island sizes, Irwin (1991) claimed that some of the routes hypothesised by Birdsell (1977) were more likely to be chosen than others. He argued that the northern route was more likely chosen than the southern. His argument was based on intervisibility between the islands, and this vanishes at the end of the southern route, especially between Timor and Northern Australia. This argument is actually challenged by the fact that there are many small island groups off northern Australia that emerged when the sea level decreased. During the Last Glacial Maximum and as far as back 60,000 years ago, there would have been more than 60 small emergent islands to the south of Timor, mostly flat continental shelf islands stretching along the edge of the Sahul shelf for 750 km. Butlin suggests two different routes from islands south east Asia to Northern Australia via the southern route: the first route is by crossing the sea to Rote - Ashmore Reef -Cartier Island – South Bonaparte; and the second route is from East Timor - Troubadour Marine Shoal - Bathrust Island (see figure 1.3 (Butlin 1989, Mulvaney & Kamminga 1999: 110).

These islands could have been used as stepping stones to reach northwest Australia. As targets, they would have been easier to reach than single a small isolated island, especially when navigation was still simple (see Keegan and Diamond 1987 on the 'configurational effect').

Bellwood (1993) is in agreement with Butlin (1989) in arguing that the route via Nusa Tenggara was very attractive, since the main obstacle people had to face was crossing Lombok Strait. Once they succeeded in crossing this, prehistoric seafarers could perhaps have walked to Alor during periods of glacial low sea level.

One topic focused upon in the many writings about this issue is that of the magnitude and chronology of sea level change during the Pleistocene and Holocene. There is often an assumption that the first migration across the sea was likely to have occurred when the water gaps were at a minimum, in periods of low sea level. But Chappell (1991) believes that the absolute widths of the water gaps might not have been the main factor in encouraging or discouraging migration during the Pleistocene. Chappel also argues that it is easier for humans to cross the sea from Timor to Northern Australia when the sea was rising (Chappel, 2000: 89-90).

Based on his research on the Huon Peninsula of New Guinea, John Chappell has produced a sea level curve covering the last glacial cycle. From this curve it can be seen that, at about 120,000 years ago, the sea level was higher than it is now, then it gradually fell to reach its lowest level at about 20,000 years ago, during the Last Glacial Maximum (figure 1. 4).

But archaeology shows clearly that humans had reached Sahul long before 20,000 years ago. Accepted dates for the

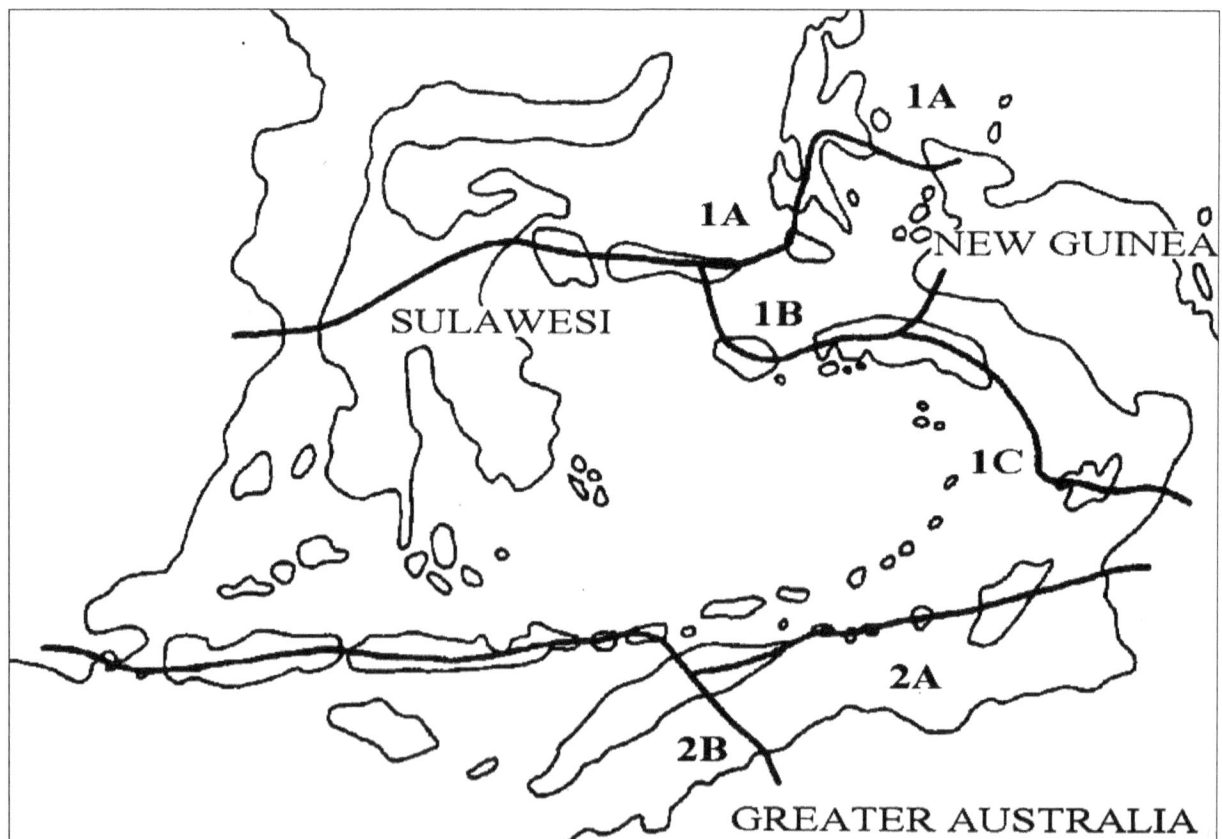

Figure 1.2: The shortest routes across Wallacea during the Pleistocene, according to Birdsell (1977).

oldest humans in Sahul are now at least 42,000 to 48,000 years ago (Gillespie 2002) as suggested by carbon dating results. Some scholars, however, believe that humans reached Sahul between 53,000 and 60,000 years ago (Robert *et.al.* 1998). During this period the sea level was 50 m below the present sea level so the water gaps between islands were wider than during the Last Glacial Maximum, when the sea level was 120 m below the present. This indicates that Chappell's arguments can be accepted, although humans would still presumably have chosen the easiest available routes.

1. Issues highlighted by archaeological studies in Nusa Tenggara

The question of when the first human settlers arrived in the Wallacean islands, especially Nusa Tenggara, is still a very central one. In 1970, stone tools claimed to be in association with *Stegodon* bones were reported from central Flores by Maringer and Verhoeven. The stone artefacts consisted of pebble tools, retouched flakes and one small bifacial axe (Bellwood 1997:67, Maringer and Verhoeven 1970). Then, in 1991-1992, an Indonesian-Dutch expedition reexamined the sites visited by Maringer and Verhoeven and excavated more stone tools from a location near Mata Menge (Bergh *et.al.* 1996; Bellwood 1997). Together with the *Stegodon* bones, some tools of chert and basalt were also found, and claimed to be human-made. At Tangi Talo, a village near the first findings by Verhoeven and Maringer, an older deposit yielded bones of a pygmy *Stegodon,* a large tortoise and Komodo dragon (*Varanus komodoensis*), but without stone tools or other indications of a human presence. If the palaeomagnetic dating is to be believed, the evidence from Mata Menge would indicate that hominids arrived in Flores 750,000 years ago (Bergh *et.al.* 1996).

On Timor, several large retouched flake tools have been found in the Ainaro gravels, which also contain two extinct forms of Stegodon. As Stegodon was alive during the Pleistocene, Glover presumed that these stone tools were also of Pleistocene age (Glover 1970). Most recently, Morwood (1998) has recovered more *Stegodon* fossils in central Flores

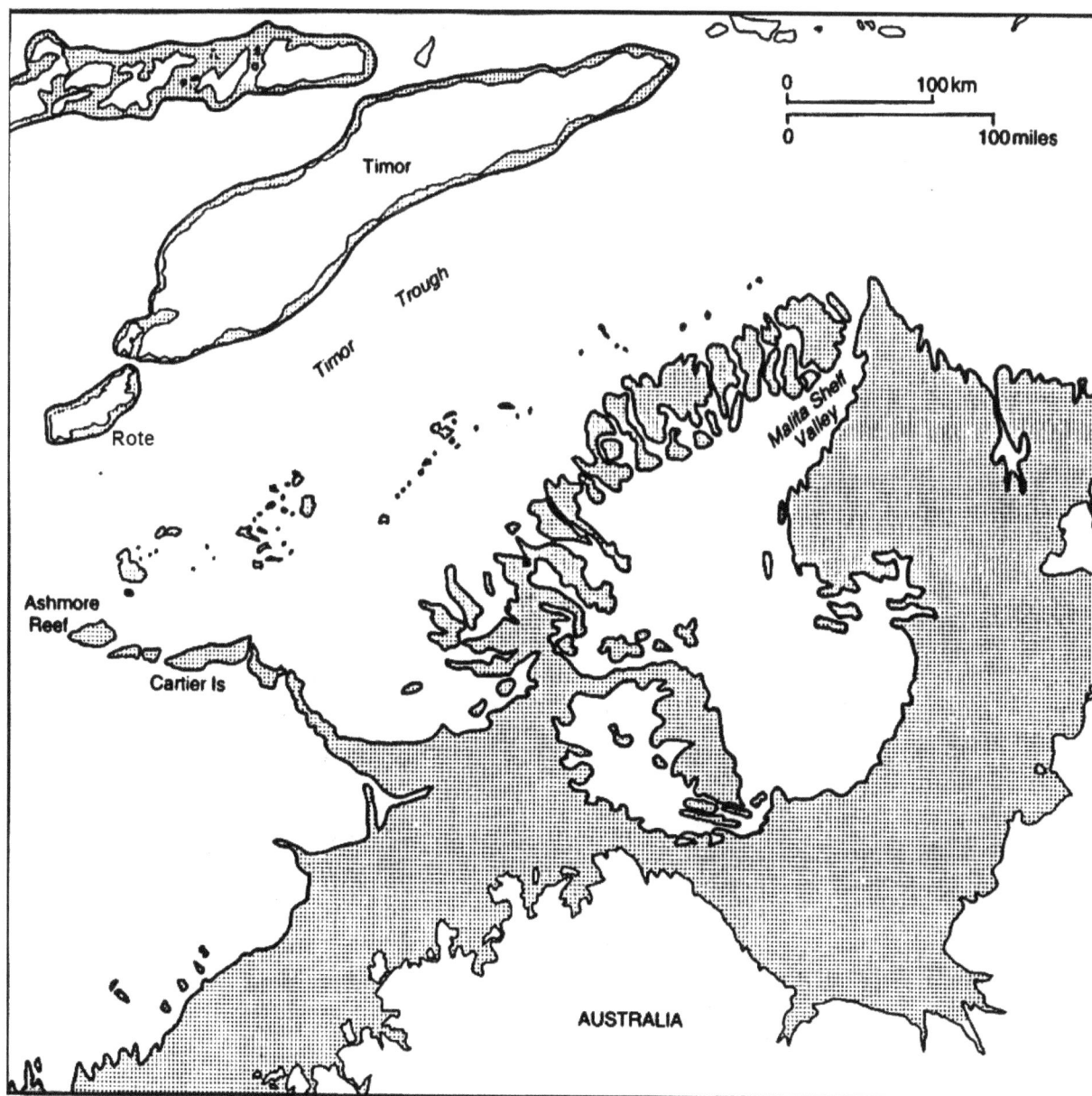

Figure 1.3: Sahul's northwestern coast opposite Timor and Rote during times of low sea level, Reconstructed from present-day bed topography (after Mulvaney and Kamminga 1999)grey shade: estimated border of Pleistocene coast line.

in association with human-made stone flakes. Fission track dating at Mata Menge also dates this assemblage to about 800,000 years ago, suggesting that *Homo erectus* arrived in Nusa Tenggara during the Middle Pleistocene.

Archaeological research in the cave of Liang Bua (Flores) in 2001-2002 by Morwood and his team is claimed to have strengthened this hypothesis. Excavations that reached 8.5 m in depth have yielded signs of replacement of early hominid populations by modern humans (Michael Morwood 2002, lecture given at Gadjah Mada University).

While the evidence that *Homo erectus* reached Nusa Tenggara seems to be getting stronger, the evidence from other regions of eastern Indonesia does not yet extend earlier than the Upper Pleistocene and the presence of humans of anatomically modern morphology. At Leang Burung in South Sulawesi, humans had arrived by 31,000 BP (Glover 1981). Based on the results of recent excavations, the arrival of humans occurred at least 27,000 years ago on Aru island (O'Connor & Veth 2000), and c.35,000 years ago in Lene Hara in Timor Leste (O'Connor 2002). Morwood and Soejono are currently waiting for luminescence dates for the first arrival of *Homo sapiens* in Liang Bua, but Morwood (pers. comm) anticipates a date of 50,000 BP or earlier. If this estimate can be confirmed, suggesting an arrival of modern humans at about 50,000 years ago (as in Australia), then the arrival of *Homo sapiens* in Nusa Tenggara occurred probably earlier than in the northern Wallacean islands (e.g. 32,000 BP in Golo Cave on Gebe: Bellwood *et.al.* 1998).

The prehistoric colonisation by modern humans of Nusa Tenggara, especially Rote and Sawu, and their cultural characteristics are the central topics of discussion in this thesis.

Besides interest in the Pleistocene period, recent studies focused on Holocene archaeology in Nusa Tenggara include a study of pottery technology and function in several Flores sites (Sumijati 1994); several studies of megalithic structures; changing economic patterns in some sites in East Timor (Glover 1972); and the economic record in Oelnaik Cave, Camplong, in West Timor (Nies Anggraeni 1989).

In addition, earlier archaeological research was carried out in the Wallacean islands by Dutch scholars such as Verhoeven (1959), Maringer and Verhoeven (1970) and van Heekeren in 1952 (Heekeren 1972). Verhoeven did many excavations in caves and rockshelters on Flores, especially in

the cave of Liang Toge, from where the mammalian findings were analysed by Hooijer (1957; 1967; Heekeren 1972) and the human bones and crania by Jacob (1967). Verhoeven excavated in Liang Momer in western Flores; in Liang Panas at Longgo Dalang, Manggarai; in Gua Alo south of Liang Momer; at Aimere open site; and in the caves of Liang Bajo, Liang Boto, Liang Bua and Liang Rundung. Van Heekeren also undertook some excavations in Liang Rundung. Important finds from this site include a lozenge-shaped pendant of pearl shell and another accessory made of shell in the shape of a fish (Heekeren 1972:146).

If we look back at the progress of archaeological research in Nusa Tenggara, it can be seen that it has been centered mainly on Flores and Timor. This means that the spread of cultural traits along the whole Nusa Tenggara chain during the Holocene period is not fully understood. Take, for example, the puzzle about the spread of microlithic technology during the mid Holocene. Microlithic backed blade industries are absent in the East Timor sites according to Glover (1972). Small stone tools occur in several caves excavated by Buhler in West Timor (Niki-Niki Cave in the neighbourhood of So'e, and also the excavation by him at Baguia, East Timor), but they are not backed blade microliths. Verhoeven also discovered microlithic industries at some of his excavated sites in Flores (Meringer & Verhoeven 1970).

However, industries of this type occur in several sites in South Sulawesi e.g. at Ulu Leang and Leang Burung (Glover and Presland 1985). Whether such technologies are really absent in Nusa Tenggara currently remains unknown owing to the many gaps in exploration.

Only a few sites in Nusa Tenggara have any absolute dates, and these are mainly from East Timor (Glover 1972; 1977; 1986; O'Connor *et.al.* 2002) and Flores (Morwood *et.al.* 2002; Sumijati 1994). Pottery-associated layers are dated to 2870 ± 60 BP at Melolo on Sumba Island, and 2990 ± 160 BP at Lewoleba on Lembata Island, and pottery also occurs at Liang Bua, Flores, (Sumijati 1994). However, the C14 samples for these dates were not taken from the layers where pottery was first occurred in significant quantity in each site.

Some basal layers of the sites excavated by Buhler on Rote (Sarasin 1936), and many of the basal layers of the Flores sites excavated by Verhoeven, might be of Late

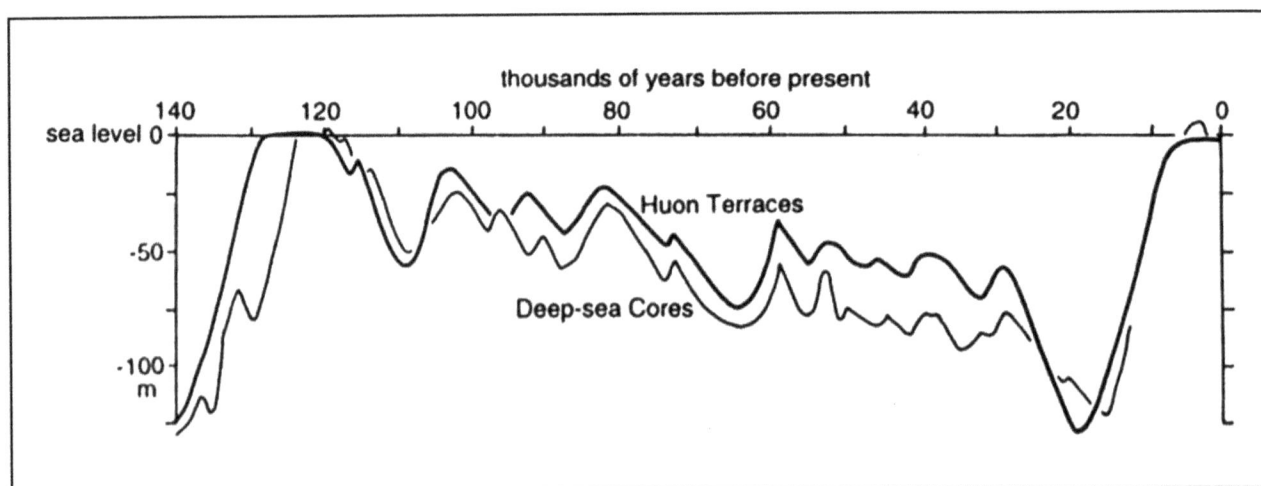

Figure 1.4: Sea level curves for the last glacial cycle, reconstructed from dated raised coral terraces on Huon Peninsula and from oxygen isotope determinations from deep-sea cores (after Chappell 1996; Bellwood 1997).

Pleistocene date, but no dating is available at the time of thesis preparation from any of these sites except for the upper layer of Liang Toge, from which bone taken from a female skeleton has been dated to 3550 ± 525 BP (Heekeren 1972:141; Jacob 1967).

Another uncertainty in relation to the spread of cultural traits through Nusa Tenggara revolves around the occurrence of tanged stone tools, which are especially characteristic of the Niki-niki cave assemblage in West Timor (Verhoeven 1959) and Uai Bobo 1 in East Timor (Glover 1986). But neither of these forms have been reported from other sites on Timor and Rote (Sarasin 1936; Almeida & Zybzweski 1967; Glover 1986; O'Connor et.al. 2002). The distributions of these two types of technology will need to be reexamined as new sites are found.

So far, most previous reports of stone artefacts from Nusa Tenggara have only presented very general descriptions of selected stone types, with little metrical analysis or technological information. (Soejono 1987; Meringer & Verhoeven 1970) However, metrical analysis has been carried out for the East Timor cave sites excavated by Glover (1972, 1986).

Despite this, current research by O'Connor (2002) in Lene Hara cave in East Timor is attempting to proceed beyond the interpretation of the site itself in order to understand the regional and interregional archaeology of Nusa Tenggara. Another aim was to investigate the utilized stone artefacts. Previous research on archaeology in Nusa Tenggara from the 1960s to the 1980s was mostly focused on restricted aspects of prehistoric life, such as the decorative motifs on the pottery from the site of Lewoleba on Lomblen Island (Bintarti 1986), or the range of shell genera exploited by the Oelnaik Cave population in West Timor (Nies Anggraeni (1989). So far, the results of these detailed studies have not been pooled to reach a fuller interpretation. Considering all the problems that still exist for archaeology in Nusa Tenggara, the crucial requirement at present is to conduct more research on those islands which remain unknown archaeologically, in order to increase the database of cultural assemblages. With this in mind, I decided to undertake archaeological research on Sawu and Rote Islands, particularly in rock shelter and cave sites. The geographic positions of Sawu and Rote in Nusa Tenggara, close to Northern Australia, cause these islands to form an interesting archaeological research focus. The study involved both survey and excavation of a number of contexts dating from the Late Pleistocene and early to middle Holocene periods. Particular attention is paid to the relationships between various technological variables and intensities of occupation, as reflected in the rates of stone artefact discard and shell food remains, frequencies of retouched tools and other spread of several technological items in Nusa Tenggara, such as the tanged points found in some Timor sites, and traditions of making and using pottery. The dates for the introduction of animal species not native to Nusa Tenggara are also considered. In particular, important questions concern the role played by Nusa Tenggara in the spread of Neolithic, presumably ancestral Austronesian cultures, within the past 4000 years or so.

2. The geological and environmental backgrounds

Basically, the Nusa Tenggara islands can be classified into an inner (northern) volcanic arc and the continental crustal fragments that form part of an outer arc to the south (Sawu, Rote and Timor). The inner volcanic arc islands are geologically young, often ringed by uplifted coral limestoneor by other sedimentary material. From west to east, the islands of the inner volcanic arc are Lombok, Sumbawa, Komodo, Flores, Solor, Adonara, Lomblen, Pantar, Alor, Atauro (off northeast Timor), Wetar, Romang, Damar, Teun, Nila, Serua and Manuk. The geological ages of these islands become younger from west to east. Within the inner volcanic arc there are two types of volcanic formations: highly eroded Tertiary volcanoes with dissected high narrow ridges, and younger Quaternary active volcanoes with conical shapes.

All the outer arc islands are part of the outer Banda arc. From west to east, they are Raijua, Sawu, Rote, Semau, Kambing, Timor, Kisar, Leti, Moa Lakor, Sermata, Luang, and Babar. The basal structure of most of these outer Banda arc Islands is derived from the Australian continental margin (Audley Charles 1993; Burrett et.al. 1991; Monk 1997), and all have complex sequences of sedimentary and metamorphic rocks. Massive fringing reef limestone is frequently uplifted many hundred of metres, especially along coastlines. These two components, the complex basement rock (including schists) and the limestone, occur in varying proportions on different islands.

Geology of Rote and Sawu

The main geological formations on Rote and Sawu, in order of age, are presented in figures 1.5 and 1. 6 (Geological Map of the Kupang-Atambua Quadrangles, Timor, published by the Geological Research and Development Center 1979):

1. The Bisane Formation (Pb) dates from the Permian and occurs in the interior of Sawu. It comprises shale, siltstone, sandstone and slate.

2. The Aitutu Formation (Tra) is the oldest formation on Rote, dating to the Permian and Triassic. It lies to the north of the excavated sites on Rote. It consists of siltstone, marl and limestone. Quartz sandstone, micaceous sandstone, chert and crystalline limestone layers are intercalated.

3. The Ofu Formation (Tko), of Cretaceous-Eocene date is located in southern Sawu and does not occur on Rote. The formation consists of deep sea sediments - pink to reddish brown calcilutite, marl and shale, with intercalations of yellowish radiolarian chert in the lower part. The chert colours are red, brown, orange and greenish yellow.

4. The Bobonaro Complex (Tb), of Eocene-Pliocene date, is located mostly in the interiors of Rote and Sawu. Lithologically, this formation consist of two principal constituents: scaly clay and exotic blocks. The exotic blocks can be micaceous sandstone from the Bisane formation, or limestone, chert and ultrabasic rock from the Noele and Ofu Formations.

5. The Noele Formation (Qtn), of Pliocene-Pleistocene age, is spread patchily around the southern coast

123°00" E

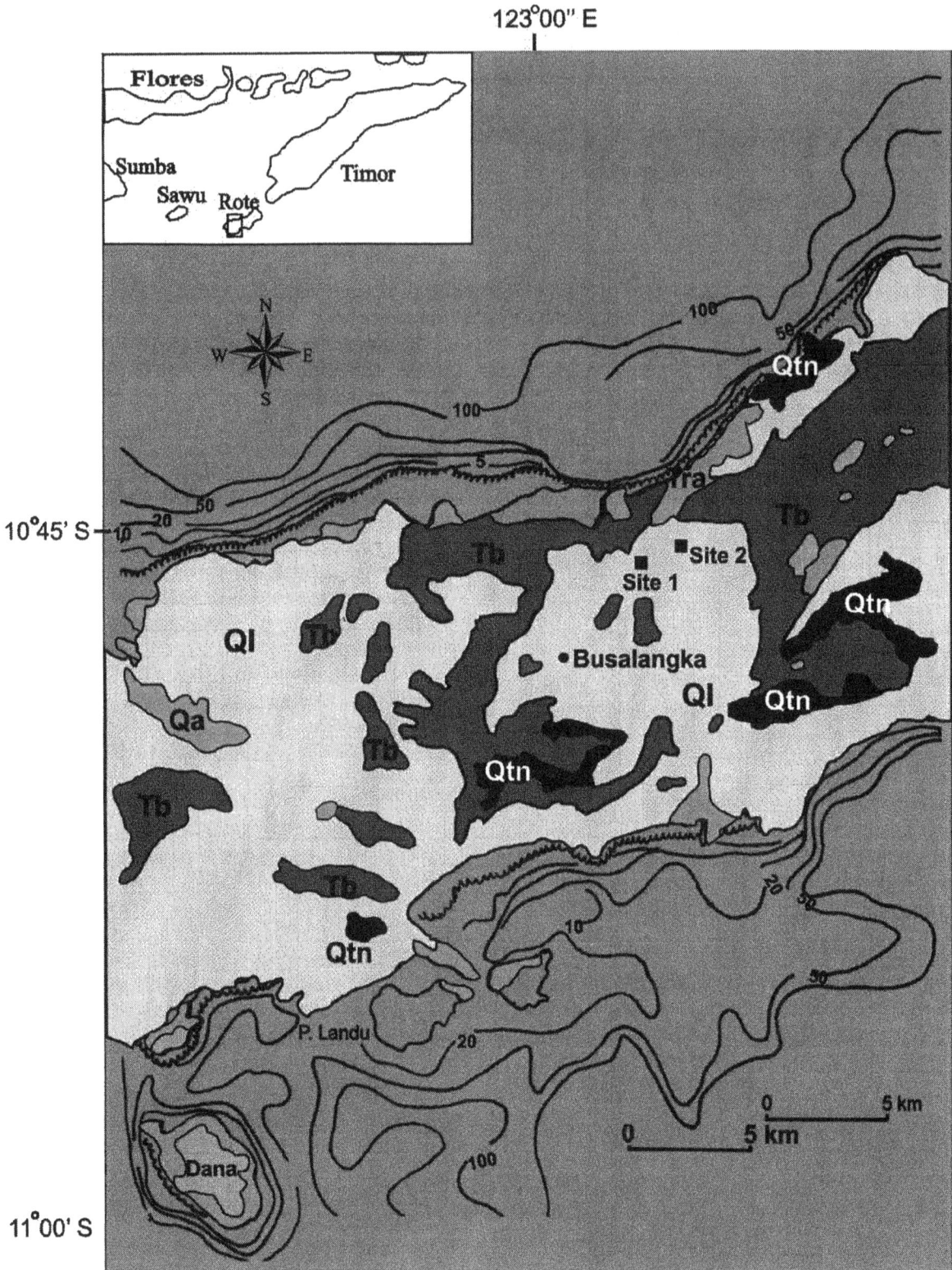

Figure 1.5: The Main geological formations on Centre Rote Island. Traced from Geologic Map of the Kupang-Atambua Quadrangles, Timor 1979

and some northeastern parts of Rote. On Sawu, this formation exists in the east. It is characterised by sandy marl interbedded with sandstone, conglomerate, and a few dacitic tuff layers.

6. Coralline limestone (Ql). This is a Pleistocene formation that surrounds Rote and Sawu, with some interior patches. It commonly consists of white to yellowish, sometimes reddish, coral

limestone and marly limestone. In East Timor this formation is called Baucau limestone.

7. Holocene alluvial sediments (Qa) in stream valleys and coastal plains, characterised by sandy clay.

6

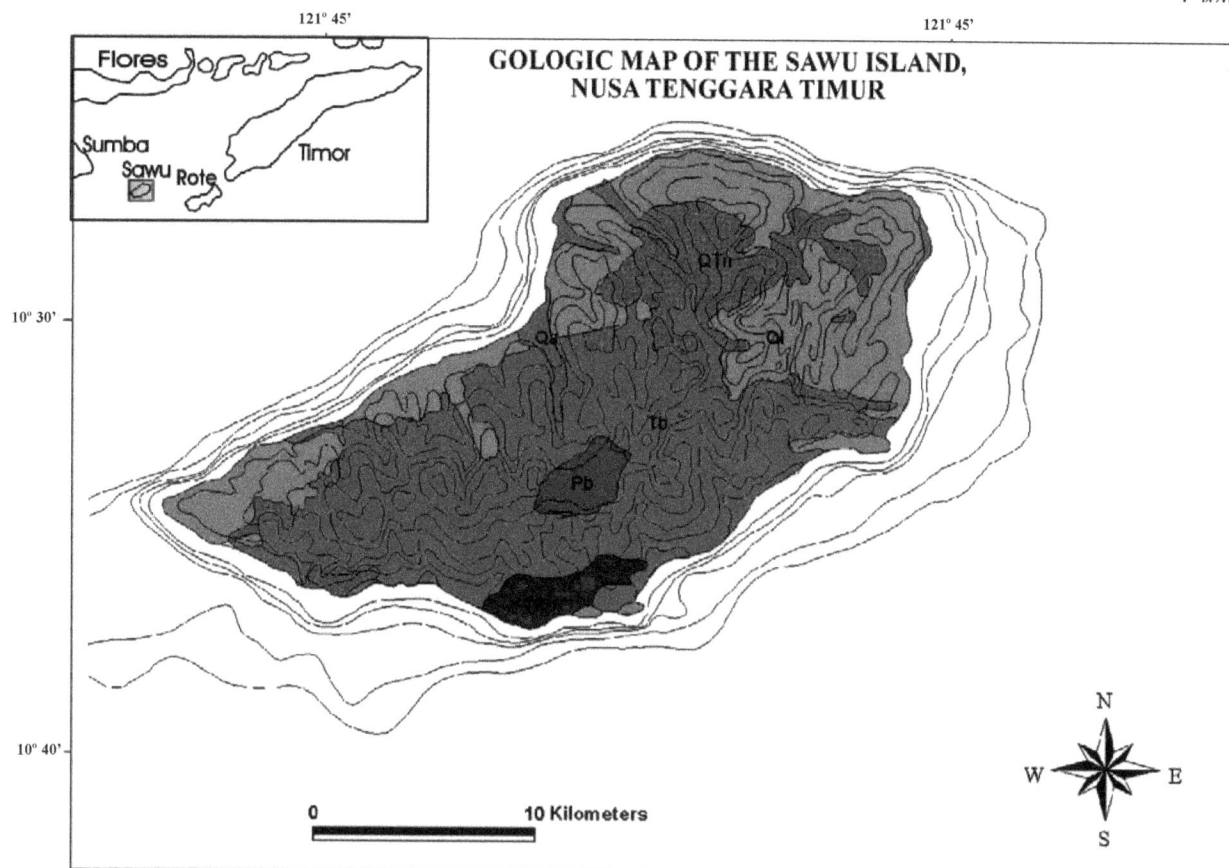

Figure 1.6: The main geological formations on Sawu Island.
Traced from Geologic Map of the Kupang-Atambua Quadrangels, Timor 1979 (Agus Tri H., 2003)

The contemporary vegetation and faunas of Nusa Tenggara

Rote and Sawu islands are located in eastern Nusa Tenggara (Nusa Tenggara Timur), the driest area in the Indonesian archipelago. Climatic factors mean that rainforest only occurs on higher ground on Flores and Timor (Monk et al 1997: 187, 234). On Rote, the interior has patches of moist decidous forest, but the coastline has mainly dry deciduous forest. All of Sawu has only dry deciduous forest, and a small area on the northern west coast is covered by thorn forest. The coastal regions of Timor have combinations of dry and moist deciduous forest, sometimes with thorn forest, whereas the interior has patchy evergreen rainforest. Sumba and Flores have evergreen forests mainly on their western ends. Tamarind savanna also occurs throughout eastern Nusa Tenggara. In Central Flores, eastward to Wetar Island, *Eucalyptus alba* savanna is dominant. West Nusa Tenggara has large savanna areas with *Albizia chinensis*, and *Melaleuca cajuputi* occurs frequently in Central Flores. *Casuarina junghuhniana* savanna is characteristic also of Sumba and Timor (Monk et al 1997: 195-202). Today, palm savanna is the dominant type of open country vegetation found on Komodo, Rote and Sawu, and on Timor, especially on the drier parts of many flat flood plains. Whitmore (1989), as cited by Monk, suggest that the present savannas and grasslands of eastern Nusa Tenggara are derived from former monsoon forest, as a result of burning (Monk *et.al.* 1997:287, 297).

Recently introduced animals in Nusa Tenggara include the Malay civet (*Viverra tangalunga*), a squirrel (*Callosciurus notatus*), murid rodents, deer, felids and pangolin. The present day native vertebrate fauna of Rote Island is relatively impoverished (Kitchener & Maryanto 1995; Kitchener & Suyanto 1996) and consists mainly of rodents, bats and reptiles. The total number of bird species on Rote is 119, compared with 230 species on Timor (Johnstone & Jepon (1997; Johnstone & Darrel 1997). Many of these are migratory shorebirds and water birds.

The Regional Palaeoenvironment during the Pleistocene and Holocene

The general trend of climate change from the Late Pleistocene into the Holocene in Nusa Tenggara can be inferred from records taken from Timor Island (Timor Trench core: Kaars 1990) and from the Lombok Ridge core (Kaars 1990; Wang *et.al.* 1999). The data from these marine cores can be interpreted largely as a reflection of the vegetation histories, and associated changes change of climate, in northwestern Australia and Nusa Tenggara.

During the last glacial period, there was a combination of drier and cooler climates in the region, as indicated by extremely low values for mangrove pollen. The pollen record from the Timor Trench indicates that grassland vegetation advanced from 38,000 to 12,000 B.P., and coastal tropical lowland forest and eucalyptus woodlands contracted. The greatest expansion of grassland took place between 19,000 and 17,000 B.P., when sea level was at its lowest. After 19,000 B.P., sea level rose again (Kaars 1990), eventually reaching its modern level during the mid Holocene.

During warmer interglacial periods, including the Holocene, as inferred from the Lombok Ridge and Timor Trench cores, higher pollen values occurred for lowland

7

rainforest taxa, pteridophytes and mangroves (Wang *et.al.* 1999). At these times, sea levels flooded the continental shelves, resulting in the coastal spread of mangroves to peak values.

Kershaw (1995) notes that the Pleistocene-Holocene transition incorporated some of the most dramatic environmental changes in global history. The whole transition spanned about 11,000 radiocarbon years, from c. 17,000 to 6000 bp, based on pollen records studied from Irian Jaya, Papua New Guinea and southern Australia. Kershaw recognises three major phases in the transition from Pleistocene to Holocene as a whole: phase 1 being the late glacial; phase 2 the Pleistocene-Holocene boundary; and phase 3 the early to middle Holocene.

Although conditions were generally dry during phase 1, the timing of the period of greatest drought varied from place to place, as suggested by studies from Atherton Tableland, Lake Carpentaria, Lynch's Crater, and Papua New Guinea. Van Campo (1982 :56) has argued that the northeast monsoon was strengthened during the last glacial maximum. The Pleistocene-Holocene boundary (phase 2) witnessed very rapid climatic change, and conditions became more humid and warm. The early to middle Holocene (phase 3) witnessed the later part of the marine transgression, and Kershaw (1995) states that this was the period of highest temperature in New Guinea, although there was some spatial variation.

Based on data from Tioman Island in the South China Sea, Tjia (1983) suggested that phase 3 sea level increased to 4 m above the present level at 6800 uncal. bp, fell temporarily at 5000 bp, then rose again to 3.5 m above present level at 4000 bp. After this it fell to +1 m at c 3700 bp, rose to +2.5 m at 3000 bp, and then declined steadily until the early years AD. The southwest monsoon was more intense before 9000 bp and rainfall was higher than at present, but the climate was getting warmer from 8000-7000 bp so evaporation would have increased. By 4000 bp, rainfall was becoming increasingly seasonal in annual distribution.

Pleistocene to Holocene Faunas in Nusa Tenggara

Based on data from Flores and Timor, it is known that large mammals lived in Nusa Tenggara during the Plio-Pleistocene, such as the pygmy *Stegodon sampoensis timorensis*. There was also a giant land tortoise, *Geochelone atlas*. Hooijer (1967) also identified an unidentified murid in association with *Stegodon* on Flores. The stegodonts had disappeared by the early Holocene, to be replaced on both Flores and Timor by a Holocene fauna dominated by murids, bats and reptiles. The living representatives of these murids in Nusa Tenggara include the Flores giant rats *Papagomys armandvellei, Papagomys verhoeveni* and *Spelaeomys florensis*. During the Holocene, another distinct genus and species of giant rat (*Coryphomys buhleri*) appeared (Hooijer 1957; Monk *et.al.* 1997).

Monk *et.al.* (1997) argue that the major factors that have affected vegetation and faunal communities in the recent past have been sea-level changes, human migrations, and agriculture. The Austronesian and Papuan language expansions brought new animals to this area. From the East Timor data, Glover (1986) notes that macaque monkeys

(*Macaca fascicularis*), rusa deer (*Cervus timorensis*), and the palm civet (*Paradoxurus hermaproditus*) all came from the west, whereas the cuscus *Phalanger orientalis* was brought from the east to as far west as Timor.

3. Past archaeological research on Rote and Sawu Islands

Previous archaeological research on these two islands has been very minimal. What we knew about the archaeology of Rote prior to my research was derived from Buhler's excavations in 1933, as reported by Sarasin in 1936 (Sarasin 1936). Buhler carried out some excavations in Dengka Princedom (West Rote), to the northwest of the lakes of Danau Anak and Danau Toea near the hamlet of Genoeng. He discovered some rock shelters about 20 minutes from Danau Anak and excavated in two of them. In shelter A, he found fragments of modern pottery, animal bones and shells in the top layer. From 20 cm down to about 1 metre below the surface, "flint" artefacts appeared. The excavation was stopped after reaching 140 cm as the finds became scanty. In another shelter (shelter B), excavation produced no results.

The report on the Rote research is very brief and further interpretation is difficult. It is not clear from the report on shelter A what kind of flint artefacts were found, or whether those from the upper level were similar to those from further down. Artefact densities are not mentioned either. Buhler also did some excavations in Lua Meol, west of Danau Anak, where he visited four caves. In one only did he find archaeological remains, in a shelter open to the south with two niches measuring 3 m and 4 m in depth, with maximum heights of 8 metres. He excavated in the two niches, and found in the top layer flint artefacts, potsherds and many marine shells, with a small pierced disc of pearl shell. Looking at the illustration, this small pierced disc is very similar to some found in East Timor sites (Glover 1986).

In 1986, several archaeological sites on Rote, including the Pia Hudale rock shelter complex in Desa Mokdale and the Tonggobatu rock shelter complex in Desa Tuanatuk, were visited by a team from the Indonesian Archaeological Research Centre in Jakarta (Bintarti *et.al.* 1986). The locations of the sites were recorded, but excavation was not undertaken. These two sites are discussed later in this thesis. Some surface Palaeolithic artefacts have also been claimed from Rote Island (Soejono 1987).

Lie Madira on Sawu was first surveyed by the Indonesian Archaeological Research Centre (Pusat Penelitian Arkeologi Nasional) in 1980 (Aziz 1980), and some stone artefacts collected there are held in the Centre in Jakarta. Except for this single visit, no archaeological research was carried out on Sawu prior to my research.

4. Research questions

Specific questions that will be approached in this thesis are:

1. What are the basic cultural features found in the Rote and Sawu rock shelter sites? Were there any major cultural changes through time?

2. Were there different intensities of site use during different periods of occupancy?

3. Were there any regional differences in cultural characteristics?

To answer these questions I will be examining the development of stone artefact manufacture, including the choice and use of raw materials in each site excavated. I will also examine whether there were differing intensities of tool use during different periods of occupancy. The changes through time in quantities and varieties of shell species and their habitats are also investigated.

The results obtained from the sites on Rote and Sawu are compared with the archaeological records from several sites in East Timor, an area with quite detailed archaeological records that are easy to access. General comparisons with other sites in the Indo-Malaysian archipelago, in order to obtain broader perspectives, especially on modern human colonisation during the Late Pleistocene and the later Austronesian colonisation, will also be undertaken.

2

ARCHAEOLOGICAL SURVEY
ON ROTE AND SAWU

1. Survey strategy

The main survey strategy was to locate as many rock shelters and caves as possible on Rote and Sawu and to determine if they were occupied during prehistoric periods.

Then, sites found were judged in terms of their potential for excavation. Priorities were allocated in terms of abundance and variety of surface finds, and also the possibility of deep deposits.

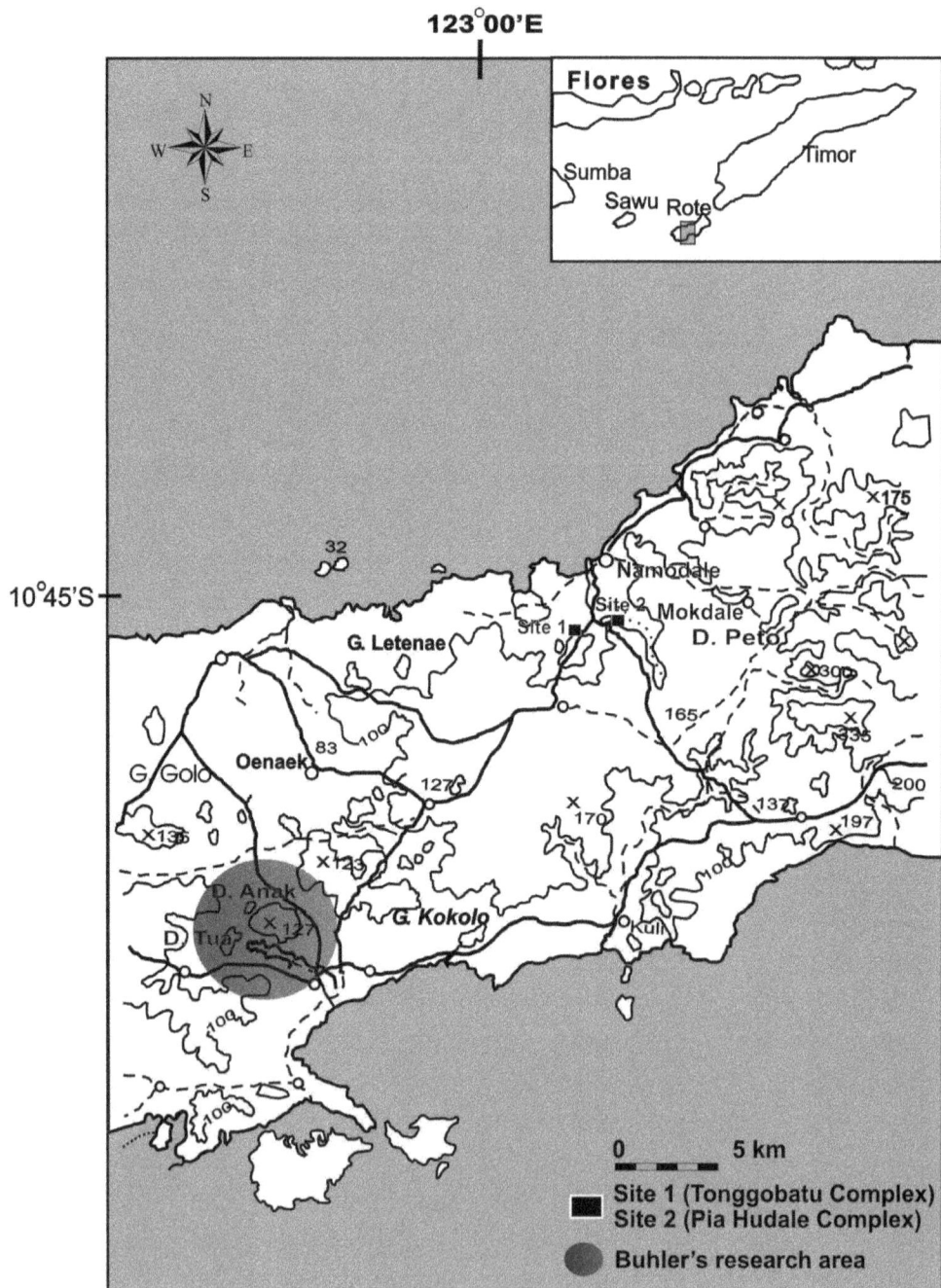

Figure 2.1: The archaeological survey region on Rote in 1997,
with locations of excavated sites and Buhler's research area

The survey was carried out based on the geological map sheet Kupang-Atambua (Geological Research and Development Center 1979). This map illustrates the geology of West Timor, Rote, Sawu and other small islands in the vicinity. Areas with limestone formations in which rock shelters and caves can be commonly formed were identified for survey. These data were then combined with information from inhabitants living in nearby villages, and with data contained in local *Departemen Pendidikan dan Kebudayaan* (Department of Education and Culture) archives, before the first field visit was undertaken.

On Rote, limestone formations occur almost everywhere except in some interior regions. Most survey was carried out in these limestone areas, including the inland Kecamatan Lobalain (Central Rote). However, in 1997 survey was not carried out around Danau Tua and Danau Anak in the vicinity of Dengka in the interior part of Rote, where Buhler did his excavations (see figure 2.1).

On Sawu Island, raised coral reef limestone occurs around the coast of much of the island. Owing to time constraints, survey was only carried out along the northern and southern coastal areas of West Sawu. East Sawu was not surveyed.

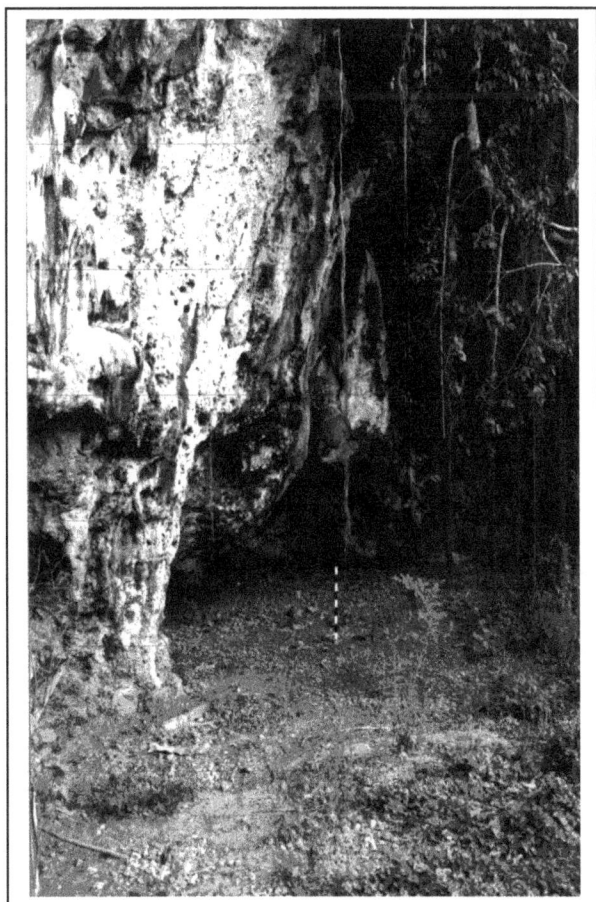

Figure 2.2: Shelter D in the Pia Hudale rock shelter complex

Survey on Rote Island
Lobalain District

Lobalain District is situated in the middle of Rote. Near one of its villages, Desa Mokdale, there is a long raised coral reef complex with several rock shelters and a cave. People in the village call this complex Pia Hudale (see figures 2.2). It is situated 90 metres above sea level and lies about 3 km from the northern coastline. The site is ideal for habitation, being close to a permanent stream that provides fresh water through the dry season and that today flows north to the coastal village of Namodale.

At present, this long raised coral reef complex is separated into two parts by a road that goes to the airport. On the west side of the road there are some shelters, and at the end of the west cliff line is a large cave with a water source in the middle of its always-inundated floor. All the rock shelters have dry floors and two stay dry during heavy rain. The east side of the complex has no shelter.

On the floor of most shelters of this complex, marine shells and stone flakes were found during survey, but the densest evidence for human activity was found in shelter D, the largest shelter in the complex, that faces northwest. An abundance of cultural remains consisting of flakes, cores, shells and several potsherds were spread on its surface. According to a local inhabitant, Pia Hudale was used for hiding during the Second World War, so human trampling certainly took place in the recent past. Besides, old people used to collect chert scattered on the shelter surface to use as strike-a-lights to make fire. This means that some chert flakes and cores, especially those of larger size, will have been removed from the site.

Limestone roof fall is plentifully spread on the shelter surface, especially at the rear. The present shelter floor and its surrounds are flat. Small shrubs, coconut trees, lontar palms, *Celtis* and *Agathis alba* grow in front of the shelter, while above its roof the roots of *Ficus sp* dangle down along the drip line and through fissures.

In Dusun Oemau Lain, in Desa Tuanatuk, another complex of raised coral reef with several shelters was found. Local people call this rock shelter complex Tonggobatu. It lies about 4 km from the northern coast of Rote (figure 2.3). Unlike the shelters in Pia Hudale that lie below the general level of the surrounding terrain, those in Tonggobatu are situated on a hill.

Tonggobatu has several rock shelters that face northwest, and several smaller ones on the opposite side of the hill. Only in those (a total of five) that face northwest were abundant stone flakes and shells found on the surface. The densest surface scatters were found in two shelters called Lua Manggetek and Lua Meko. Lua Manggetek is the largest and the most conveniently-placed shelter, with a domed roof.

Lua Meko is not very large, and only stone flakes and no sherds were scattered on its surface. Here, it was predicted that a deep deposit would survive in the area close to the inside wall of Lua Meko, where preservation is good and the chance of soil sliding outside the shelter only very small.

The present environment of the Tonggobatu shelters is very dry, with external vegetation consisting of *Agathis alba, Ficus* sp, grass, and cotton trees. However, in front of the raised coral reef complex there is a small seasonal stream that only carries water during the rainy season.

11

Figure 2.3: The Tonggobatu limestone massif on Rote Island (white arrow) as seen from Mokdale-Busalangga road.

Tonggobatu also has some east-facing shelters but these are very damp within and some are partly filled with massive blocks of roof fall. Except for a few sherds, no artefacts were found on the surfaces of these sites. The eastern side also has one deep vertical cave which is not suitable for human occupation.

In Dusun Nggefa, in Desa Holoama, there is another raised coral reef complex, with three big shelters facing northwest about 4 km from the northern coastline. The surrounding area is a flat lowland where shrub vegetation grows, dominated by *Agathis alba*. This group of shelters was most likely used for habitation, although no surface artefacts were found when the survey was carried out and the deposits looked thin. In front of this shelter complex there is a large block of sandstone with an impression that looks like a human foot (figure 2.4) and rows of small hollows. In Maluku Utara, similar features are still used by local people to crush canarium nuts.

Figure 2.4: A large block of sandstone with an impression like a human foot and lines of small hollows, Dusun Nggefa, Desa Holoama.

Western Rote District

Several raised coral reef complexes with very small shelters were also found in Western Rote District. In the Boa Peninsula and Oe Seli, in the southern coastal area, there are several raised coral reef complexes. However, most of the shelters are very close to sea level and waves can sometimes enter. Some other rock shelters were situated in the mangrove area, difficult of access. No artefacts were found around any of these. However, some sherds were found on the surfaces of several small rock shelters in the northern coastal area, west of Baa, but no stone artefacts were found

in these shelters. Many are wet inside during the rainy season.

2006 achaeological survey on Rote

In 2006 a survey was carried out along the rivers near the Tonggobatu rockshelter complex to the coast direction.The purpose was to see the spread and varieties of chert material. It was found that most red and yellowish-colour chert occur in boulder sizes, along the river beds and on the ground (figure 2.5 and 2.6).

Survey was also carried out around Danau Tua and Danau Anak and Bokae Region to alocate sites with possible older occupation. In Bokae region, East Rote we found a terrace site near Watulilok river. Geologically, the area is belong to the Bobonaro complex. Lithologically this complex consists of two principal constituents: a. scaly clay, b. exotic blocks of various sizes. Scatter of stone artefacts, consisting of flakes and cores cherts were found on the terrace surface, mostly bigger than those found in Pia Hudale and Tonggobatu rockshelters. We did not find any cave site in Bokae region.

Down to the coast, on the low hill there are stone sarcophagi used as burial container with human bones missing the head still inside. Although nowadays villages are not brave to even just touch the hill area, the old people in the Watulilok said that the head had been taken away by people in the past.

The shape of stone sarcophag look like small boats with lid of the same material in a roof shape or like the boat (figure 2.7 and 2.8). These small sarcophag have never been found yet in other part of Indonesia. Around the area, there are scatter of pottery found, but none are red –slipped pottery.

Around Danau Tua and Danau Anak in East Rote where Buhler carried a series of excavation in 1930s. Many small rockshelters were found, but we did not find any artefact on the floor. On the biggest shelter, Lua Meol, there are some pottery scatters on the surface but no stone artefact.

Sawu Island

An archaeological survey were carried out in West Sawu District (figure 2.5). On the way from Seba (the Sawu capital) to Mesara village on the western peninsula there are outcrops of raised coral, but none are high enough to form rock shelters. On the northern side of western Sawu, in Desa Raedewa, there is a long raised coral reef complex called Lie Da, containing at least three big shelters with abundant

Figure 2.5: A River in Dusun Oemaulain, Rote , possible source for yellow and red cherts

Figure 2.6: Yellow chert boulder scatters on the ground, 0.5 km from Tonggobatu Rockshelter complex.

scatters of cultural remains. The biggest shelter had been exploited for bat dung fertilizer in the past. This practice stopped in 1940s, according to interviewed old people. When the survey was carried out, there were trace of three fertilizer mining pits up to 1 m deep, indicating heavy disturbance. The cave deposits were originally more than 1 metre deep. Many stone artefacts from these pits were scattered on the surface, but no pottery was found.

The site with most potential for excavation is the cave of Lie Madira in Desa Daieko. Lie Madira is situated 264 m inland from Roa Lie beach on the northern coast of Sawu, a popular beach for collecting crabs and shells and evaporating sea water for salt. The area around the cave supports coastal vegetation such as lontar and coconut palms, *Pandanus sp.* and shrubs.

Lie Madira has two entrances. One leads into a narrow and long cave used for habitation. The other leads into another deep and long cave which goes down for about 20 m to a source of fresh water used by the Desa Daieko villagers. A cement staircase has been built down to this water source. In the other cave, used for habitation, many stone flakes and some sherds were found scattered on the surface, especially around the mouth. Some stone flakes were also found outside the cave. No artefacts were found in the inner water-filled part of the cave.

The present maximum height of the roof of Lie Madira

in the habitation area is 3 m. The length of the cave is 15.50 m from the mouth to the back, and the maximum width is 4.5 m. The present cave mouth is 3 m wide and 1.25 m high. The front has no rock fall, but the inner area is piled with limestone rubble. The cave inside is very dark and sun cannot reach very far in. However, the cave is dry enough for habitation.

Another cave visited was Ratu Monepidu, in the southern coastal area. A few land snails were found inside this cave but no stone artefacts. In the middle of the cave there are two very large piles of roof fall that make it very difficult to examine the entire surface of the cave and to conduct any excavation. No river exists near this site, but people make gardens around it, suggesting that it could have been used for habitation in the past.

Figure 2.7: Small sarcophagus on Bukit Watu Lilok

Figure 2.8: Small sarcophagus on Bukit Watu Lilok

2. The modern tradition of pottery making on Sawu

Data on locally-made Sawu pottery can be obtained from the central market in Seba. Based on interviews with local people and traders in Seba, I discovered that all the pottery that is sold in the market is brought from Mesara, a small village provides all the pottery needs for the island. The potters' male family members often sell the pottery in the central village on the northwest side of Sawu Island. People also said that Mesara is the only pottery making village in Sawu. Nowadays, potters prefer to sell pottery to Seba market rather than selling it door to door. People also travel to Mesara to buy pottery directly from the local potters.

All pots sold in the market are plain, non-red-slipped cooking pots. Interviews with local people who often visit Mesara informed me that open air firing processes are used, but I could not gain other useful details from the interviews because people could only give very general statements. However, from the physical appearance of the pottery sold in the market, it can be inferred that the formation processes are similar to those used in Dusun Oenitas on Rote. For comparative purposes I purchased several specimens.

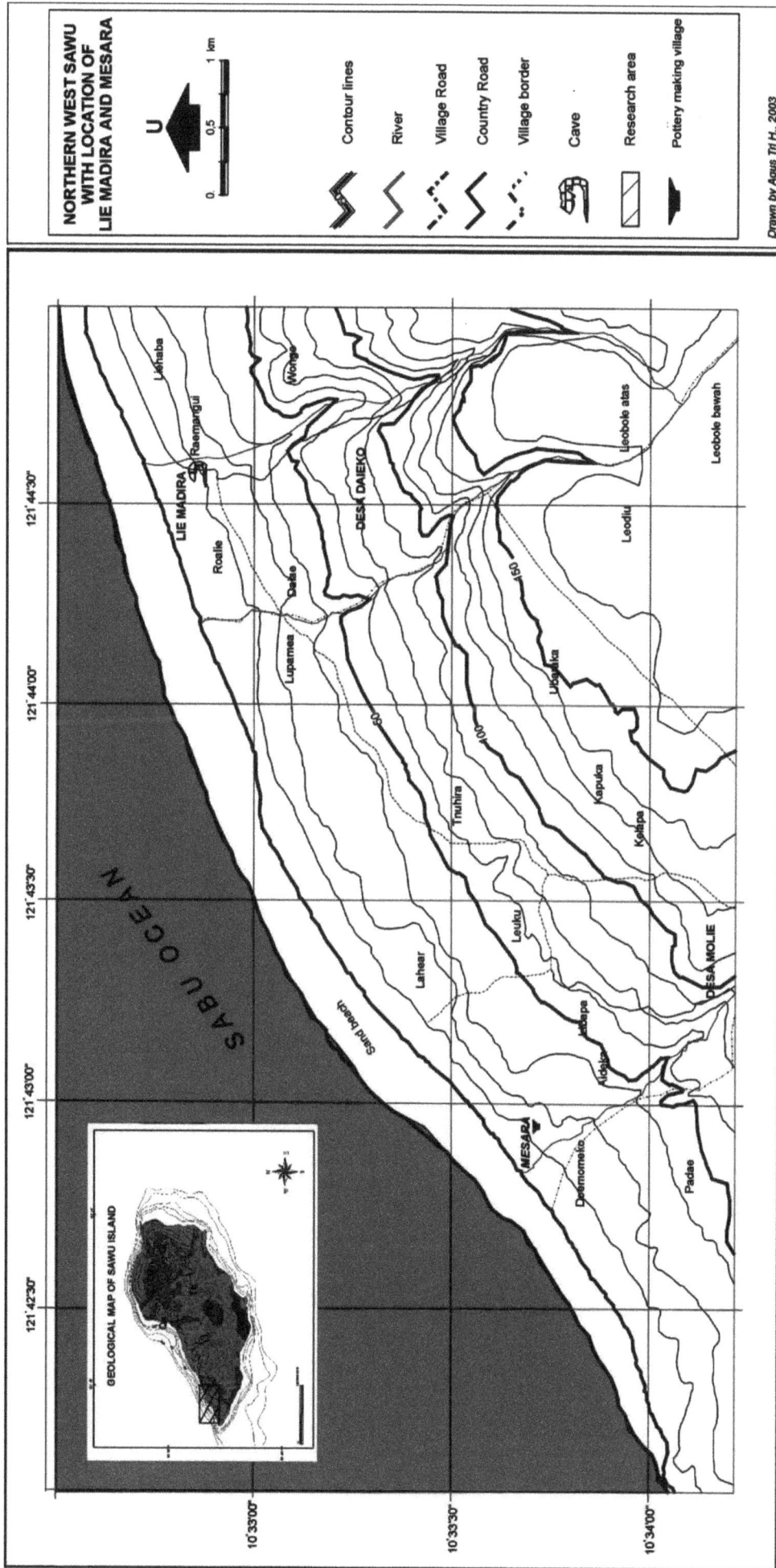

Figure 2.9: Northern West Sawu, with the location of Lie Madira (drawn by Agus TH., 2003)

3

EXCAVATION AND LABORATORY METHODS

This chapter describes all the excavation and recording procedures and techniques of analysis and laboratory methodology applied to investigate the problems identified in chapter I.

1. Excavation and recording procedures

Generally, in large rock shelters, a grid of one metre square was laid out first, and then individual squares were chosen for excavation. Squares were chosen for excavation within the grids based on consideration of the possibility of finding deep deposits, lack of disturbance, and as little root penetration as possible. For small rock shelters and caves, the locations for test pits were chosen individually.

During excavation, the depths of all spits and major finds were measured below a datum point established at the ground level of the first square to be excavated. Before scraping the first spit, artefacts, bones and other archaeological remains found on the surface were collected, after their locations were recorded. Excavation was carried out by 5 cm spits. Because of the dryness of the sediments, all excavated soil was dry sieved through first a 4 mm sieve and then a 0.5 mm sieve, the latter to catch very small remains such as fish and small animal bones, and glass and shell beads.

In the field, all archaeological finds were classified into stone artefacts, sherds, bones, shells, and ornaments, all kept separately for each spit. Bones were then separated in the laboratory into human and animal bones. Sediment samples were collected from each layer from the excavation sections after excavation was completed, starting from the bottom of each profile in order to ensure no mixing as a result of particles falling from above.

After the excavation was completed for each square, a section drawing of the visible layers was carried out, pH was measured, and the soil colours were determined with a Munsell color chart in both moist and dry conditions. A pinch of soil from each layer was then matched with a standard texture chart. Texture was recorded using the finger rubbing method following Limbrey (1975). Structures and boundaries between layers were also recorded as sharp or merging in the field.

2. The identification of transformation processes in caves

Archaeological assemblages uncovered from excavation in caves often do not represent direct *in situ* discard by the humans who occupied the sites in prehistoric times. During the thousands of years between original discard and the time when an archaeologist decides to survey and excavate, there are several processes that can change the distribution of data in a cave site, either horizontally or vertically. In relation to the occupation sequence, identifying any vertical transformation, either natural or cultural, that has taken place in a site is crucial (Rowlett and Robbins 1982). Due to vertical transformation, items originally deposited in one level can eventually be placed several layers apart vertically. As a result, a single deposit can contain the products of many different depositional cycles. It is thus very important to identify the processes responsible for the formation of each depositional unit within a site.

To identify the occurrence of transformation processes and disturbance in each site, several strategies were applied. The topography of the site was considered, layers were examined for evidence of disturbance, conjoining or refitting analysis of stone artifacts and potsherds was undertaken, and the degrees of weathering and mineralization of human bones were identified in the laboratory, together with the total number of individuals represented by all bone fragments recovered in a site. For the rock shelters considered here, ploughing activity is clearly not a problem. But animal and human trampling have to be considered; although likely to have been minimal, an experiment by Schiffer (1987; Limbrey 1975) shows that large objects tend to move upwards, while small objects tend to move downwards as a result of trampling.

The effects of trampling depend on several factors, including the quantity of cultural material on the ground surface, the intensity of the trampling, and the nature of the surface sediments. Furthermore, the penetrability of a surface sediment is determined to a degree by its cultural content - dense lithic and ceramic debris beneath the ground surface is resistant to applied force by trampling (Schiffer 1987:126). In a sparse and soft deposit, however, animal and human trampling can mix up the original sequence of archaeological remains.

Underlying the use of refitting analysis for identifying disturbance is the assumption that fragments of an individual artefact deposited in different places will represent a single time of manufacture. This type of analysis was pioneered by Burg (1959), and later by South (1977:291), to establish contemporaneity for ceramic and glass artefacts. Lithic refitting has been pioneered by Villa (1982), and Schiffer (1987: 285-287) has evaluated the potential of this activity to identify transformation processes. Basically, the refitting of stone artefacts can be classified into two activities: refitting flakes detached from the same core, and refitting fragments of tools (although any piece of stone broken by human activity can of course be refitted to a matching piece). By refitting, Richardson (1992) was able to demonstrate that substantial vertical artefact movement had occurred between layers, with consequent implications for interpretation, in Kenniff Cave, Queensland.

Refitting of both stone artefact fragments and potsherds was carried out for the Rote sites, but the results were not very satisfactory. Only a small number of sherds were recovered from my excavations and none could be joined, although there is a possibility that two small sherds found in Lua Meko came from the same pot. The difficulties arise because the sherds found in the deposits average only 3.5 cm in maximum dimension, all have rounded edges, and only five have rim profiles.

Apart from refitting, analysis of the degree of mineralization, especially in human bone, was also carried out. The occurrence of different degrees of mineralization in bones found in the same layer, especially in the case of finds of fairly fresh human bone underlying highly weathered ones, signifies the occurrence of disturbance. This analysis was assisted by David Bulbeck at the Australian National University, in conjunction with his morphological analysis of the human bones (appendix 1). In addition, the occurence of bones of introduced animals in pre-pottery layers also demands attention, as they may also be an indication of site disturbance.

As well as pottery, the refitting of stone artefact fragments also did not produce very good results in my sites. No fragments could be refitted across different layers, except for two pieces from Lie Madira which were separated by 5 cm vertically. But although only one such case was found, this need not guarantee that vertical movement of archaeological finds did not take place. Refitting of flakes from the same cores did not produce good results either. Some grouping of flakes of the same colour chert can be done, but these do not necessarily come from the same nodule. Conversely, a single chert nodule can sometimes be multicoloured.

3. Analysis of Archaeological Finds

For the purposes of analysis of each site, the archaeological assemblages were divided into several horizons (or analytical levels) based on combinations of radiocarbon dates and changes in assemblages by depth. Examples include changes in shellfish species, the appearances of pottery, and animals brought from Sundaland, and changing densities of stone artefacts and shells. If some human bones from different spits could be regarded as possibly from one individual, all of the other archaeological finds recovered in those spits were treated as belonging to a single analytical level.

Stone artefact analysis

The analysis of stone artefacts includes:

1. Plotting the varying densities of stone artefacts in each rock shelter through time, in order to plot changing intensities of site occupation. The varying proportions of unretouched and modified flakes (retouched or with hafting modification) can also give an indication of the nature of site use at any particular time.

2. Technological examination of raw material selection, mode of reduction, secondary working and types of modification, and the distributions of variation through time.

3. Functional analysis, via the investigation of use wear. Without use wear analysis, unretouched flakes that were actually used can be mistaken for debitage. Use wear analysis allows understanding of the choices involving the sizes and shapes of flakes detached from a pebble or nodule to make tools with identified functions. These choices will often depend on the characteristics of the material that was being worked (e.g. hard, medium or soft, and coarse or fine grained).

Initially, all stone assemblages were classified using a combination of the schemes of Sullivan and Rozen (1985, 1989) and Andrefsky (1998). Their strategies were modified slightly to suit the specific data from the excavated sites on Rote and Sawu. The first division of all chipped stone artefacts into tools and non tools (debitage), as suggested by Andrefsky (1998), was considered suitable for the purposes of my study.

Low powered microscopic examination, normally up to 40X, but sometimes up to 100X magnification, was applied, rather than just using the naked eye or magnifying to only 10X, as carried out by Andrefsky. Although utilised stone tools with very minimal signs of use wear can still be categorised wrongly as debitage even under a high powered microscope, the use of a higher magnification can help to minimize the possibility of error.

Classification proceeded according to a number of successive steps. Firstly, all chipped stone pieces were separated into tools and debitage. Chipped stone artefacts that had signs of modification through human intent, such as retouch, backing, hafting modification, or thinning (Young and Bonnichsen 1984), and/or have clear signs of use wear under 40X magnification, such as striation, gloss and edge damages, were classified as stone tools. Chipped stone artefacts that did not have any of the above indicators were classified as debitage.

Stone tool can also be classified into bifacial and non-bifacial tool. Bifacial tools are worked from both ventral and dorsal surfaces, whereas non-bifacial tools are worked only unifacially. Non-bifacial tools are classified into flake tools with secondary working and those that have only use wear. The definition of retouch used here is that flake scars should be at least 3 mm long from any margin.

During analysis, stone artefacts in the debitage category were classified into complete flakes, broken flakes, flake fragments, flake shatter, and debris. Flakes were classified as complete if they have bulbs of percussion and complete distal and proximal ends, and as broken flakes if only proximal or distal ends survive (not both). Debris includes chipped pieces which do not have a bulb of percussion or a striking platform, and are irregular in shape ("chunks"). For inter-assemblage comparison, only complete flakes and broken proximal ends of flakes were measured while end s of flakes were examined qualitatively.

Based on this classification, there are three types of flaked implement in the sites analysed - tools with some secondary working, tools without secondary working, and non-tool flaked debitage. Comparison of size attributes between these three categories will be useful for answering questions concerning choice of flake sizes for use as tools.

Use-wear analysis

Types of use wear that can be identified, following the guidelines of Kamminga (1982), include edge damage, striation, polish/gloss, and dulling. Since not all types of striation can be identified with low magnifications below 40X, magnifications up to 100X were used when necessary to identify faint traces of wear, although this is still classified as a low power approach by Odell and Vereecken (1980).

Odell and Vereecken (1980) did a blind test to check the reliability of lithic use-wear interpretation applying a low power microscopic approach. They found that it is difficult to identify exactly the material worked, especially on a retouched edge. However, they were able to reach between 61 and 68% accuracy in terms of grouping worked materials into soft, soft medium, hard medium and hard.

Odell's replicative experiments suggest that use damage can also be classified by type of motion; longitudinal to the working edge (cutting, sawing, slicing and carving); transverse (scraping, planing, adzing, whittling); or of intermediate or different directionality (graving, boring). To differentiate between longitudinal and transverse motion relative to the working edge is not difficult when striations can be identified.

However, some characteristics of use-wear that can differentiate between the types of motion are often difficult to identify. Both cutting and sawing produce scarring on both surfaces of an edge, alternating from side to side and developing with use into denticulation of the lateral margin, with striation near the edge and parallel to it. The only difference is that sawing (two-way motion) does not produce unidirectional scarring, unlike cutting (one-way motion). Snap fractures (half moon shaped) only occur on relatively thin edges; these can be indicators of longitudinal motion as they often occur when cutting or sawing with an unretouched edge. In the cases of slicing and carving, the angle of the tool to the worked surface and the direction of motion can change during the course of a stroke.

Scraping leads to damage that is exclusively unifacial, or almost so, that occurs over a relatively wide area depending on the nature of the contact between the tool and the worked material. Striations, if present, are transverse to the working to the edge, on the surface opposite the scarring. Projections are more easily worn down. Planning is another example of transverse motion, defined by a pushing rather than a pulling motion. Nevertheless, the wear characteristics of scraping and planing are similar. Whittling is a transverse motion in which that portion of the edge that first makes contact with the worked material remains in contact throughout the length of the stroke. Penetration and horizontal movement of the tool edge result in the removal of slices, or shaving from the substance being worked. This activity results in predominantly unifacial removal.

Adzing is basically a transverse motion that also results in unifacial scarring and striations perpendicular or oblique to the edge. When the edge is symmetrical (double-bevelled), damage is usually bifacial. Another type of transverse motion is graving, in which the principal damage occurs on the tip of the tool. Boring is a complex movement that includes downward pressure and lateral twisting. The downward pressure roughens and scars the tip. The twisting results in the removal of small flakes from the lateral edges that lead to the point. Hafting can also leave use-wear, of either an abrasive or dislocatory (scarring) type.

The first stage in use-wear analysis should be to separate damage due to utilisation from damage caused by trampling and other causes. Guidelines for doing this are provided by Tringham (1974), who experimented and found that accidental damage tends to be unpatterned, not favouring one part of a tool over any other. Striations tend to be multidirectional and not correlated with particular edges. Polish and edge rounding are usually unassociated with particular edges and may be a result of extreme battering and crushing. Damage by trampling usually produces scars also that have no fixed orientation or size, and usually a random distribution.

Terminations of scars are grouped as feather, hinge, step and snap (or bending according to Kamminga 1982). Ideally, different scar terminations and sizes should correlate with specific activities and worked materials, but, in practice, individual attributes can overlap if a tool is used for more than one purpose. Since this study applied a low power approach, polish other than gloss cannot be identified and so different types of polish were not recorded.

Types of striation are classified into sleek and furrowed. Sleek striations have smooth and regular margins while furrowed striations have irregular margins. Sleek striations usually occur on sickle blades, but under 100 X magnification it is not possible to differentiate these two types. Therefore, the main information to be derived from striations concerns the direction of motion during use.

The formation of use wear patterns is determined by the material, shape and weight of the tool; the applied load (pressure) and the duration of use; the cross-section and profile of the working edge and its edge angle; and the abrasive environment. The edge angle is defined as that between the ventral surface and the retouched or utilised edge. Edge angle can determine the last function of the edge, if the tools were used for more than one function, because edge angle contributes to tool suitability for a given task. It can be functionally diagnostic when correlated with other variables. For example, an acute edge angle is not suitable for scraping bone, because it will be easily broken after a short period. Thickness can also limit the functions of tools. For example, a thin-ended scraper on a blade is more likely to break from a percussion action such as chopping than a thicker and more robust tool. Gloss can occur on the ventral edge or on both ventral and dorsal edges, sometimes as diffuse polish, other times as a localised, very bright gloss. It may occur on the corner of a flake or chunk, or in the centre of a sharp margin.

Because most stone tools from excavated sites on Rote and Sawu are of chert, only the signs of use-wear that occur on the chert and flint materials in Kamminga's experiments (Kamminga 1982) will be used for comparison. Vereecken (Odell and Vereecken 1980) used obsidian for their experiments, and this does not occur on Rote. Only the positions of scars and striations on stone tools, and the directions of the striations, will be compared to infer stone tool functions.

Analysis of manufacturing technology

Since the target of this analysis is to understand several aspects of prehistoric stone manufacturing technology, several variables need to be synthesised together. The numbers of bifacial tools, of flake tools with secondary working other than retouch, of flake tools with retouch only, and flake tools without secondary working but with signs of use wear, are recorded for each level of occupation. Then, the characteristics and technology of each tool category are examined and compared between the levels of occupation. Examination is focused on metric variables and ratios (length, width, proportion of length to width). Possible varieties of secondary working are also examined, together with the types and positions of retouch.

Comparison of stone tool data between sites was then performed, and the results integrated with other factors such as physical environment. Comparisons were also carried out between the lower and upper layers in sites, and whenever possible with other cultural changes.

Aspects of raw material selection were carried out by macroscopic identification to gain data about the types of material used, the possibility of selection of certain size ranges of raw material, and preferences for using outcrop sources or secondary sources such as river beds. Raw materials were identified macroscopically and include chert, dacite, and silicified limestone. Sources were guessed from the nature of cortex and degree of rolling (Flenniken and White 1985), together with local geological information as a guide. Selection of size ranges of raw materials can be inferred from cortex analysis; cores that still have cortex can often have their original sizes estimated. Some flakes with cortex on 75%-100% of their dorsal surfaces can also indicate the relative sizes of the original cores.

Data to answer questions concerning mode of reduction are obtained from a range of cores and flakes simultaneously. Theoretically, there are several modes of core reduction depending on constraints such as raw material, time or skill (Hayden 1996). Each mode has its characteristics and suitability for different raw materials, knapper skills and intended tasks. Blade reduction can waste raw material since systematic blade production requires the preparation of cores and the removal of many preparation flakes. Moreover, skill, training and time are necessary to systematically produce blades. Blade production needs specific sizes and shapes of raw material, Thus, there is an increasing procurement cost of raw material. Bipolar reduction produces a great deal of shatter and small flakes and would be wasteful of large core material in the production of knives, but the bipolar technique is also believed to maximise the use of raw materials when applied to small cores. Expedient core reduction is the removal of flakes without planning to produce certain types of detached flakes. Direction of flake removal can be random, and the skills needed are few and suited to any sizes of raw material.

To determine which mode of core reduction has been applied, the first step of analysis is to identify and classify all the cores found in the assemblage. Core variables include number of platforms and arrangement of flake scars, allowing classification into multidirectional platform cores, prismatic or single platform cores, and bipolar cores. Multidirectional cores usually result from casual reduction techniques, whereas prismatic cores can give an indication of the application of blade technology. Bipolar cores are more difficult to recognise in the assemblage since they often shatter, but usually the broken pieces are identifiable. Commonly, bipolar cores are characterised by crushing from opposing ends (Andrefsky 1998:149).

Flenniken (1981: 29 -32) states that it is difficult to characterise bipolar flake morphology since bipolar reduction has the potential to shatter an objective piece into many different shapes of debitage. Bipolar flakes have two points of percussion, with compression rings from two directions. Squat forms or flakes with compression rings and split objective pieces are among the results of bipolar flake morphology that can be recognised. Many irregular types of shatter may also be a result of bipolar reduction.

Apart from core analysis, mode of reduction can be determined from flake analysis. Blade/ bladelets have length:width ratios greater than 2:1, parallel margins and dorsal ridges, and sometimes facetted striking platforms. The occurrence of this type of flake in the deposits suggest that blade reduction was sometimes applied, although the occurrence of blades in sites without any prismatic cores is suggestive that some blades could simply be removed by expedient core reduction.

Problems can arise with bifacial tools, since it is possible that bifacial technology was used in a site even though no bifacial artefacts might be found, especially if the assemblage is not dense and the site was only used occasionally. The same goes for any other kind of trimming activity such as retouching. Bifacial flaking is discussed in context in the section on stone tools.

4. Pottery analysis

Macro-analysis consists of form analysis and surface treatment analysis. Form analysis is the reconstruction of pottery shapes based on body and mouth diameter, neck angle, rim thickness and lip modification. Several pottery form analyses carried out for Indonesian sites have applied Shepard's terminology for describing vessel shapes, based on rim profiles and the contours of the vessel body (Bellwood 1980; 1988; Ardika 1991; Sumijati 1995; Mahirta 1996). Therefore, to make the results of the form/shape analyses from Rote and Sawu comparable with those for other Indonesian sites, I also applied Shepard's terminology (see figure 3.1):

Pottery analysis can be classified into two parts: the first is macro-analysis and the second is the micro-analysis of pottery paste. Through the latter, it is possible to detect the number of pottery making centres represented by the sherds found in the caves, and to detect whether the red-slipped and non-slipped pottery was made in the same locations. The assumption underlying such analysis is that each pottery making centre has uniform characteristics in term of raw material use and the technology applied to pottery manufacture. At present, only one pottery making village survives on Rote, at Dusun Oenitas, and one on Sawu at Dusun Mesara. At Oenitas some potters still produce red-slipped pottery today. The results of this analysis are presented separately in chapter VII.

Other attributes of pottery form such as lip profiles are also described, since these can often differ and characteristise local styles of pottery (Ardika 1991). Surface decoration is rare in the Rote and Sawu sites.

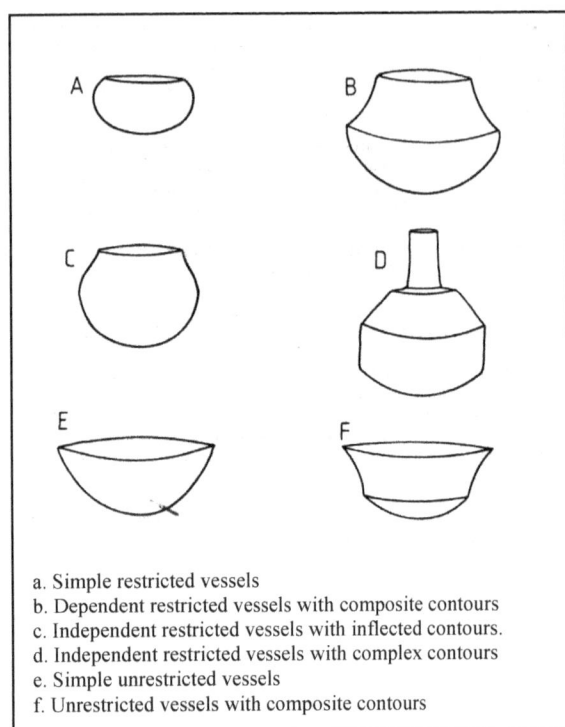

a. Simple restricted vessels
b. Dependent restricted vessels with composite contours
c. Independent restricted vessels with inflected contours.
d. Independent restricted vessels with complex contours
e. Simple unrestricted vessels
f. Unrestricted vessels with composite contours

Figure 3.1: Classification of vessel shapes according to Anna Shepard (simplified from Shepard 1974).

Micro-analysis of pottery paste was performed using an electron microprobe on both clay and mineral inclusions. With the electron microprobe, it is possible to discriminate between pottery inclusions and the clay matrix (Freestone 1982; Summerhayes and Walker 1982; Anson 1983; Hunt 1989; Hunt 1993, Ambrose 1992; Tite 1992).To undertake electron microprobe analysis, sections from selected sherds are sliced and set in an epoxy resin pellet, from which a thick section is taken for analysis (details of sample preparation are in an appendix 2). This thick section is put in a specimen holder within the sample chamber. The sample can be viewed through an attached video camera and points can be selected for analysis by moving the specimen holder.

Four different points in the clay matrix were analysed for each sample to ascertain the level of variability. Chemical analysis of mineral inclusions was also undetaken, by pointing directly at different inclusions in the specimen. For both the clay matrix and mineral inclusion analyses, 8 elements (Mg, Al, Si, Ca, Ti, Fe, Na, and K, as oxides) were chosen. Both energy and wavelength dispersive spectometry were used - the former to obtain a spectrum to detect whether the spot for analysis was part of a mineral inclusion or part of the paste, and the latter for quantitative analyses. I used the Scanning Electron Microscope (JEOL 6040) in the Research School of Biologicall Sciences at ANU.

Before a large number of samples was analysed, a test of the sensitivity of the method was carried out. Two recent potsherd samples from known sources (one from Mesara village on Sawu and three samples from Oenitas village on Rote) were analysed and shown not to cluster together, despite the presence of some overlap. The data of clay composition for each sample were then analysed with the Canonical Variate Analysis (CVA) with the statistical package GenStat to identify clusters.

A number of authors (Rye 1981;52; Shepard 1954:161-162) have suggested various criteria for distinguishing natural mineral inclusions from human additives in pottery. Rye (1981:52) favours an examination of shape and size distributions. Grains with rounded edges result from natural erosion and transport, whereas grains with sharply angular edges result from crushing. A presence of the latter generally implies purposeful addition by the potter, whereas in the former case there is a possibility of natural addition to the clay. The presence of two sets of minerals of differing origin can also be a definite indication of tempering.

To describe the shapes of inclusions, Power's Scale of Roundness was used. Thus, the inclusions can be very angular, angular, sub-angular, sub-rounded, rounded or well rounded. Classification was carried out by matching inclusions with a standard chart arranged by Power (Barraclough 1992), and also an inclusion sorting chart (Barraclough 1992).

Macroscopic analysis of pottery from East Timor was not carried out. For comparison purposes, data on surface treatment and vessel form are taken from Glover's report on East Timor sites (Glover 1986). However, microscopic analysis of pottery pastes from East Timor sites has been undertaken since no data on this have been previously published.

5. Shell analysis

Non-artefactual shell analysis

The primary purpose of the analysis of food shells is to find out which habitats were exploited and to what extent the people who occupied a given site practised selectivity in their collection. The results of shell abundance analysis will also be compared between assemblages.

The stages of shell analysis are as follows:

1. Shell artefacts are first separated from other shells.
2. All food shells (of all species including complete, broken and small fragments) are weighed by spit or layer, to plot changing intensities of shell exploitation during site occupancy.
3. Shell species are identified and allocated to habitats.
4. Shell abundance analyses by species are undertaken.

Identification of shell species was carried out using the reference collection available in Archaeology and Natural History, RSPAS, ANU, backed by shell reference books. In doing MNI (mean number of individuals) analysis it is important not to double-count fragments that originally came from a single individual. But because different shell species are prone to different patterns of fragmentation, not imposing a uniform method of counting for MNI is important (Heffernan 1980). In this study, the MNI counting method was to count umbones on bivalves and apices on some gastropods (*Turbo*, *Trochus* and *Conus*). *Terebralia* apices are more fragile so characteristic columelar plicae in the aperture were counted. Labial sections were counted on *Nerita*. After counting, all bivalves were divided by two. Chitons were counted for only the proximal valve, rather than by dividing the total number of valves found found by eight, as done by Heffernan (1980).

The shell abundance measures used in this study are both absolute and relative abundance. Absolute abundance is MNI (Minimum Number of Individuals) of shells untransformed, while relative abundance is the percentage values. The use of both types of abundance analysis is suggested by Thomas (1995). Relative abundances of each shell species per spit are counted by MNI for each species divided by the total number of all shell species X 100%.

Shell weights were not used because of bias due to differing degrees of calcification with depth, and due to difficulties in identifying very small pieces of shell for certain species. Relative frequencies are a commonly encountered statistic generated for shells in sites with more than one species present (Claassen 1998). The calculation used here to compare counts among different levels was chosen following Begler and Keating (1979). The total count for each species per site is computed, and then the proportion per level is calculated. This allows comparison of one shell species with another within each level. Percentages are then compared across the excavation unit to reveal information about habitats, human behaviour, or formation processes (Claassen 1998).

Shell artefact analysis

Shells artefacts include ornaments, tools and other modified pieces identified from traces of cutting. Shell ornaments include beads and other shell ornaments. All of the shell ornaments recovered from Rote and Sawu are simple in both technique and form. The first stage is to identify any traces of fracture or retouch on pieces of shell that can signify usage as tools. For instance, in Pulau Mare, Maluku Utara, *Anadara* scrapers are used for thinning pot walls. The second stage is to identify other signs of human modification, such as grooving and snapping.

6. Bone analysis

The animal bones have been identified by Dr. Ken Aplin (CSIRO, Canberra). The results give data on the animal species exploited and changes in these species over time. It is also important to try to detect the arrivals of introduced wild and domestic animals from other places. Faunal data can also throw light on intensity of occupation, as well as environmental change.

The human bone analyses were carried by David Bulbeck (School of Archaeology and Anthropology, Australian National University) and the results are presented in an appendix at the back of this thesis. The human bones were cleaned by dry brushing and soaking in distilled water. Except for Lie Madira, all the sites excavated contain human bone fragments, and their conditions vary from fragile to heavily encrusted with calcium carbonate. All were found in fragmentary conditions and none were articulated - we found no complete skeletons as burials.

The analysis of human bones is focused on numbers of individuals and their gender. No parts of human skulls were found during excavation, so that population affinities are difficult to determine (as discussed in the appendix by David Bulbeck). Apart from identification of the number of individuals represented and their sex, an analysis of the degrees of calcium carbonate concretion on the bones was carried out by David Bulbeck. This latter can help to identify site disturbance in cases where bones with significantly differing degrees of calcification occur in the same spit. A full version of Dr Bulbeck's report is presented in an appendix (Bulbeck 2000).

4

THE PIA HUDALE ROCKSHELTER COMPLEX

All the rock shelters in the Pia Hudale raised coral complex have flat floor surfaces, and one cave at the end of the complex is inundated with water. It was decided to excavate shelter D in the Pia Hudale complex. This is the largest shelter in the complex and provides the most convenient place for habitation, being close to a permanent fresh water source (see figure 2.1 in chapter 2). The distance from the back wall to the drip line is sufficient here to provide reliable shelter. Also, shelter D had an abundance of surface finds, consisting of chert flakes, shells and several pottery sherds.

1. The Pia Hudale shelter D excavation

In Pia Hudale shelter D, five 1X 1 m squares within the survey grid (B2, C3, D3, E4, and F4) were opened for excavation. Squares D3 and C3 were situated in the middle of the shelter, B2 was close to the drip line, and E4 and F4 were situated close to the wall (figure 4.1).

Bedrock was reached in all squares excavated, except in E4 where the excavation stopped at the same level as F4 (at spit 8, 40 cm below the surface). Square E4 ran into sterile deposit at about 30 cm below the surface, and there were signs of bedrock in spit 8. Elsewhere, bedrock was reached at 65-75 cm below the surface, except closer to the wall, where it was reached at 40 cm in F4. Excavation in E4 hit sterile at about 30 cm below the surface. Live *Ficus* roots penetrate up to 40 cm below the surface in squares B2 and C3.

Stratigraphy

The excavation uncovered three stratigraphic layers as follows (see fig 4.2):

Layer 1 is a humus layer, a mixture of dark brown sand (10 YR 4/3) with goat dung and dried leaves. This loose layer varies from 2 to 10 cm thick, but average thickness is about 5 cm. In square B2, the thickness of this dark brown sand layer reaches 10 cm. Sediment samples contain lots of chert micro debitage and shell debris.

Layer 2 is a dark yellowish brown (10YR 4/4) sandy sediment. It contains pebble to boulder size limestone roof fall. Goat dung is also present, but not dense. Thickness varies from 7 cm in squares E4 and F4 to 25 cm in squares C3, D3 and B2. According to microscopic examination, dried roots are still present. Micro-debitage suggest that lithic manufacturing activities were quite intensive during the formation of this layer.

Layer 3 is a compact dark reddish brown silty clay (5 YR 3/4) with graded bedding that becomes coarser toward the bottom, suggesting some water action. Thickness is up to 50 cm in squares D3 and C3. Between layer 2 and 3 there is a thin layer of dark greyish brown (10 YR 4/2) sand that contains charcoal. This thin layer only appears on square E4 and F4 section.

Archaeological finds from the Pia Hudale excavation (see tables 4.1 to 4.5 for details).

Square B2 produced the richest variety of archaeological remains, including several hammerstones, and a shell ornament in the shape of a fish in spit 5. From spit 6 down to bedrock the finds became very sporadic, consisting of mostly small stone debitage and fragments of land snails.

Square C3 was similar to square D3. Special finds from this square were a broken bone needle 3 cm long found in spit 5, and one shell bead from spit 3. In square D3, stone artefacts, shells, human and animal bones and one sherd were found. The pottery was found at the surface, while stone artefacts and shells were recovered from the surface down to 65 cm (spit 13), below which lay sterile soil. The densest finds occurred from the surface down to spit 5, at 25 cm.

Square E4 was located close to back wall of the shelter. This square had the lowest density of stone artefacts and shells, although some large stone artefacts with signs of secondary working were found on the surface. Culturally sterile deposit was reached 40 cm below the surface, but actual bedrock was not reached.

The only red-slipped sherd found in Pia Hudale was that recovered from spit 2 in square F4 (10 cm below the surface). This square also produced several human bones, including a long bone.

In terms of vertical distribution, archaeological finds are most concentrated in layers 1 and 2, while layer 3 had sporadic finds and most stone artefacts consist of only small debitage. Other finds in layer 3 include small animal bones and land snail fragments. Pottery was only found in layer 1, shell artefacts in layers 1 and 2, and human bones were found scattered in layers 1 and 2 only, being absent in layer 3 in all squares excavated.

Radiocarbon dating

Four C14 dates have been obtained from the ANU laboratory for Pia Hudale. All are on marine shells, and are distributed from 10 cm below the surface to just above bedrock at 55 cm. The results are listed in table 4.6. All four dates fall close together at the end of the Pleistocene, suggesting that the site reflects a short intensive Palaeolithic occupation with only superficial Neolithic activity.

Furthermore, it is possible that there have been vertical post-depositional transformations of shells and lithics in the site. Pottery is very rare and only occurs down to 10 cm below the surface.

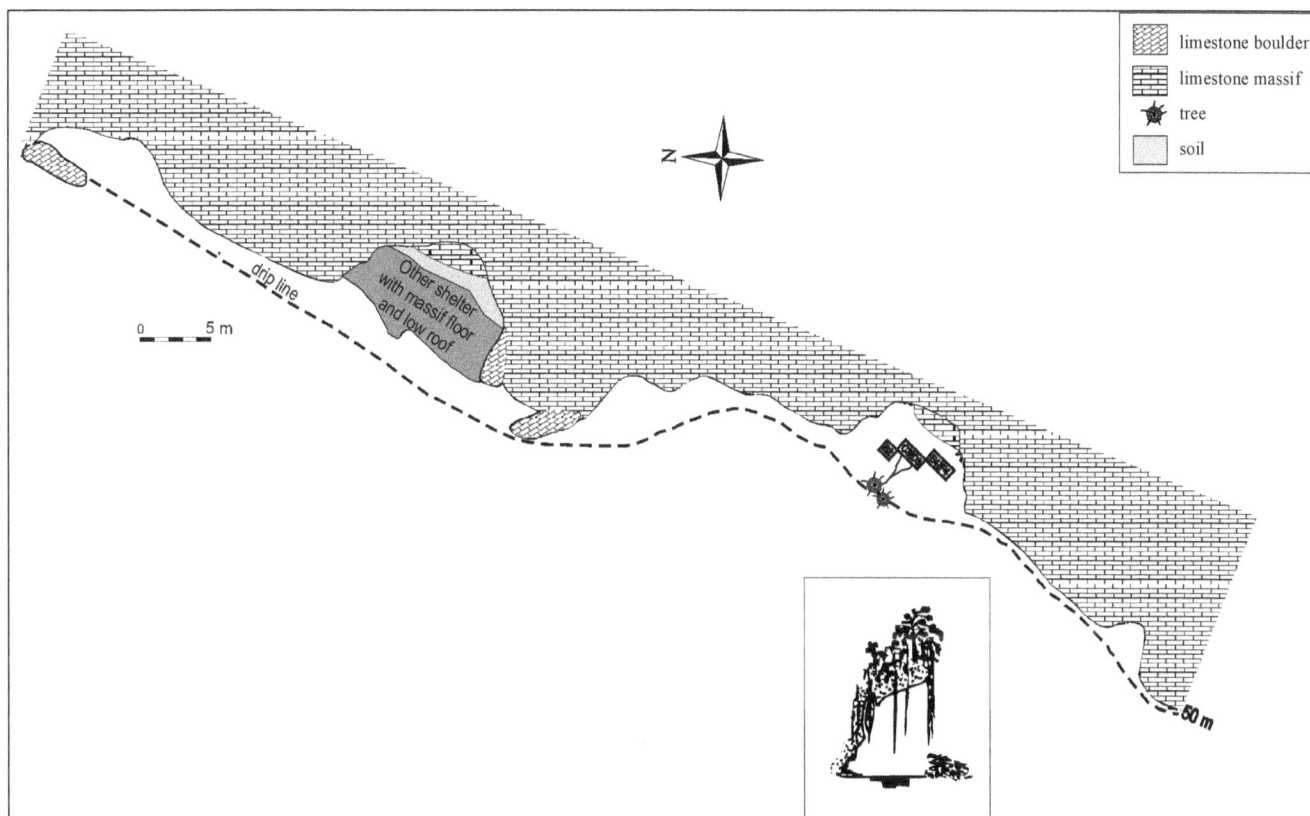

Figure 4.1: Plan of the Pia Hudale rockshelter complex, showing the excavation square in shelter D

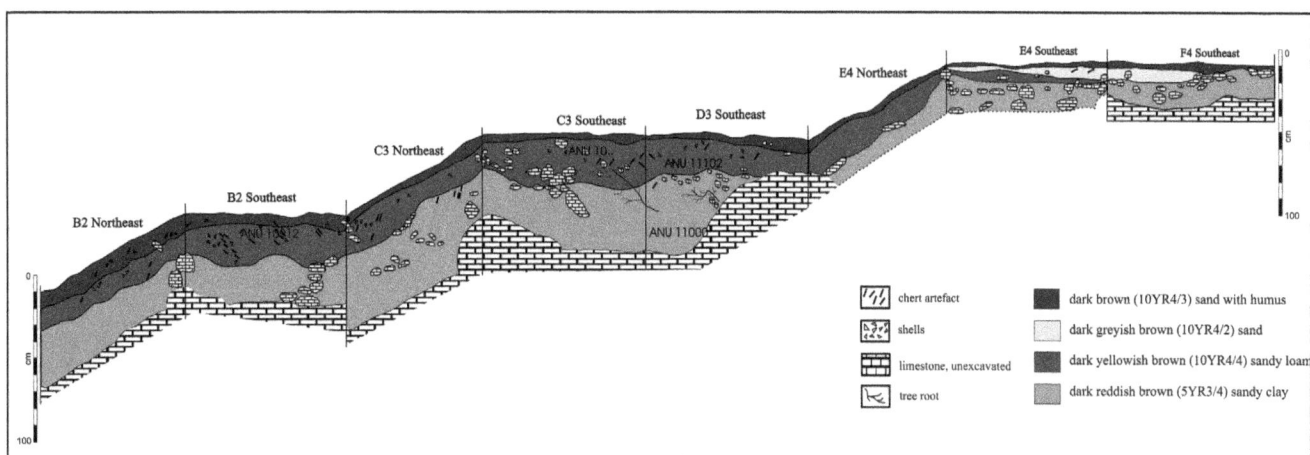

Figure 4.2: The Stratigraphy of Pia Hudale

Table 4.1 Distribution of archaeological finds in square B2, Pia Hudale

spit	0		1		2		3		4		5		6		7		8		9		10		11		12		13	
Material	no	gr	no	gr	no	gr	no	gr	no	gr	no	gr	no	gr	no	gr	no	gr	no	gr	no	gr	no	gr	no	gr	no	gr
pottery																												
glass fragments	1	5																										
stone artefacts:																												
hammer stones			1				3																					
cores	3	124	2	250	8	280	5	175			2	75	1		1		1	30										
retouched & debitage	68	1085	774	1850	783	1705	783	1650	806	1405	441	1060	171	195	151	255	174	135	55	30	57	35	29	10				
shells:																												
shell bead							1	0,3																				
perforated oliva shell																												
other shell ornament											1																	
shell tool																												
non artefactual shell*	27	115	95	1106	380	1124	317	533	311	580	62	175	8	25			11	45	9	25								
crabs			3	1	2	0,5																						
human remains:																												
bone			1	7			3	10			1	5	4	10														
animal bones	32	8,5	42	16	50	10,5	34	17	30	7							38	11										
plant seed									2	1	1	0,5																

Note: * complete and fragments

Table 4.2 Distribution of archaeological finds in square C3, Pia Hudale rocksheter

spit	0		1		2		3		4		5		6		7		8		9		10		11		12		13		14/15	
Material	no	gr	no	gr	no	gr	no	gr	no	gr	no	gr	no	gr	no	gr	no	gr	no	gr	no	gr	no	gr	no	gr	no	gr	no	gr
chinese ceramic	2																													
pottery			1																											
glass	1																													
stone artefacts:																														
hammer stones																														
cores	3	95	7	80	5	230	3	185	2	200	1	143	1	140	1	65	1	165	2	190										
retouched & debitage	10	65	1015	2015	998	1900	1015	2195	279	675	75	212	126	425	99	325	83	100	27	75	83	25	84	24	20	4	13	5		
shells:																														
shell bead							2	1			1	7																		
perforated oliva shell																														
other shell ornaments			2																											
shell tools																														
dentallium																														
non artefacts	23	265	155	803	181	450	149	275	53	145	10	40	24	40			7	15	3	12	2	10								
other mollusc																														
human remains																														
bone			3	30	3	14			1	5																				
animal bone			1	1	43	18	19	8,5	5	3	5	3	15	4,6			1	0,5	3	2			12	5						
plant seed			2	0,5																										

spit	0		1		2		3		4		5		6		7		8		9		10		11		12		13		14/15	
Material	no	gr	no	gr	no	gr	no	gr	no	gr	no	gr	no	gr	no	gr	no	gr	no	gr	no	gr	no	gr	no	gr	no	gr	no	gr
chinese ceramic	1																													
pottery																														
glass	1																													
stone artefacts:																														
hammer															1															
cores	3		7		5		3		1		1		1		3		1		2											
retouched & debitage	82	263	776	2315	1201	2125	572	1750	559	1250	782	1775	564	2652	663	1425	185	455	58	237	33	70	70	15						
shells:																														
shell bead							2																							
perforated oliva											1																			
other shell ornament			2																											
shell tool																														
dentallium																														
non artefacts	71	410	321	630	166	515	233	625	140	475	127	355	88	245	13	30			2	5	2	10								
other mollusc																														
human remains																														
bone			1	4			5	14			2	7	1	7																
bone artefact											1	2																		
tooth																														
animal bone	10	14	60	10	8	2	83	16	42	7	28	6	55	11	31	8	2	0,2	1	0,2			14	2			10	1		

Table 4.3 Distribution of Archaeological finds in square D3, Pia Hudale rockshelter

spit	0		1		2		3		4		5		6		7		8	
Material	no	gr	no	gr	no	gr	no	gr	no	gr	no	gr	no	gr	no	gr	no	gr
pottery	5	90																
stone artefacts:																		
hammer stones					2		2											
cores	4	300	1	85	2	65												
retouched & debitage	29	635	226	850	161	450	61	110	38	75	129	125	30	18				
shells:																		
non-artefactual shell*	15	210	15	135	72	405	27	95	79	550	34	70	12	5				
human remains:																		
bone	1	5	5	20			4	19			1	10	2	12				
tooth											1	6						
animal bone			3	1	5	3,5												

note: * complete and fragments

Table 4.4 Distribution of archaeological finds in square E4, Pia Hudale rock-shelter

spit	0		1		2		3		4		5		6		7		8	
Material	no	gr	no	gr	no	gr	no	gr	no	gr	no	gr	no	gr	no	gr	no	gr
retouched & debitage	51	445	229	835	187	100	49	380										
Pottery			1	5	1	10												
shells:																		
perforated oliva shell			1	5														
non-artefactual shell	4	16	6	18	10	35	2	10										
other mollusc																		
human remains																		
bone	2	120	3	12	1	3												
animal bone			4	1	16	24					5	3						

Table 4.5 Distribution of Archaeological finds in square F4, Pia Hudale rockshelter

Lab. No	spit	depth	layer	square	sample	uncalib 14C age (years BP)	cal BP
ANU-11102	2	10 cm	1	D3	*Turbo opercula*	10,440±500	12,912 (12,410) 11,474
ANU-10912	4	20 cm	2	B2	*Turbo opercula*	11,290±150	13,427 (13,250) 13,087
ANU-11270	5	25 cm	2	C3	*Gafrarium sp.*	10580±80	11,085 (10,990) 10939
ANU-11000	11	55 cm	3	D3	*Melanoides feniculus*	11,160±220	13,355 (13,120) 12,900

Table 4.6: Carbon dating results from Pia Hudale. Melanoides feniculus is a fresh water mollusc species.

Human bones occur down to spit 6 (30 cm below the surface), but not below that level. The degree of calcium carbonate concretion of the human bone is not in orderly sequence from top to bottom of the deposits, as noted in analysis by David Bulbeck (see Appendix 1). Tidal mudflat and sandy intertidal shellfish species also never occur below spit 6, these being species that appear to have increased in numbers with Holocene sea level rise.

These observations suggest that vertical transformations have taken place in the site in Holocene times, down to spit 6, connected with burial activity. These disturbances occurred before the arrival of pottery, since the lowest sherds are only from spit 2 in square F4.

Owing to these observations, the Pia Hudale deposit is divided into two analytical levels, based mainly on the presence of large quantities of *Anadara* and *Gafrarium* shells, and human bones, from spit 6 upwards (table 4.7).

Analytical levels	spits	natural layers
Lower	7---15	3
Upper	1,2,3,4,5,6	1, 2

Table 4.7: The correlations between analytical levels, spits, and natural stratigraphic layers in Pia Hudale, Rote.

2. Analysis of archaeological finds, Pia Hudale:

Human remains

Apart from identification of the number of individuals represented in Pia Hudale, and their sex, an analysis of the degrees of calcium carbonate concretion on the bones was carried out by David Bulbeck. As noted, this can help to identify site disturbance in cases where bones with significantly differing degrees of calcification occur in the same spit. In this chapter I summarize some important points only.

Human bone fragments were found from spits 1 to 6 in squares B2, C3 and D3. All were found in pre-pottery contexts, that is from the second stratigraphic layer downwards. The human bones are very fragmentary and heavily calcified, similar to those from Lua Meko and Lua Manggetek in the Tonggobatu rockshelter complex.

The analysis of the bones by Dr Bulbeck gave information on sex and age, and the numbers of individuals represented in the excavated area. The degree of calcification is quite varied, and heavily calcified bone occurs from the surface down to spit 5. Based on the sequence of degree of calcification, the deposit in square B2 seems to be a little disturbed (see table 1 in Dr. Bulbeck's report). It is suggested that the burial characteristics, which frequently include extremity bones, are 'inconsistent with the practice of secondary burial' (Bulbeck, appendix 1). He suggests that some of the burials were originally primary, but secondary burial was also practiced in the shelter, perhaps with removal of the cranium and mandible beforehand.

Dr Bulbeck suggests that several individuals are represented in the site at least one adult male, one adult female and one teenager. There is betel-nut stain on a tooth from spit 5 in square E4. Betel-nut chewing is a common habit on Rote today, and is widely present in Island Southeast Asia and Melanesia.

Animal Bones

Animal bone fragments were found mostly from squares B2, C3 and D3, and were identified by Dr. Ken Aplin at CSIRO Wildlife Division in Canberra. He found cow/horse remains only on the surface, while rat bones were spread throughout the deposit. No *Rattus exulans* bones were found, but extinct rat species occurred through all layers. Also present are freshwater turtles, marine fish (the most numerous bones), rats, bats and birds (table 4.8 to table 4.12).

Fish bones occurred from spit 1 down to spit 5 in square B2, from spit 1 down to spit 3 in square C3, only in spit 2 in square D3, and in spit 1 in square E4. Individual species cannot be identified, but all are medium to large sized fish (more than 1-2 kg). Fresh water chelonid turtle occurred only once, in spit 5 in square B2. There is an endemic long-necked turtle species on Rote, *Chelodina* sp.

Rat remains occur in all stratigraphic layers in squares C3, D3 and B2, while in square F4 they only occur in the upper layer. In square B2, rat bones occur from spit 1 down to spit 8, in square C3 from spit 1 down to spit 13, and in square D3 down to spit 11 (table 4.8). From the jaws and teeth, Aplin thinks that these bones belong to so-far undescribed species of quite large and robust rodents, estimated to weigh about 200-300 grams, that could relate to members of the Australian *Rattus sordidus* complex. He is also certain that these *Rattus* remains from Pia Hudale are different from the giant *Rattus* species found on Flores and Sumba.

This robust *Rattus* species is more common in spits 1-6 than in spits 7–15. 180 specimens from all squares combined were found in the upper layers, and only 36 in the lower. Most identified specimens are unburnt, and only three were burnt. Because terrestrial meat must have been scarce prior to the Neolithic in Rote, it is likely that these rats were consumed by the Pia Hudale occupants, just as many people eat rice field rats in Southeast Asia today.

27

spit	B/U	number of specimens	weight
1	U	13	2
1	B	1	0.1
2	U	17	5.1
3	U	21	4
4	U	16	5
5	U	8	1
8	U	1	0.1

Table 4.8.a: distribution of rat bones, square B2, Pia Hudale (B: Burn; U: Unburn)

spit	B/U	number of specimens	weight
1	U	5	2
3	U	11	2
4	U	3	0.2
4	B	1	0.1
5	U	10	3
5	B	3	0.5
6	U	12	3
8	U	9	1.5
9	U	2	0.2
11	U	5	0.2
13	U	2	0.2

Table 4.8.b: distribution of rat bones, square C3, Pia Hudale (B: Burn; U: Unburn)

spit	B/U	number of specimens	weight
2	U	12	3
3	U	1	0.2
4	U	5	3
5	U	5	3
6	U	11	4
7	U	3	0.5
9	U	2	1
11	U	3	1
11	U	8	1

Table 4.8.c: distribution of rat bones, square D3, Pia Hudale (B: Burn; U: Unburn)

spit	B/U	number of specimens	weight
2	U	3	1
5	U	1	0.5
1	U	1	0.1
2	U	6	3.1

Table 4.8.d: distribution of rat bones, square E4 & F4, Pia Hudale (B: Burn; U: Unburn)

spit	square	B/U	N	weight (gm)	remarks
1	B2	U	10	3	ribs
1	B2	B	1	0.1	long bone shaft fragments
2	B2	U	9	5	long bone shaft fragments
3	B2	U	9	5	long bone shaft fragments
3	B2	B	1	0.1	long bone shaft fragments
4	B2	U	11	3	lower jaw fragment of a small *Pteropus* sp.
8	B2	U	1	0.5	shaft fragment
1	C3	U	5	3.2	long bone shaft fragments
1	C3	B	4	1	long bone shaft fragments
1	C3	C	2	1	long bone shaft fragments
3	C3	U	10	4	shaft fragments
4	C3	U	2	0.5	shaft fragments
4	C3	U	9	3	long bone fragments
5	C3	U	8	1	long bone fragments
5	C3	B	4	0.5	long bone fragments
6	C3	U	19	4	long bone fragments
8	C3	U	6	2	long bone fragments
8	C3	B	1	0.1	long bone fragments
11	C3	U	1	0	long bone shaft fragments
1	D3	U	1	1	long bone shaft fragments
2	D3	U	9	5	long bone shaft fragments
2	D3	B	4	1	long bone shaft fragments
6	D3	U	1	0.1	long bone shaft fragments
7	D3	U	3	0.3	long bone shaft fragments
2	E4	U	1	1.5	dentary of large *Pteropus* sp.
1	F4	U	3	0.5	long bone shaft fragments

Table 4.9: Distribution of bat bones per spit, all squares Pia Hudale

site/square	shell artefacts	provenance	description, information
square B2	1 shell bead	spit 3	round, flat, with one hole (figure 4.3)
square B2	1 shell pendant	spit 5	fish shape pendant (figure 4.3)
square C3	2 shell bead	spit 3	round, flat with one hole
square C3	3 shell ornaments	spit1	modified gafrarium shell (figure 4.4)
square C3	1 shell scraper	spit 1	unmodified anadara shell
square C3	1 perforated oliva	spit 5	unmodified (figure 4.3)
square E4	1 ornament	spit 2	squre preform for a pendant
square E4	1 shell scaper	surface	denticulated
square F4	1 perforated oliva	spit 1	unmodified

Table 4.10: Distribution of possible bat bones, all squares, Pia Hudale

spit	square	B/U	N	Weight gm	description
1	B2	B	1	0.1	spine of medium sized fish
2	B2	U	1	0.1	spine of medium sized fish
3	B2	U	3	0.5	spine fragments
4	B2	U	2	1	cranial fragments
5	B2	U	1	0.3	humerus of fresh water turtle
1	C3	B	1	0.1	spine of medium sized fish
1	C3	U	1	0.2	vertebra of medium sized fish
2	C3	B	1	0.1	vertebra of medium sized fish
3	C3	U	1	0.5	vertebra of medium sized fish
2	C3	B	1	0.5	vertebra of medium sized fish
1	E4	U	1	0.1	spine of medium sized fish
2	F4	U	1	1	spine of medium-large sized fish

Table 4.11: Distribution of fish and freshwater turtle bones, Pia Hudale

spit	square	B/U	No	Weight	description
1	B2	U	2	0.4	two molar fragments of cow/horse
0	C3	U	1	1	shaft fragments of large mammals
2	D3	U	1	1	distal tibiotarsus of medium-sized bird
3	D3	U	2	1.5	vertebra and proximal femur of medium-sized bird
5	D3	U	2	2	distal tibiotarsus and coracoid of medium-sized bird
9	D3	U	1	1	medium-sized vertebrate
2	F4	U	4	9	medium-large vertebrate
2	F4	B	1	3	proximal ulna fragments of deer?

Table 4.12: Distribution of animal bone in Pia Hudale

spit	B/U	N	weight
1	U	16	4
1	C	1	0.1
2	B	2	1
2	U	29	7
3	U	15	5
3	B	1	0.1
4	U	23	14
5	U	21	5
8	U	4	1

Table 4.13: Distribution of possible terrestrial vertebrates in Pia Hudale, Square B2.

spit	B/U	N	weight
1	-	-	-
2	U	9	2
2	B	3	0.5
6	U	3	0.8
7	U	4	0.5
7	B	1	0.1
8	U	1	0.1

Table 4.14: Distribution of terrestrial vertebrates in Pia Hudale, Square D3.

spit	B/U	N	weight
1	U	2	0.8
4	-	-	-
5	U	2	0.8

Table 4.15: Distribution of terrestrial vertebrates in Pia Hudale, Square E4.

spit	B/U	N	weight
0	U	1	1
0	B	1	0.2
1	U	26	2
1	B	3	0.1
2	U	7	1.5
2	B	1	0.1
3	U	23	3
4	U	20	1.5
4	B	4	0.1
5	U	30	4
5	B	6	0.2
6	U	21	2
6	B	1	0.1
6	C	2	0.1
7	B	1	0.1
8	U	13	1.5
8	-	-	-
9	U	1	0.2
10	-	-	-
11	U	7	1.5
11	B	1	0.1
12	-	-	-
13	U	8	0.2

Table 4.16: Distribution of terrestrial vertebrates in Pia Hudale, Square C3.
B/U = Burn/Unburn

Small rats such as *Rattus exulans* are absent in this site.

Bird remains occur mostly in the upper layer. From the more complete bones, Ken Aplin states that all are of chicked-sized birds, and probably of native origin.

Bats are the most common animals in the deposits and occur in all spits. There are at least two and possibly three species, probably including *Pteropus* or *Acerodon* fruit bat species that roost in trees/mangrove. Since these bat species do not live on the cave naturally, they were presumably brought into Pia Hudale for human consumption.

The occurrence of domesticated animal close to the surface of the site is certain, based on the presence of two molar fragments of bovid or horse. It is likely that the shaft fragment of a large mammal found on the surface belonged to a domesticated animal too. One needle-sized bone point was found in spit 4 in square C3 in Pia Hudale. This is the same spit that produced the shell pendant in square B2.

Shell remains

All molluscan remains recovered are classified into shell artefacts and food shells. The variety of shell artefacts in Pia Hudale can be seen in figure 4.3 and 4.4 below.

Shell artefacts

Several ornaments and one shell tool were recovered. One shell bead and one fish-shaped shell pendant were found in square B2, spits 3 and 5 respectively (figure 4.3). One shell artefact (figure 4.3, third from left) that looks like a square preform for a pendant was found in square E4 spit 2. Two shell beads were found in square C3 spit 3 and three leaf shaped *Gafrarium* shells, that might have functioned as ornaments (figure 4.4), were found in square C3 spit 1. Fish shaped shell pendant was also found in Leang Rundung (Flores) (Heekeren 1972:146) but there is no picture to compare with shell pendant recovered from Pia Hudale.

Non-artefactual shell remains

Throughout occupancy, at least 17 different shell families were brought into Pia Hudale, consisting of freshwater, mangrove and marine shells (Table 2 in appendix). Despite the possibility that every square had been disturbed by burial activities, there seems to be a pattern of shell distribution. Thiaridae freshwater shells were the most common species brought to the shelter. Since their first appearance in spit 12, the numbers increased dramatically and reached a peak in spit 1. The second most common species were Veneridae, from both tidal mudflat and sandy

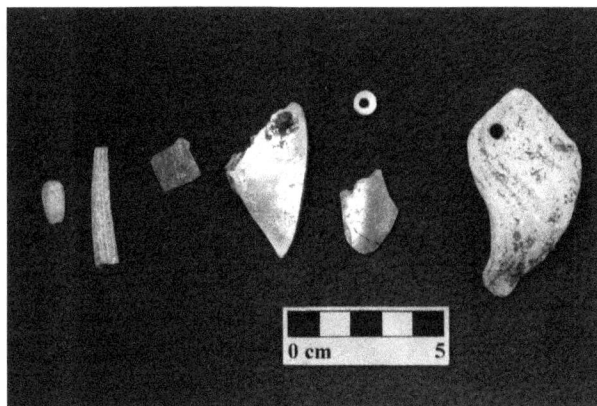

*Figure 4.3 Shell bead and shell ornaments
from Pia Hudale*

Figure 4.4 Shaped Gafrarium shells

intertidal habitats. These preferences are clear from the results of both absolute abundance (MNI) and relative abundance analyses (figures 4.5 and 4.6).

In the earlier period of occupancy (around 13,000 years ago), represented by the shells from spits 15 to 12, only two shell families, each consisting of one species, were found in the site. These are Neritidae (*Nerita undata*) and Thiaridae (*Melanoides funiculus*), from upper reef and freshwater

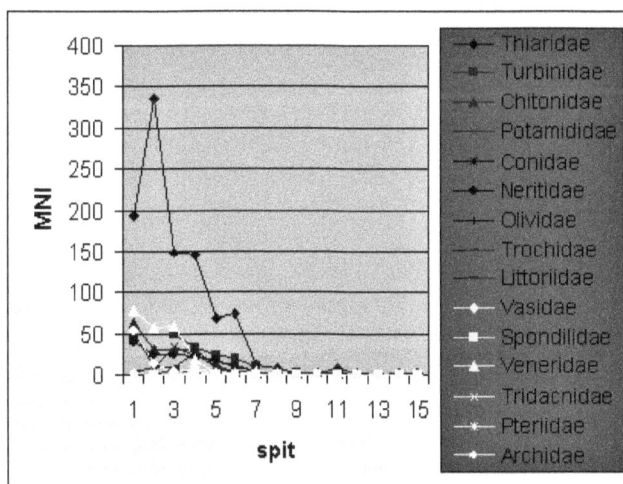

*Figure 4.5: Absolute abundance of shell families,
all squares combined, per spit. Pia Hudale*

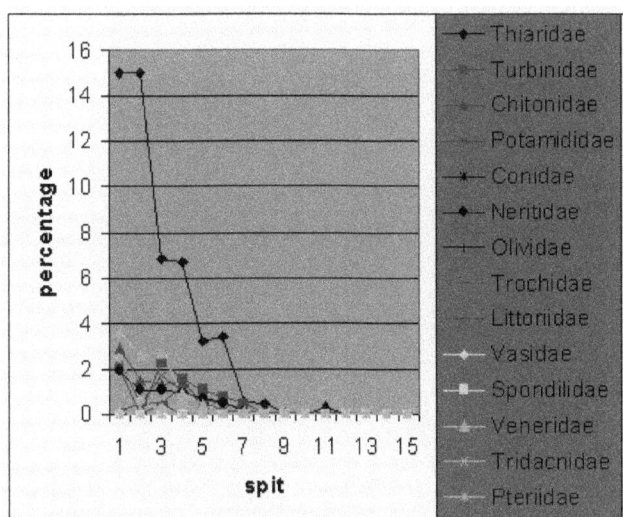

*Figure 4.6: Relative abundance of shell family,
All squares combined, per spit. Pia Hudale*

habitats respectively.

Toward the end of the earlier period of occupancy, represented by shells from spits 11 to 7, new species of Veneridae, Chitonidae and Turbinidae were brought into the site. All are represented by only one to two individuals, except for *Melanoides funiculus*, which reaches 7 individuals in spit 11. During this period, tidal mudflat/mangrove species seem to have been exploited, although the number is small in spit 7.

In the later period of occupancy, the range of shell species brought to the site varies even more, even though the layers that represent this period of occupancy have been disturbed. For example, Veneridae, which first appear in spit 7, are represented there by only one species, *Gafrarium pectinatum*. In the later period of occupancy, two new species appear in spit 5 - *Tapes litteratus* and *Tapes hiantina*. The Neritidae family was represented by only two species in the lower layer (*Nerita undata* and *Nerita albicilla*), but in spit 6 and above there are four species of Neritidae, with the addition of *Nerita planospira* and *Nerita costata*. Freshwater Thiaridae *(Melanoides funiculus)* also show a dramatic increase in number from only 11 in spit 7 (lower level), to 332 in spit 2.

Shells from tidal mudflat/mangrove habitats also increase in number upwards. They first appear in spit 7 with only one species, *Terebralia palustris* (Potamididae). This species does not occur in spits 8 to 15, perhaps due to environmental changes on the coastline. Spit 7 then has 14 of them and they rise to 11 in spit 6 and 14 in spit 5. Apart from Potamididae, two other shell families (Veneridae and Arcidae*)* from sandy intertidal and mangrove/tidal mudflat areas seem to have become an important source of food. Veneridae first occur in spit 9 with only 1 individual. But from spit 5 upwards the numbers increase greatly, with 14 in spit 5, 8 in spit 4, 9 in spit 3, 57 in spit 2, and 79 in spit 1 and on the surface.

Chitonidae occur from the earlier period, although not as early as Neritidae. They first appear in spit 11 but never become very important above, peaking in spit 4 with 21 individuals.

Turbinidae were not much exploited in the earlier period. Only one occurs in spit 9, and then 9 in spit 7. From spit 6 to the surface, this family increases significantly, with 24 in spit 5, 39 in spit 4, 34 in spit 3, 51 in spit 2, and 43 in spit 1 and on the surface.

Strombidae were not exploited at all in the earlier period, and first appear in spit 5 with 8 individuals, 19 in spit 4, 3 in spit 3, 10 in spit 2, and 6 in spit 1 and on the surface.

Trochidae appeared in spit 11 with only 1 individual, then appears again in spit 6 (1 individual), 8 in spit 5, 16 in spit 4, 10 in spit 3, 9 in spit 2 and 3 in spit 1 and on the surface.

Arcidae (*Anadara granosa* and *Anadara alinea*) first appear in spit 8, and then occur from spit 6 to the surface. Numbers increase steadily and peak in spits 1 and 2, where they are represented by 54 and 56 individuals respectively.

Littoridae also only occur in the later period of occupancy, in spit 3 with 8 individuals. Other families such as Olividae, Vasidae, Conidae and Pteriidae only occur rarely in spits 1 and 2, suggesting that they were brought to the cave not for consumption but for manufacturing purposes. One *Oliva* shell was found with a hole, but it is not clear if it was purposefully produced.

Examining the distribution of shells found in Pia Hudale, it can be inferred that the number of families exploited increased over the period of occupancy, from only one species of one family in the earliest stage to 14 shell families in the later period of occupancy. Significant increases in Thiaridae and Potamididae in the later period of occupancy suggest that they became favourite shellfish in the diet, and also that the mangrove habitats where these shell families lived were becoming easier to exploit and perhaps more extensive. In the later period the tidal mudflat and mangrove shells became much more important, possibly reflecting Holocene sea level rise and the progressive drowning of shallow coastal environments.

Stone artefact analysis

A huge number of flaked stone artefacts (a total of 18,938) were recovered from the 5 squares excavated in Pia Hudale. Only those from squares B2, C3 and D3 were examined and 1,500 pieces were analysed quantitatively. Those from squares E4 and F4 were analysed only qualitatively. Except for hammerstone, chert was the only raw material used in Pia Hudale, the most common chert being yellow.

Non-retouched utilised flakes

The utilised flakes from Pia Hudale assemblage are classified as in the other sites.

The distribution of stone artefacts in the upper analytical level is very dense, suggesting that the site was used more intensively in the later period of occupancy. This may relate to the location of the sites increasingly closer to marine resource.

Glossed flakes

Only 14 glossed flakes were recovered from Pia Hudale (see table 4.17). Some of the glossed flakes are drawn in figure

4. 7). All came from the upper analytical level, 12 from stratigraphic layer 1 and two from stratigraphic layer 2. Four of the items are bladelets. Maximum dimensions of the glossed pieces vary from 28 to 40 mm. Commonly, the spread of gloss is only on a small portion of the working edge, and generally is more intense on one side suggesting a scraper action. Only two flakes have gloss on both sides, suggesting use as knives.

Some flakes with gloss have clear striations. On 12 they are transverse to the working edges, suggesting a scraper mode of action. Probably, two of them were used for whittling, as indicated by the forms of their edges, distributions of gloss and types of micro edge scars. Scalar terminations of micro scars suggest that these flakes were used to scrape soft materials which contain silica.

Other signs of use wear

Thirty-seven stone flakes (including broken flakes) from Pia Hudale have edge damage. These flakes were found from the surface down to spit 5 (25 cm below the surface), but most were found from spit 3. As with the glossed flakes, most were used in a scraper mode of action. These flakes are varied, with percussion lengths between 21.51 and 56.51 mm. The forms of the utilised edges vary. There is a tendency for concave and convex working edges to have higher edge angles than straight working edges. Flakes with straight working edges commonly have micro scar edge damage and small scars less than 1 mm in size, with feather terminations and one or two small shallow step terminations. Step terminations are more common on concave and convex working edges, but the sizes are also small, not bigger than 2 mm.

Some of these flakes have striations with a uniform orientation, suggesting that these simple flake tools had a single function, most likely used once and then thrown away. Reuse of the same flake, even for the same function, would have resulted in traces of slightly different orientations of the striations.

Stone manufacturing technology
Retouched flakes

A total of 61 retouched flakes was recovered, 31 complete and the rest broken. Only two came from the lower analytical level (one from spit 7 and another from spit 8, while the rest occurred from spit 6 up to the surface, with a

Level of analysis	spits	retouched	unmodified	unmodified	Waste	core	all stone
		flake	glossed flake	used flake	Flake		artefacts
Lower	7---15	59	—	—	1884	8	1951
Upper	1,2,3,4,5,6	2	14	37	16860	74	16987
	total	61	14	37	18744	82	18938

Table 4.17: Distribution of stone artefacts, Pia Hudale squares B2, C3 and D3

concentration in spits 2 and 3.

Retouched pieces from the Pia Hudale assemblage can be classified into three major groups :

1. Flakes that have retouch only on the working edge, probably for resharpening.

2. Retouch applied finely on the edge to correct minor irregulaties of the natural shape of the flakes. One flake in Pia Hudale has this type of retouch on its distal edge, most likely to improve the sharpness of its hinge termination.

3. Retouch that covers not only the edge of the flake, but also spreads to the middle. This type of retouch was most likely applied for shaping purposes, and occurred only on the surface of the site. Two items

clearly show hafting modification, and two others have bifacial retouch. Each has large retouch scars which spread to the middle, giving the impression that they are truly bifacial like a hand axe (figure 4.8).

Only two rejuvenation flake edges were found in the deposit, suggesting that rejuvenation was not a common practice to resharpen the working edge. Rather, resharpening the working edge was carried out by applying retouch.

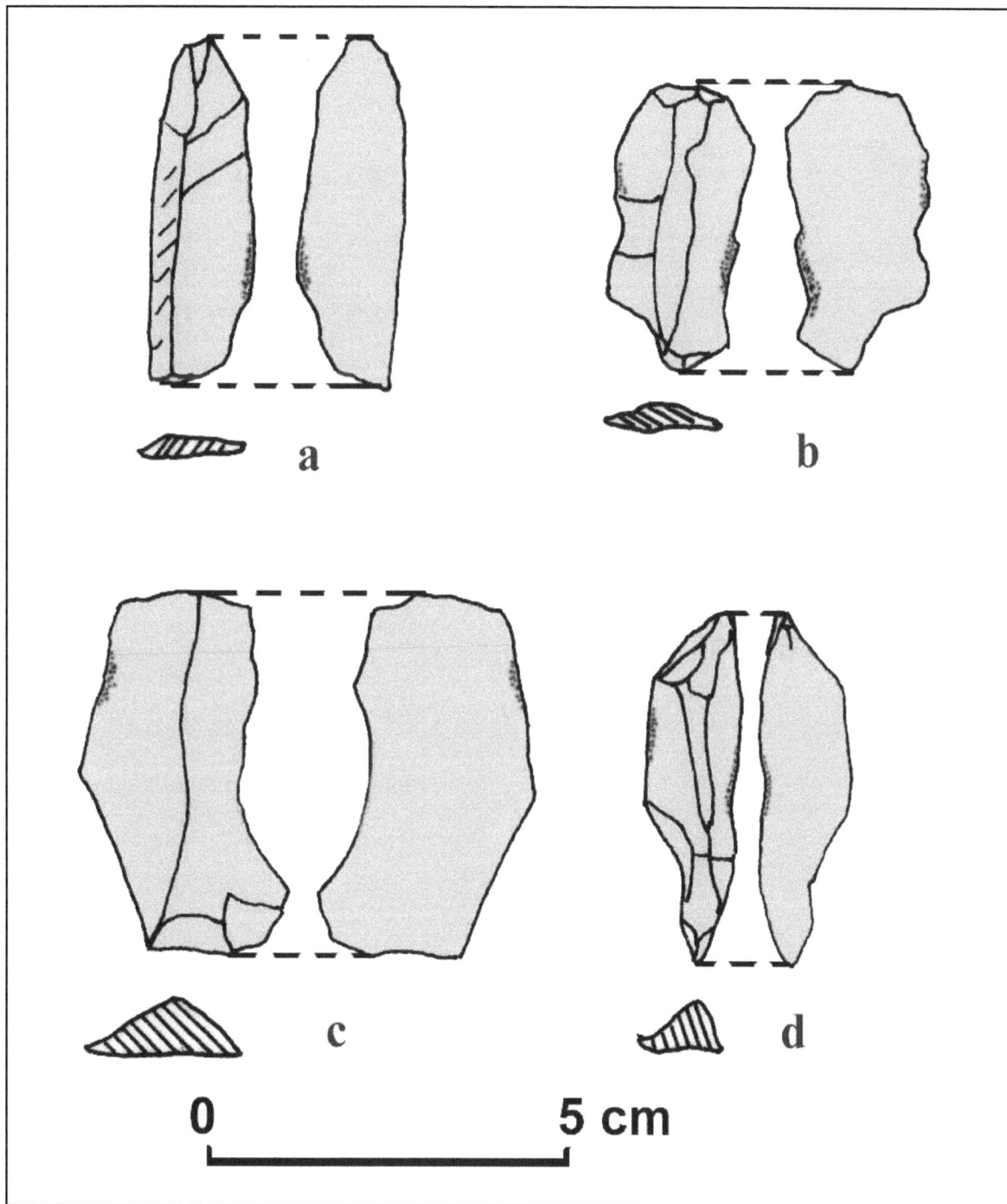

Figure 4.7: Glossed flakes from Pia Hudale, all from spit 2
a from surface; b from square B2 spit 8; c from square B2 spit 6; d from surface. Stipples show the glossed area.

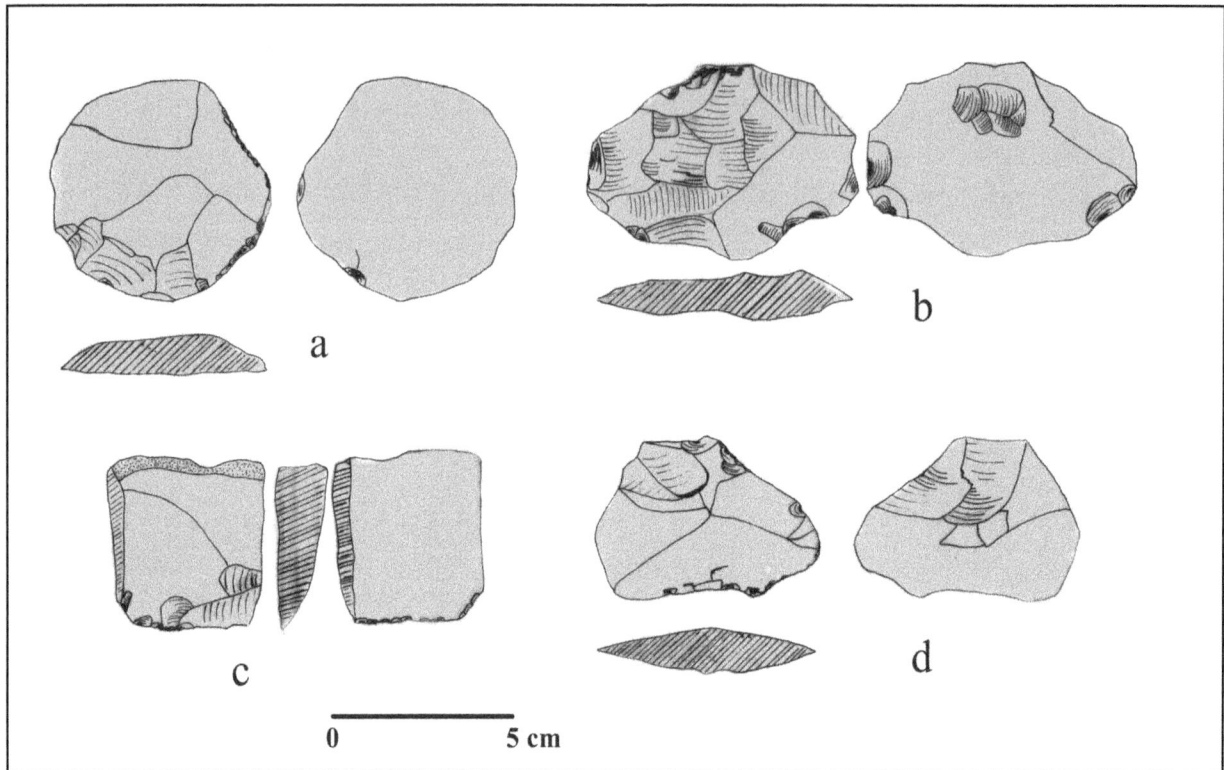

Figure 4.8: Selected stone artefacts showing 'shaping retouch' from the Pia Hudale.
a with unificial retouch; b,d with bifacial retouch; c adze-like form. a, b, c. surface finds, d. from spit 1 square D3

More of the first type of retouched pieces were found than other types of retouched pieces, and most clustered in layer 1, with occasional examples found below (see table 4.17 above). Eleven flakes have the first type of retouch applied on their distal and side edges, one has it all around its edges except for the distal end. 27 are retouched along their long edges, seven are retouched on two sides, and one flake has two clusters of retouch along a single edge.

Mode of reduction

Mode of reduction can be inferred from core characters found in the deposit. A total of 82 cores recovered from the Pia Hudale excavation. All cores characters indicate that the mode of reduction is parallel core reduction (following Andrefsky 1998). Most cores are of multi-platform type. Among the cores found, 74 were recovered from the upper layer (from spit 1 down to spit 6), and the remaining 8 from the lower layer (spits 15 to 7). Only 5 cores have a single platform, and these still retain most of their cortex on their surfaces, which gives the impression that the reduction process from these single platform cores was unfinished, or that the flakes detached from these cores were not suitable for use as tools.

From these cores can also be reconstructed the sizes of the original nodules - average dimension would have been about 6 cm, with a range from 3.5 cm to 8 cm. On average, the core size (measured as the largest dimension) from the Pia Hudale assemblage is 28 mm. Comparison of the mean maximum dimension for 74 cores from the upper layer (from the surface down to spit 6) with that for the sample of only 8 cores from the lower layer (from spit 7 down to spit 15) does not indicate any statistically significant difference. However, the occurrence of very small rounded cores measuring between 20 and 29 mm only in the upper layer suggests two possibilities. Either the core reduction process was more intense in the later period of occupancy, or smaller nodules were used in the later period than in the earlier one.

Examining the sizes of the last flakes to be detached from the cores, it can be inferred that multiplatform cores were reduced until the flakes were about 27 mm long, after which cores were discarded.

The abundance of multiplatform chert cores in Pia Hudale, some very small and rounded, gives a strong indication that stone tool manufacture in this site emphasized the production of flake tools. Clearly, the core reduction process was intended for flake production, whether they were to be modified further or not. Even though some rather big bifacial tools and adzes were found on the surface of the site, from the technology it is apparent that they were made from flake blanks rather than from pebbles (figure 4.8 above).

Debitage analysis

Flakes which do not carry signs of use wear are considered as debitage, which consisted of flakes (including broken flakes) and flake shatter. A total of 1500 flakes of varied size was measured. In the upper layer (spits 1-6), the debitage is bigger than in the lower layer, being 40.67 mm in average dimension, while in the lower layer the debitage size is 21.91 mm on average. The data violate the stringent assumption of an independent group t-test, so it is decided to perform a Mann-Whitney U-test (non-parametric test) (Coakes and Steed 1999, 202-203). The result of Mann-Whitney U-test equivalent to the independent groups T-tests shows that there is significant difference here, in flake sizes between the lower and upper layers.

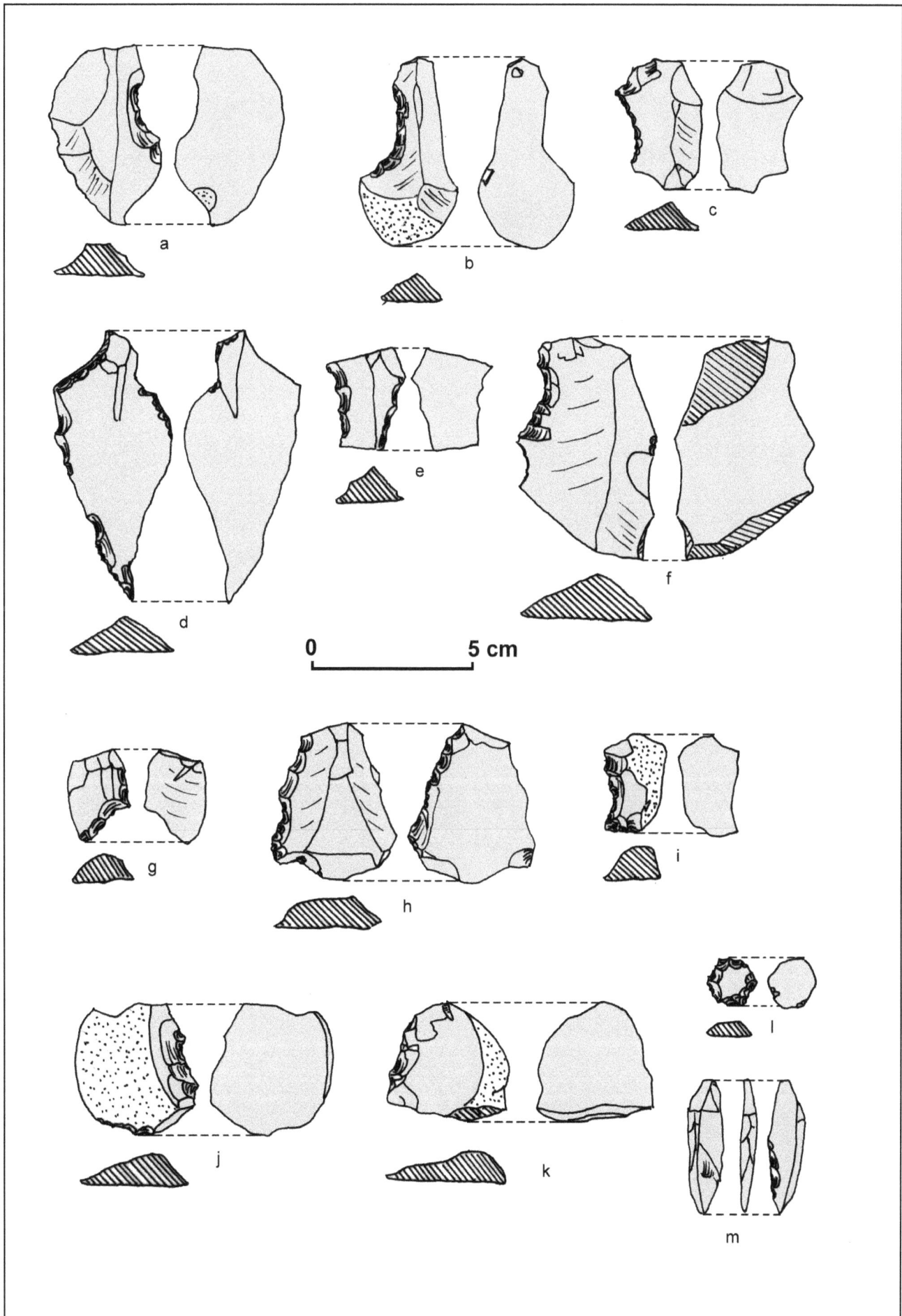

Figure 4.9: Retouched pieces, Pia Hudale. A. from spit 3, b. from spit 1, c. from spit 2, d from surface, e. from spit 1, f. from spit 6., g. from spit 6, h. from spit 1, i. from spit 6, j. from spit 3, k. from spit 4, l from spit 2, m from spit 1

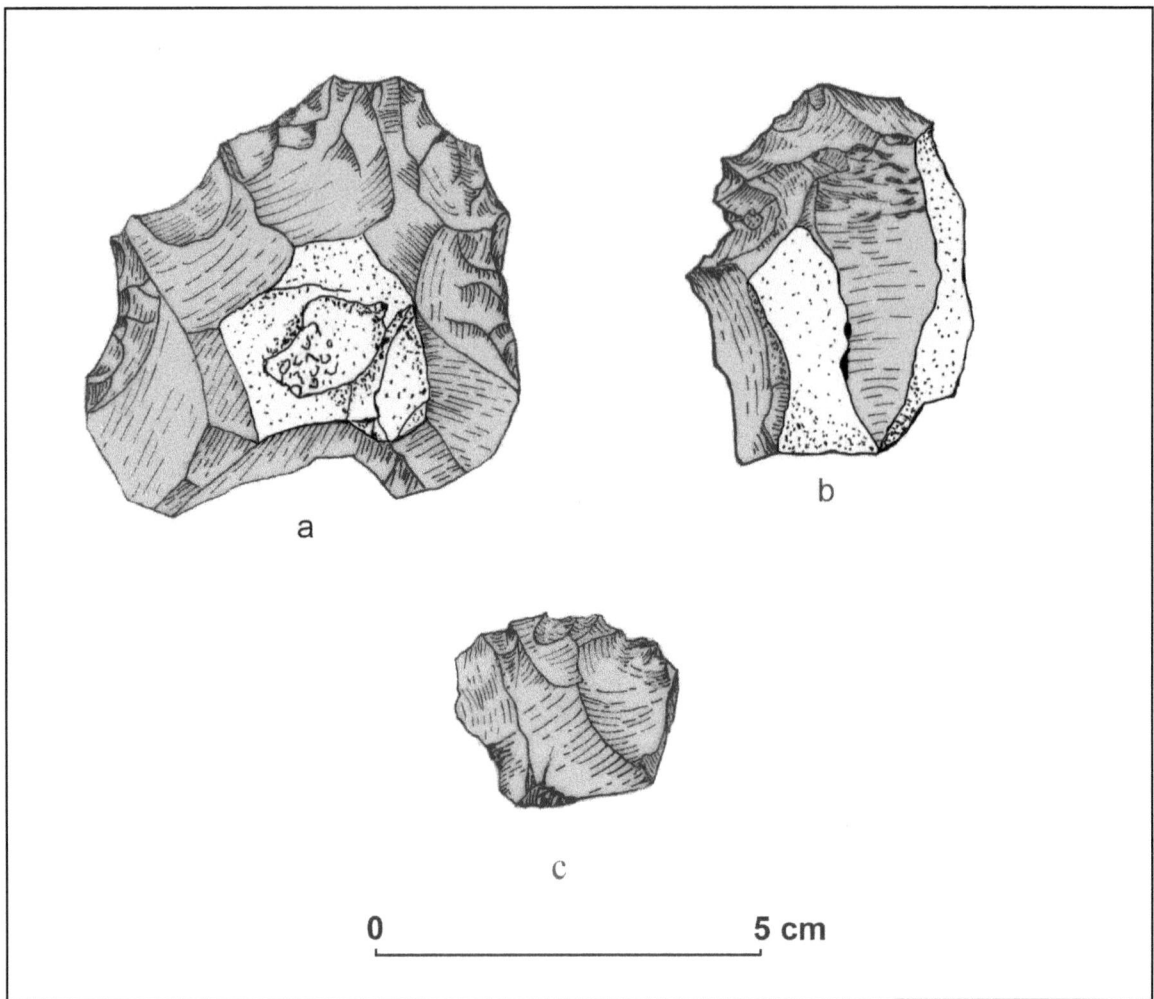

Figure 4.10: Cores found in Pia Hudale.
a from square D3 spit 5; b from square D3 spit 3; c from square D3 spit 6

Especially in flake length, and platform thickness (table 4.18).

None of the debitage found in either layer indicates the use of true blade technology. Only a small number of flakes (199 out of 1500 flakes measured or 13.26%) have an elongation index of more than 2 indicating a length more than twice the width. Moreover, only 7 of these blades have parallel sides. Indeed, short flakes are the most characteristic item from Pia Hudale.

In the lower layer, apart from the small flakes, more than half the debitage consists of flake shatter and other small debris. Flakes of larger size were evidently already taken out for tools, leaving only flakes of very small size which were not suitable for further use. Several cores found in the lower

layer suggest that core reduction processes to produce flakes did take place occasionally, but production was not very intensive.

Some flakes with 75 to 100% of cortex on their dorsal surfaces do occur in the lower layers, although in very small number compared with those occurring in the upper layers. The occurrence of these cortexed flakes in the lower layers implies that the first stage of core reduction also took place in the site at that time.

In the lower layer, apart from the small flakes, more than half the debitage consists of flake shatter and other small debris. Flakes of larger size were evidently already taken out for tools, leaving only flakes of very small size which were not suitable for further use. Several cores found in the lower

Test Statistics[a]

	LENGTH	WIDTH	PLATWIDT	PLATTHIC
Mann-Whitney U	85125.000	94716.500	93880.500	75293.500
Wilcoxon W	956985.0	105156.5	955208.50	926153.5
Z	-2.187	-.127	-.660	-4.386
Asymp. Sig. (2-tailed)	.029	.899	.509	.000

a. Grouping Variable: UNIT

Table 4.18: Mann-Whitney U Test for flakes recovered
from level of analysis /unit 1(lower) and 2 (upper)

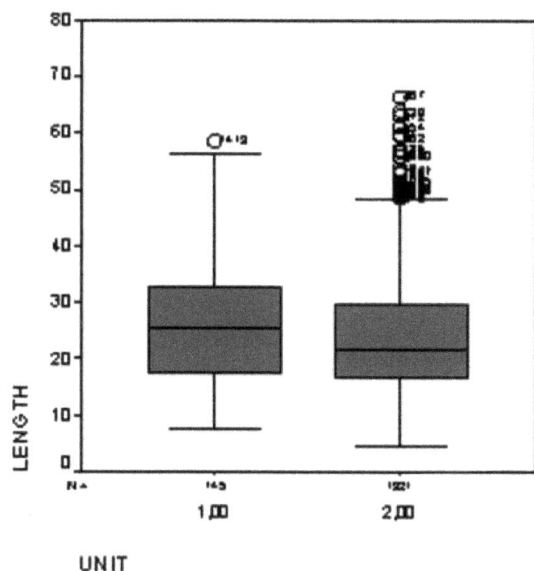

Figure 4.11: Box plot showing the spread of flake length recovered in level of analysis / unit 1 and 2, Pia Hudale

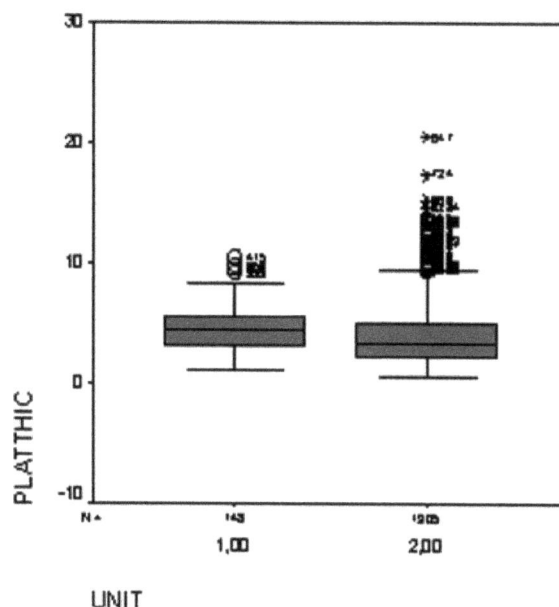

Figure 4.12: Box plot showing the spread of platform thickness of flakes recovered in level of analysis / unit 1 and unit 2, Pia Hudale

layer suggest that core reduction processes to produce flakes did take place occasionally, but production was not very intensive.

Some flakes with 75 to 100% of cortex on their dorsal surfaces do occur in the lower layers, although in very small. The occurrence of these cortexed flakes in the lower layers implies that the first stage of core reduction also took place in the site at that time. This is because on Rote, chert often occurs in boulder sizes. It is likely that , people in the past had to flake the material at the sourcing area and brought nodule size chert to the shelter. As a consequence, only a few flake retain cortex.

Pottery Analysis

Pottery form and surface decoration

Only three sherds were recovered from this site during excavation. Two are red-slipped, one being part of a cooking pot rim with a simple lip, 2.3 mm thick, found in F4 at 10 cm below the surface. It is difficult to reconstruct the vessel size since the sherd is very small. The other red-slipped sherd is a body part only. Another potsherd found in spit 1 in square D3 is a non-slipped part of a globular vessel body.

Several sherds were recovered from the surface of Pia Hudale, including three red-slipped. One surface find outside the shelter is a shoulder of a cooking pot, with simple shell-

impressed decoration and red slip. All other surface sherds have plain surfaces without red slip. There are no carinations, as on Sawu. Today, all cooking pots made in Oenitas Village have globular bodies and some have red slip.

Pottery sourcing analysis of Pia Hudale pottery is presented together with pottery from other sites in chapter VII.

3. Summary

Several kinds of evidence recovered from excavation suggest that Pia Hudale has been disturbed, especially in the upper part of the deposit. According to C14 dating from the lowermost deposit, the site was occupied from at least 11,160 ± 220 uncal BP. Since the initial occupation, the occupants used mostly chert to produce simple types of tools. Retouch technology was only used in the later period of occupancy.

There is increased intensity of site use in the later period of occupancy, as reflected by increased numbers of stone artefacts (retouched flakes, unmodified glossed flakes, unmodified used flakes and waste flakes). Increasing intensity of site use is also reflected in the increasing MNIs for each shell species. The exploitation area was becoming more varied in the later phases of occupation. However, Pia Hudale seems not to have been occupied after the arrival of pottery and domesticated animals.

5

THE TONGGOBATU ROCKSHELTER COMPLEX

In the Tonggobatu rockshelter complex, two shelters were excavated - Lua Manggetek and Lua Meko (see locations on site plan, figure 5.2).

1. The Lua Manggetek Excavation

Lua Manggetek (figure 5. 1) is quite a large shelter. After grids were laid out with an orientation to 320°, one 2 X 1 metre trench (C3D3) and one 1 X 1 metre square (F3) were opened for excavation. Several squares, closer to the outer slope rather than to the back wall, were then selected for excavation (the area close to the back wall is occupied by an outcrop of bedrock). On the surface of Lua Manggetek, several manuports and stone artefacts were collected.

Initially, square C3 was dug in 5 cm spits until spit 6 was reached, 30 cm below the surface. But from the observed stratigraphy there was a strong indication that this area had been disturbed, as shown by loose deposits with quantities of leaf litter. Because of this, it was decided to open up square D3 to see if intact deposits could be found. Both of the squares (C3D3) were dug together to bedrock, which was reached in spit 13, 65 cm below the surface.

The excavation of square F3 was carried out in 5 cm spits until spit 9, 45 cm below the surface. After reaching archaeologically-sterile deposits in spit 7, almost the whole area of the square was already filled by sloping bedrock.

The stratigraphy of Manggetek

The excavation uncovered several stratigraphic layers as shown in figure 5.3.

Layer 1. This consists of very loose goat dung and dried leaves with almost no soil, about 10 cm in maximum thickness. Microscopic analysis shows that this layer contains tiny shell fragments, stone micro-debitage, dried leaves and roots.

Layer 2. This consists of loose brown (10 YR 4/3) dark soil with goat dung but no dried leaves, 10 cm in maximum thickness. It is characterized by much limestone rubble measuring about 10 to 15 cm in size. Microscopic analysis of the sediment again reveals stone micro-debitage and tiny shell fragments.

Layer 3 is dark grayish brown (10 YR 4/3) and contains fewer stone artefacts. It has a maximum thickness of 12 cm. Microanalysis of this sediment reveals lots of small roots and dried leaves.

In square F3, the boundary between layers 2 and 3 cannot be recognised. This is either because the sediment has been totally disturbed, or more probably, since the surface of this square is higher, layer 2 has been eroded or has slid downslope.

Layer 4 is a dark brown (7.5 YR 3/2) sediment containing mostly sand and clay. It has a maximum thickness of 20 cm and contains no roots or dried leaves, although some dried roots were recognised during micro-sedimentary analysis.

Layer 5. This layer is the thickest, starting from 40 cm below the surface and then going down through spits 8 to 13 in trench C3D3 until bedrock, which here is almost flat. The colour of this unit is reddish brown (5 YR 4/4). Micro-sedimentary analysis reveals micro stone debitage and shell fragments.

Archaeological finds

Archaeological finds in trench C3D3 mostly consist of shells and stone artefacts with only a small number of bones. Potsherds were found at the surface down to 15 cm below the surface. Pottery was not found below that level except a single occurrence in spit 9. The densest artefacts and shells occurred from spits 1 to 8, after which the deposit becomes sparse. The archaeological finds diminish further down, but when the excavation reached spits 11 and 12, the quantity of small debitage increased significantly until spit 13, when bedrock was reached (table 5.1).

Square F3 produced a number of small sherds down to spit 9, 45 cm below the surface. One of the sherds (in spit 6) was red slipped. Bones and charcoal were found at the same level. Most stone artefacts and non-artefactual shell were found down to spit 5 (table 5.2).

In terms of vertical distribution, archaeological finds are most concentrated in layers 1 (goat dung, sub surface), 2 and 3 in trench C3D3. They consist mostly of marine shells, especially *Anadara sp.*, and flaked stone artefacts. Glass fragments were found at the surface only, together with non red-slipped pottery. In layers 4 and 5 the archaeological finds were very sporadic, although human bone only occurs in the lower layers. A charcoal concentration was found on the bed rock. In square F3, sherds occurred in layer 1 and the upper part of layer 2. Shell artefacts were found in layer 2, but human bones were again absent in the upper layers. Generally, square F3 had lower concentrations of archaeological remains than trench C3D3.

Figure 5.1: Lua Manggetek shelter in Tonggobatu rockshelter complex, Tuanatuk, Rote

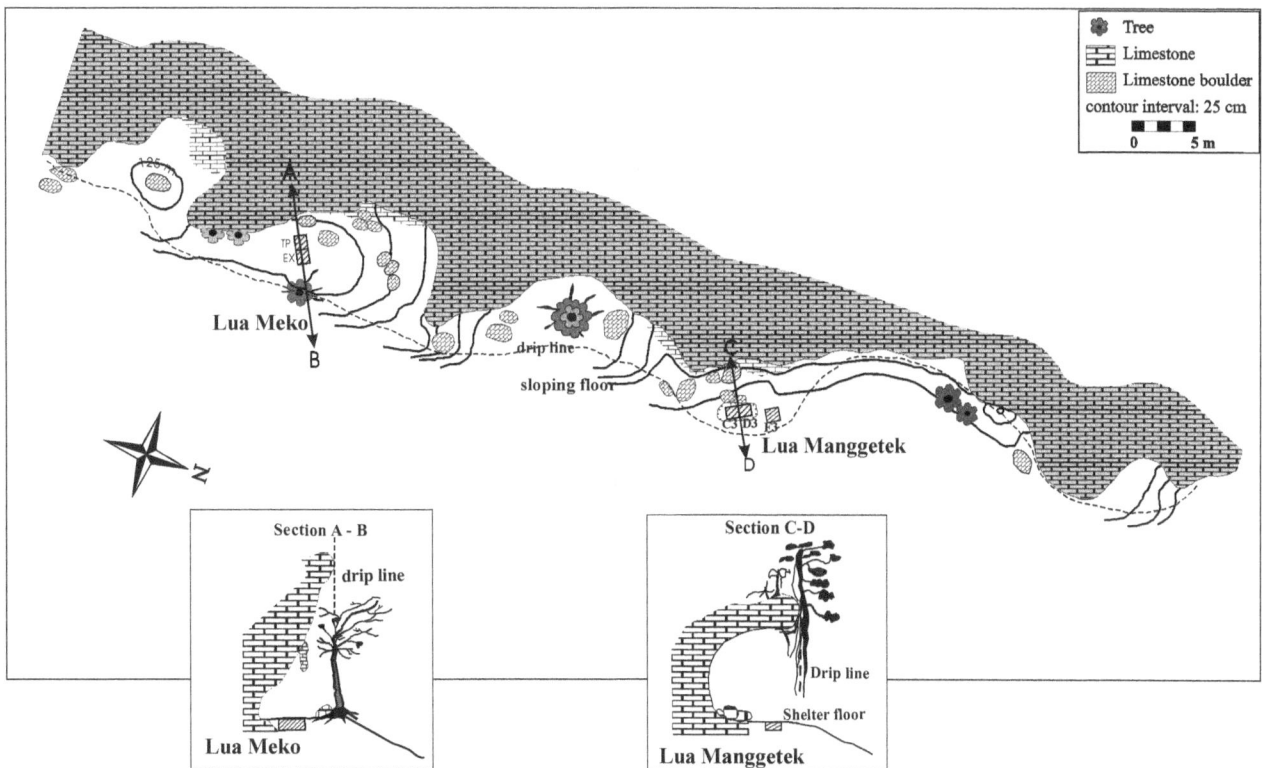

Figure 5.2: Plan and section of the Tonggobatu rockshelter complex

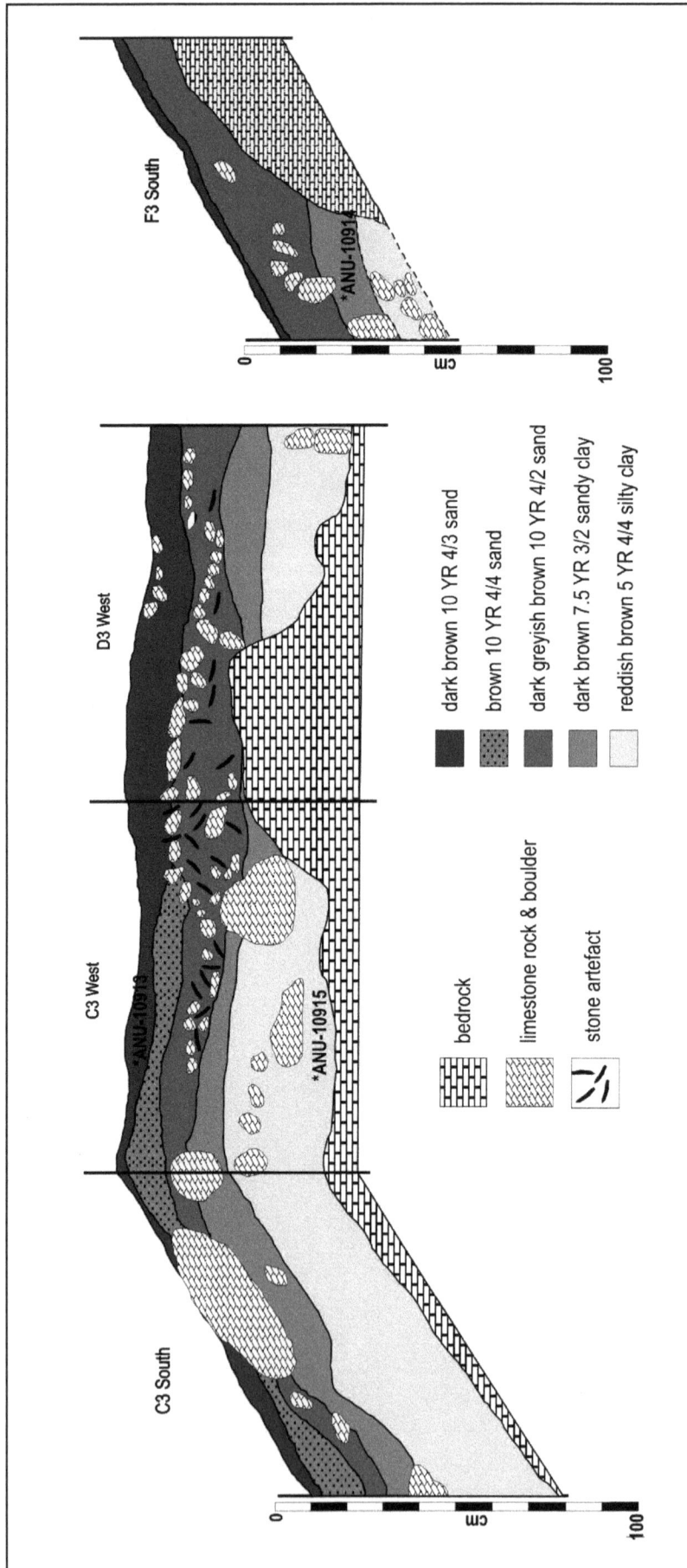

Figure 5.3 Section of the trench C3-D3 and square F3 Lua Manggetek

spit	0		1		2		3		4		5		6		7		8		9		10		11		12		13	
Material	no	gr	no	gr	no	gr	no	gr	no	gr	no	gr	no	gr	no	gr	no	gr	no	gr	no	gr	no	gr	no	gr	no	gr
pottery	6	40	7	10			6	17											1	5								
stone artefacts:																												
hammer stone															1				1									
cores	4	85	7	85	18	700	9	230	6	160	1	50	3	175	3	165	1	45					4	85			1	
all debitage & tools			81	1080	80	115	128	1185	130	1235	430	625	73	400	529	855	480	1080	559	580	133	440	430	550	717	802	1030	505
shells:																												
shell bead			1	0,5			2	2																				
perforated oliva	1	3																										
shell tool											1	3																
non-artefactual shell*			45	275	33	280	16	135	7	80	27	165	6	165	24	50	19	90	10	5	6	20	15	50	64	215	89	150
other mollusc																												
human remains																												
bone			4	244											17	90	4	78	9	21	2	2	2	10	37	20	8	20
animal bones	3	2									1	6					1	3	9	10			2	2	8	4	2	0,2
plant seed																												

Table 5.1 Distribution of arcaheological finds in Trench C3D3, Lua Manggetek, Tonggobatu complex

spit	0		1		2		3		4		5		6		7		8		9	
Material	no	gr	no	gr	no	gr	no	gr	no	gr	no	gr	no	gr	no	gr	no	gr	no	gr
pottery					1	2							1	2	1	2	1		1	3
stone artefacts:																				
cores					1	100					5	125								
all debitage & tools			202	500	12	180	22	245	32	255	14	125	8	10	5	15				
shells:																				
non-artefactual shell*	15	140	33	184	12	153	17	108	5	18										
human remains																				
bone											2	10			2					
animal bone													2	0,5						

Table 5.2 Distribution of arcaheological finds in square F3, Lua Manggetek, Tonggobatu complex

Chapter 5

Lab no.	spit	depth	layer	square/ trench	sample	uncalib 14C age (years BP)	Cal BP
ANU-10913	1	5 cm	1	C3D3	*Anadara sp.*	7,050±80	7980 (7910) 7826
ANU-10914	6	30 cm	3	F3	charcoal	880±180	956 (760) 660
ANU-10915	13	65 cm	5	C3D3	charcoal	13,390±430	16,580 (16,010) 15,362

Table 5.3: Carbon dating results, Lua Manggetek (Tonggobatu complex)

Radiocarbon dating of Lua Manggetek

Three samples for radiocarbon dating were submitted to the ANU laboratory. A sample of *Anadara granosa* from spit 1 in square D3 comes from the disturbed layer. A charcoal sample comes from a concentration of charcoal on the bed rock (spit 13) trench C3D3. Another charcoal sample comes from spit 6 in square F3. The results are presented in table 5.3 with calibration using the Calib 3 bidecadal 1 tree ring dataset to 9440 BC, and the coral dataset to 20,000 cal BC for ANU-10915. A marine reservoir effect substraction of 450 years was applied to the *Anadara* sample before calibration (table 5.3).

Disturbance in MGT above and including spit 6 is clearly visible in the presence of leaf litter in the deposits, although conjoin analysis of pottery does not work owing to the limited number of potsherds recovered. Conjoin analysis of flaked stone artefacts does not work either.

The occurrence of several sherds from spit 6 down to spit 9 in square F3 suggests that all the deposits in this square are disturbed. Therefore, the Manggetek cultural sequence is not judged from the sequence of archaeological finds in square F3. Compared with square F3, there is a degree of stratigraphic integrity in the lower part of trench C3D3, although a small potsherd was found in spit 9. Furthermore, the Lua Manggetek human remains found between spits 6 and 13 show regularly increasing degrees of calcification with depth (see the appendix for details). It is inferred that only the upper part of C3D3 has been disturbed, as indicated by the shell date of 7,050±80 yr BP from near the surface of the site.

As with Pia Hudale, there seems also to be here a phase of shelter usage in the Terminal Pleistocene and Early Holocene associated with C14 samples ANU 10913 and 10915, although these two dates are much further apart than those in the Pia Hudale series. Recent occupation with pottery then occurs on top of the sequence. Whether the site was occupied between ANU 10913 and 10914 is uncertain owing to the considerable degree of disturbance of the upper deposits.

For analytical purpose, spits 13 to 7 in C3D3 are grouped as the lower analytical level, and spits 6 to 1 as the upper analytical level that corresponds with a high density of stone artefacts and esturarine bivalves (*Anadara* and *Gafrarium*). Only the lower analytical level contains human

Level of analysis	spit	natural layer
Lower	7-13	5
Upper	1-6	1-4

Table 5.4: The correlations between analytical levels, spits, and natural stratigraphic layers in Lua Manggetek,

remains (table 5.4). As will be noted again below, C3D3 clearly reveals an overall stratigraphic integrity in terms of its succession of environmental markers, even though individual instances of disturbance can be noted.

2. Analysis of archaeological finds found in Lua Manggetek

Human bone remains

Human bone fragments were found in spits 6 and 7 in square F3 and from spits 7 to 13 in trench C3D3. They occurred spread out, not concentrated in one area. The condition of the bones was very fragmentary. The degree of calcification increased smoothly with depth, suggesting a stratigraphic integrity for the lower layers. The vertical distribution can be seen in Dr. Bulbeck's report. All the bone was found below the upper disturbed layer in trench C3D3 and below the pottery finds. But in square F3, human bone was found at the same level as charcoal dated to 880±180 BP, in association with red-slipped pottery.

Although no repetition of specific bones occurred, the bone fragments do not represent one individuals because there are different degrees of bone calcification. Age and stature are difficult to estimate owing to the condition of the bone, but one femur head diameter is 38.33 mm, suggesting a female individual. The junction between the head of the femur and the shaft, that could allow estimation of whether the skeleton is of mature age (above 16 years old) or younger, is unfortunately not complete.

Based on degree of calcification, it seems that there were two periods when Lua Manggetek was used as a burial place. The younger period comprises spit 6 in square F3, and the bones here represent an adult male individual. The early period corresponds to the human remains from spits 7 to 13. The remains from square F3 represent a child. Dr Bulbeck is not certain whether these older remains represent one individual or two. They could represent a male, with bones from spits 8 to 13, and a female, with bones from spits 7 to 13. However, given the lack of duplication, all of these older bones could be from one individual - an adult of uncertain sex. Extremities bones also occur frequently in the assemblages, suggesting that primary burial was practised.

Animal bones

Compared with the number of animal bones from other sites, the remains from Lua Manggetek are rather few (table 5.5). They consist of rats, bats, fish and pig, with the addition of snake. No turtle bones were found in Lua Manggetek.

Bat bones occur from the subsurface down to spit 5 and belong to fruit bats, like those from Pia Hudale and Lua

spit	square	Taxon	B/U	N	Weight (gr)	Remarks
5	C3D3	Pig	U	1	6	right dentary fragment of immature pig, no teeth
6	F3	Fish	U	1	0.1	vertebra from medium-sized fish c.20 cm-30 cm long
11	C3D3	pteropodid	U	1	1	long bone shaft fragment
12	C3D3	pteropodid	U	2	1	long bone shaft frogment
12	C3D3	Snake	U	1	0.1	vertebra of c 0.50 m long snake
12	C3D3	Murid	U	1	0.1	left humerus shaft fragment
13	C3D3	Murid	U	1	0.1	left humerus shaft fragment

Table 5.5: The distribution of animal bones in Lua Manggetek, Tonggobatu B: burn; U: unburn

Level of analysis	Spit	retouched flakes	Unmodified gloss flakes	unmodified used flakes	waste flakes	cores	all stone artefacts
Lower	7-13	2	–	–	3888	9	3899
Upper	1-6	12	4	20	1176	54	1266
Total		14	4	20	5064	63	5165

Table 5.6: The distribution of stone artefacts by analytical level in Manggetek

Meko. One snake vertebra was found close to bedrock, and belonged to a circa 0.5 m long snake.

One vertebra of fish was found in spit 6 in square F3. It is of a medium-sized marine fish, circa 20 - 30 cm long. Pig was positively identified from spit 1 in trench C3D3, and no pig bone was found below the upper zone with pottery. *Rattus exulans* is absent, as in the other sites.

The stone artefacts from Manggetek

A total of 5165 flaked stone artefacts was recovered from this site. Rates of stone artefact discard during the site occupation are difficult to establish since there is a strong indication that the deposit is disturbed.

Raw Materials

The raw materials used in Lua Manggetek mostly are chert, with minor igneous rocks. Yellowish brown and reddish brown cherts were the most frequent, with some minor white chert. Only 5 non chert stone artefacts were found, consisting of silicified sandstone and dacite. They occurred from the bottom layer of square C3D3 to the surface and consisted of one manuport, one core tool, one core, and stone flakes with very thick patination (figure 5.4).

The closest formation that contains chert is the Aitutu formation situated in the Namodale area on the northern coast of Rote (see map in chapter 1). Recent survey finds that yellow and red chert boulders are available sporadically along several river beds near Tonggobatu rock-shelter complex in Dusun Oemaulain. Chert also occurs sporadically on Rote Island. It occur as exotic blocks of various sizes in

Level of nalysis	spit	Ratio waste flakes to retouched pieces
Lower	11-14	1944
Upper	1-6	98

Table 5.7: Rratio of waste flakes to retouched pieces

the Bobonaro formation and in the lower part of Aitutu formation (Geological map of the Kupang-Atambua Quadrangle, Timor).

Identification of utilised flakes with signs of use wear

The utilised flakes recognised from Lua Manggetek consist of gloss-bearing flakes, flakes with edge striations, and flakes with patterns of edge damage in the form of flake scars.

Only 8 glossed flakes were found, all from the upper analytical level (table 5.6 above). In all cases, the gloss was unifacial, and it occurs on both retouched and unretouched flakes. Combinations of striation and edge flaking occur on 20 pieces, all with one short edge. It appears that these tools were used in a scraper mode of activity, and only for short periods.

One utilised flake has bifacially-symmetrical microfracturing and striation, which suggests use with a longitudinal cutting motion as a knife. All other utilised flakes have asymmetrical microfracturing and striation, typical of edge-transverse scraping motions. Two flakes were found with black residue together with small microfractures (less than 1 mm) and striations. This black residue is perhaps a kind of plant gum.

Stone manufacturing technology

A total of 350 chert flakes from trench C3D3 was measured for statistical analysis. To see if there was any change in the technology of stone tool production through time in the site, a Mann-Whitney U test, equivalent to the independent groups t-test were undertaken. These show that the assemblages from the lower and upper analytical levels are statistically different in size. The statistics results indicate that there is significant differences in flake length, width, platform width and platform thickness between lower and upper analytical unit (table 5.8).

Test Statistics[a]

	LENGTH	WIDTH	PLATWIDT	PLATTHIC
Mann-Whitney U	6106.500	4646.000	8516.500	8846.000
Wilcoxon W	22216.500	19871.000	24269.500	25317.000
Z	-8.454	-9.715	-4.780	-4.723
Asymp. Sig. (2-tailed)	.000	.000	.000	.000

a. Grouping Variable: UNIT

Table 5.8: Mann-Whitney U test results for flake recovered in lower (unit 1) and upper level (unit 2)

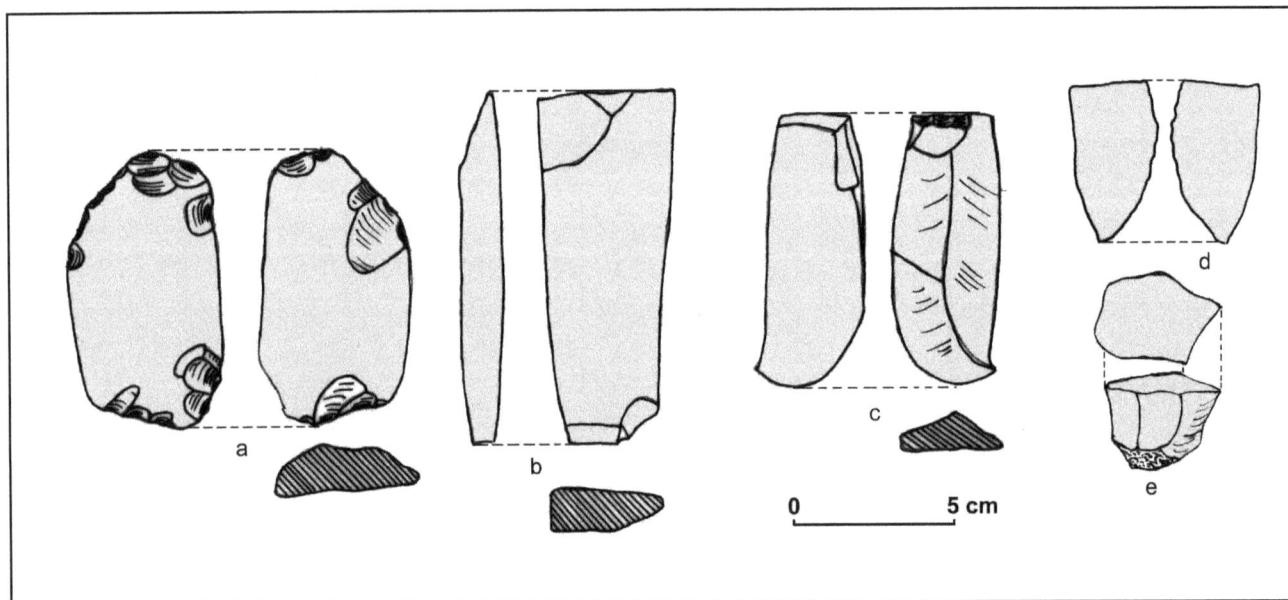

Figure 5.4: Non-chert flaked stone artefacts, Lua Manggetek
A from spit 6; b from surface; s,d,e from spit 13

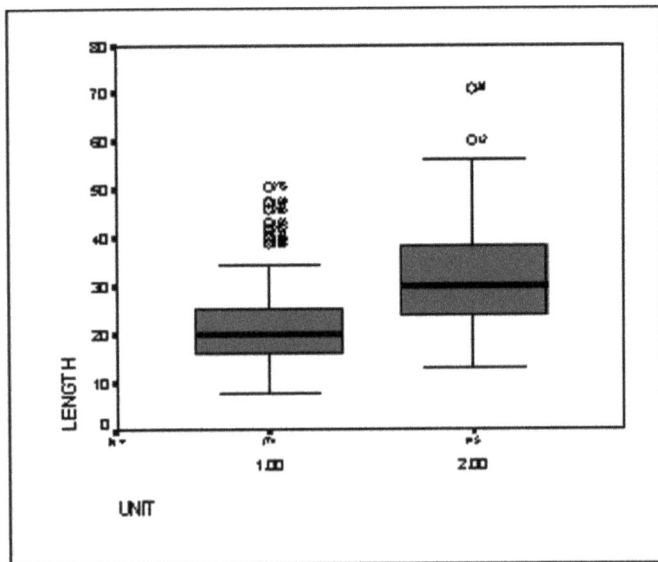

Figure 5.5: Box plot shows the spread of the flake length for each level of analysis, Lua Manggetek

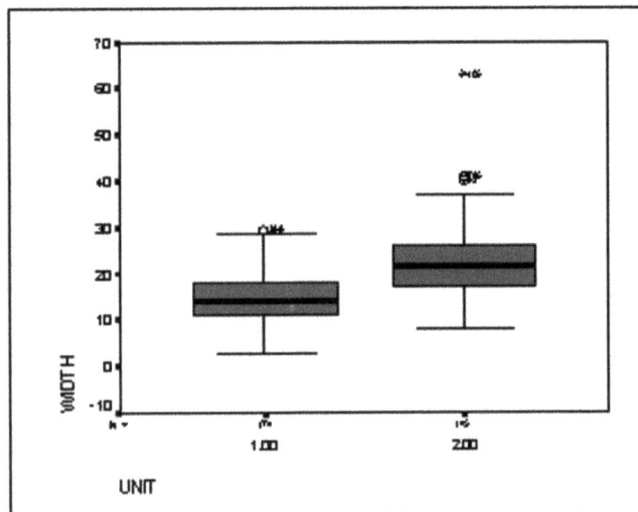

Figure 5.6: Box plot shows the spread of the flake width for each level of analysis, Lua Manggetek

The mean length of stone flakes from the lower analytical level is 21.56 mm, and for those from the upper analytical level is 30.95 mm. The mean width of the stone flakes from the lower level is 14.86 mm, and for upper level is 22.46 mm. Thus, the upper layer flakes are bigger than the lower layer flakes. However, the statistical results should be interpreted carefully. Although there are differences in the sizes of flakes between the lower and upper levels, as shown by p-value, I argue that the differences are merely a reflection of transformation processes, rather than a reflection of any major change in technology.

Retouched flakes

The proportion of retouched flakes (14 pieces) is very small compared with the total number of flakes found in the assemblage. In the lower level, the ratio of waste to retouched flakes is much higher than in the upper (table 5.7),

The location of retouch varies (see figure 5.4), and most is unifacial. Usually, the part of the flake which is retouched is a small portion of a long edge, but there can also be retouched both on the long edge and/or on the striking platform end of the flake.

Striations are sometimes denser on the unretouched edges of some pieces than inside the retouch itself, suggesting that some retouch was produced to resharpen the edge after it became dull because of use. No backing retouch is found in this assemblage. The technique of forming retouch was certainly hard hammer percussion, as indicated by big and deep negative scars on flake edges. Small, shallow and thin scars of the kind produced by pressure flaking are not found in the assemblage.

All chert tools retouched are of the common conchoidal flake type. There are no blades or bladelets with retouch in the deposit. One non-chert retouched tool (from spit 6) is a dacite pebble, retouched bifacially. (figure 5.3 a above). One manuport, of silicified sandstone (from the surface), is not retouched but has crushing on one end suggesting use for indirect percussion. One flake of silicified sandstone was found in spit 6. This has perimeter scars on its proximal end but has not been retouched. One small dacite core also occurred in the lower level.

Mode of reduction

A total of 63 cores was recovered from Lua Manggetek - 54 from the upper analytical level and 9 from the lower level.

In the lower analytical level, one single platform and 8 multi-platform cores were found, suggesting that both blade reduction and expedient core reduction modes were applied, with expedient core reduction being the more common practice. The single platform core still retains half of its cortex, but the size of the last complete bladelet detached is very small (30.42 mm).

The percentage of flakes with blade proportions is also low in both analytical levels. Only 9 of the total 350 flakes measured are classified as having blade proportion. It can be interpreted that blade reduction mode, especially with preparation, was rarely practiced. An overhang removal strategy to detach flakes from cores was also applied evenly in the earlier and later periods of occupancy, while most platforms lacked any special preparation. Less than 1% of platforms reveal any facetting.

Five small cores with some crushing may be bipolar cores, but the precise percentage of bipolar flakes is difficult to assess. Some angular shattered fragments would appear to be the result of this technique.

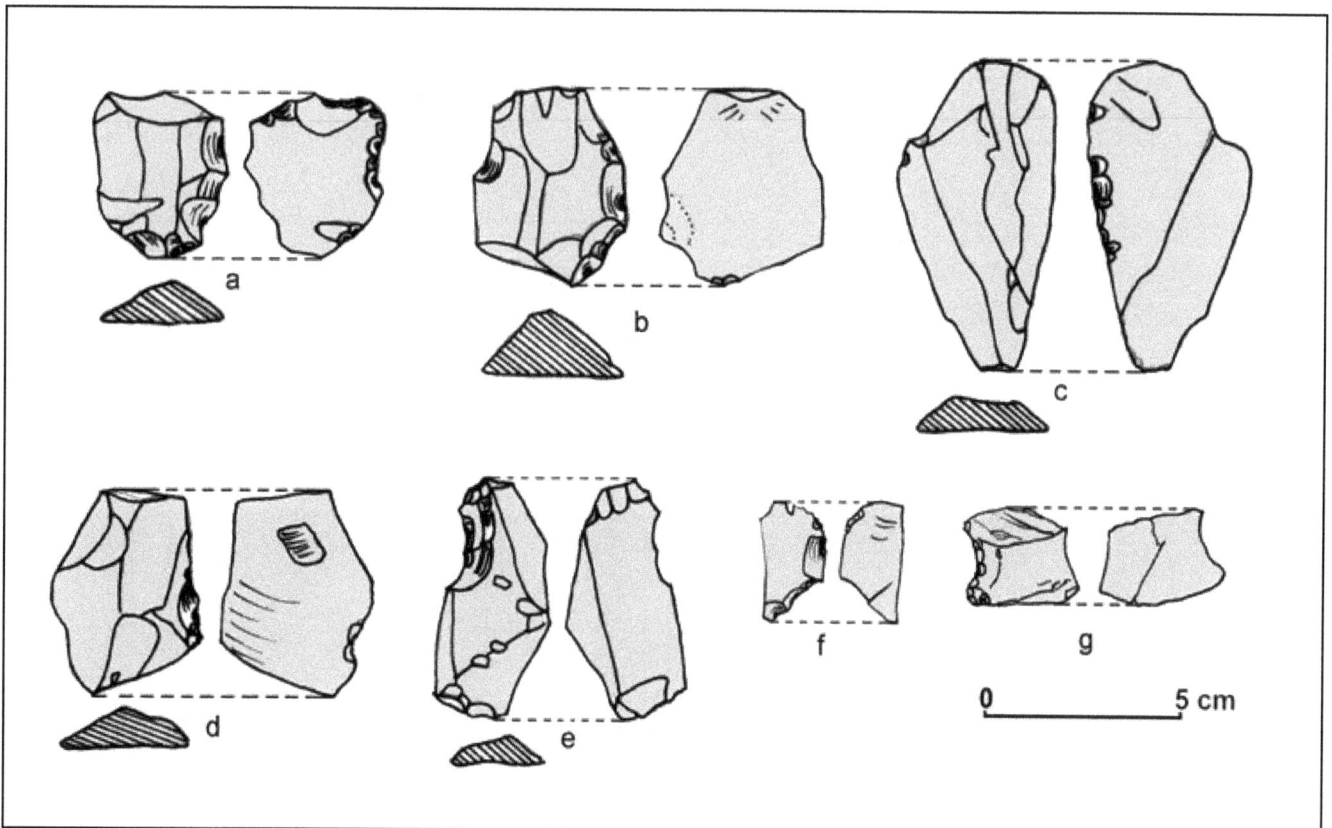

Figure 5.7: Retouched pieces from Lua Manggetek
a-c from spit 1 trench C3D3; d from spit 2 trench C3D3; e from spit 6; f from spit 8; g from surface

45

Trimming activity

Based on debitage size range analysis, it seems that the intensity of trimming for retouching or thinning was higher in the lower analytical level. But the fact that only very rare retouch occurred in the lower level, plus the absence of bifaces, led me to examine qualitatively the characteristics of those small flakes from Lua Manggetek that bear signs of trimming activity. Such trimming flakes have feather flake terminations, narrow faceted striking platforms, alip, little or no cotex, and a diffuse bulb of force (Andrefsky 1998: 118). Only a few flakes are identified as trimming flakes. This suggests that although more debitages occurs in the lower level, trimming activity was not intensive. This finding strengthens the argument that vertical transformation took place in the site.

Shell analysis

Shell artefacts

In Lua Manggetek, one *Anadara* scraper was found from square C3, spit 5. Shell beads were found in spits 1 and 3. One round cut *Conus* shell was found in square C3, spit 1 (figure 5. 10). In terms of the tidy breakage around its edge, this is an artefact, probably a preform for an ornament. One preform for a shell bead came from square C3, spit 1.

Perforated *Oliva* shells in Manggetek were found only on the surface. These perforated *Oliva* shells might have functioned as ornaments, since the whorl of this species is quite hard and does not break easily.

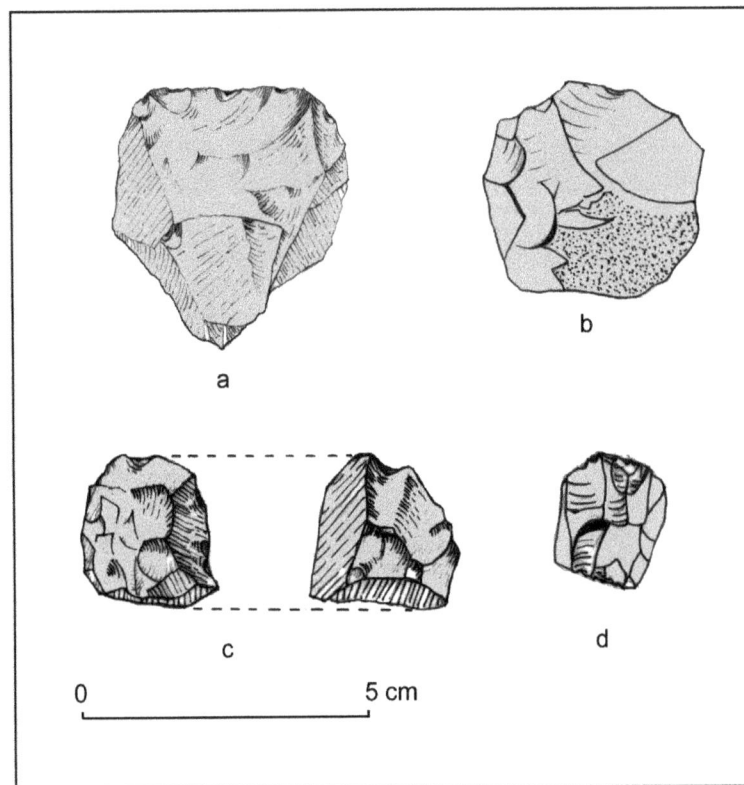

Figure 5. 8: Cores from Lua Manggetek: a) spit 2; b) surface; c) spit 1; d) spit 7. a and c are drawn by Agus Tri Hascaryo

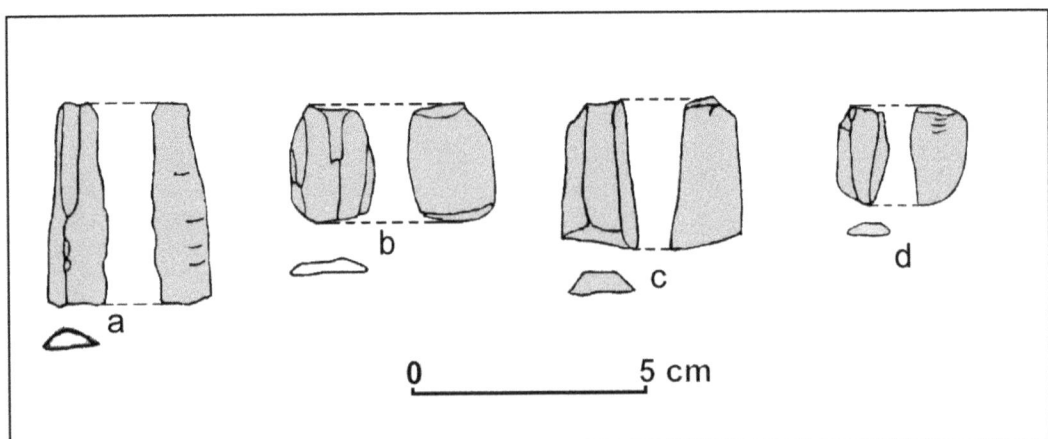

Figure 5.9: Flakes with parallel ridges, Lua Manggetek

Square	Shell artefacts	Provenance	Description, information
trench C3D3	1 shell bead	spit 1	round, flat with one hole
	2 shell bead	spit 3	as above
	1 perforated oliva	surface	Oliva oliva shell
	1 preform pendant (?)	spit 1	round and cut Conus shell (ornament preform ?)
	1 perforated oliva	surface	unmodified

Table 5.9: Shell artefact distribution by spit, Lua Manggetek

Non-artefactual shell remains

The molluscs exploited by the Lua Manggetek occupants comprised 14 families, including one freshwater family (Thiaridae, of the species *Melanoides funiculus*). The occurrence of this species in the Lua Manggetek assemblage is sporadic. It occurs firstly in the bed rock layer in considerable numbers, then occurs again in spit 7 at 35 cm below the surface, and again in spit 1, but only in small numbers. Amongst the marine shells brought back to the shelter, *Neritidae* were the most frequently brought to the shelter, followed by *Arcidae* and *Chitonidae* (see table 3 in appendix).

The distributions of these three shell families seem to follow different patterns. The *Arcidae* family, especially *Anadara granosa*, does not occur in the lower assemblage except in spit 7. It occurs in significant numbers from spit 6 to the surface. If this occurrence is plotted against the radiocarbon dates, the first time this shellfish was consumed was only a little before 7050±80 BP. *Neritidae* occur throughout all layers, but mostly in the lower layer, 65 to 60 cm below the surface. In the bottom layer of square C3, the MNI of Neritidae is 24 while, after that, Neritidae only occur occasionally, with an occurrence of 6 shells maximum per spit. The distribution of Chitonidae is similar to that for *Neritidae*. They occur throughout all layers, but mostly at 65 to 60 cm below the surface. After that, chitons only occur rarely, but steadily, in the assemblage, with a maximum occurrence of 2 MNI per spit. The distribution of *Potamididae* and *Strombidae* is very similar to the distribution of *Archidae*, although neither occur in significant quantity in Lua Manggetek. *Potamididae* and *Strombidae* were only brought in small numbers to the cave in the later occupancy period. They never occur below spit 6 (30 cm below the surface). Examining the pattern of shell

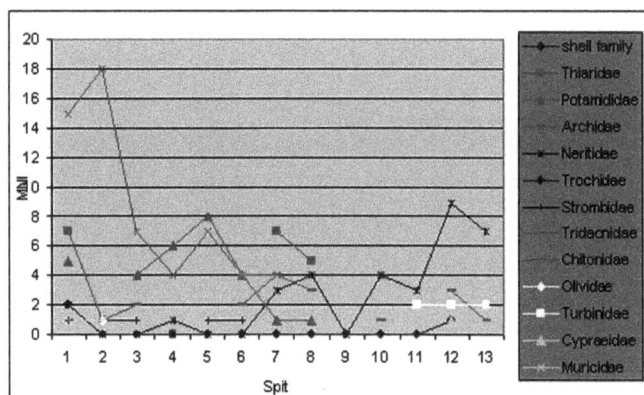

Figure 5.10: Cut Conus shell, Lua Manggetek

distribution from the Lua Manggetek assemblage, it can be seen that six different habitats were exploited regularly - fresh water, tidal mudflat, sandy intertidal, upper reef, intertidal reef and reef edge.

Since there is a strong indication of site disturbance in the upper level of analysis, the sequence of MNI of shell species that increases from spit 6 to the surface (figure 5.11 & 5.12) might not be significant. However, general comparison of shell species between the lower and upper levels of analysis indicates significant differences. I argue that these changes reflect changes in sea level. There is shell species increase during the later period of occupation.

In square F3, *Geloina coaxans* occurs down to spit 4 only. This occurrence may reflect exploitation of a new species that appeared because of the changing Holocene

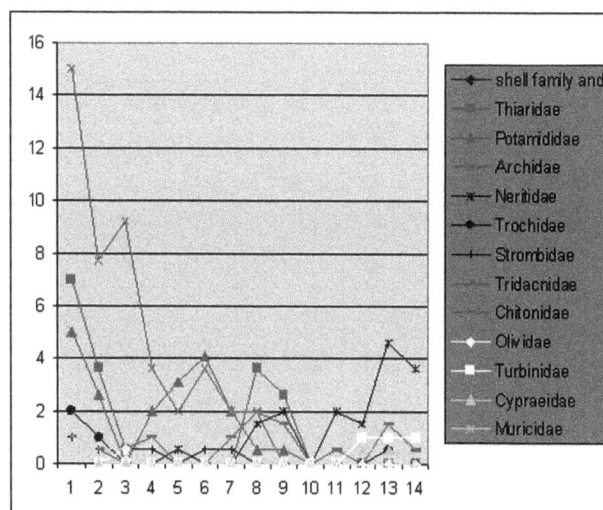

Figure 5.11: Absolute abundances (MNI) of shell families in trench C3D3, Lua Manggetek

Figure 5.12: Relative abundances of shell families in trench C3D3, Lua Manggetek.

coastal environment. The occurrence of mangrove and tidal mudflat bivalve shells such as *Anadara* and *Geloina* is much greater in the upper layers than in the lower, and the converse occurrence of Neritidae is mainly in the lower layers. By 7000 years ago, the Holocene sea level was approaching its current level and becoming stable, as opposed to the rapid changes in previous millennia. Such stability would have led to a change of coastline geomorphology from steep and rocky in the Pleistocene to a stable mudflat coastline in the mid-Holocene. These consistencies in shell distribution from bottom to top of the Manggetek sequence also suggest that, while individual instances of disturbance have occurred in the history of the site, at no time has the whole profile ever been entirely disturbed from top to bottom.

Pottery

The sherds from Lua Manggetek include red-slipped and plain sherds. In square F3, pottery was found down to 10 cm below surface, and then also from spit 6 down to spit 9. Two red-slipped potsherds were found at 10 cm and 30 cm below the surface. All the other pottery from F3 is plain without red slip.

Three red-slipped potsherds were found on the surface and at 5 cm below the surface in trench C3D3, one being part of the rim of a cooking pot with a nubbin on its lip (figure 5.13) . The size of this cooking pot is difficult to reconstruct owing to the small size of the rim piece. Non red-slipped potsherds were found down to spit 9, but their sizes are very small (1.5 cm) and they probably infiltrated down from the upper layer.

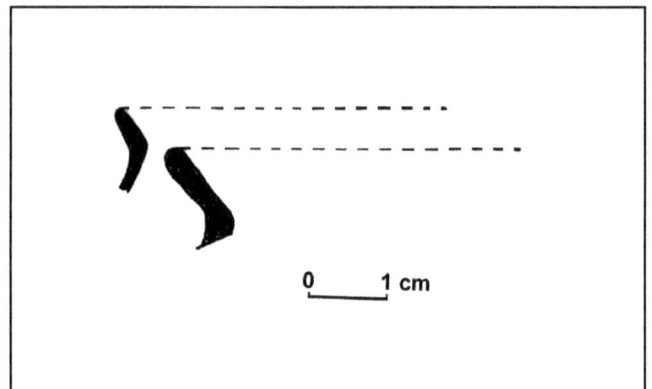

Figure 5. 13 Rim profiles of cooking pots from Lua Manggetek, one with a nubbin on the lip.

3. The excavation of Lua Meko

Lua Meko is an extension of the Lua Manggetek shelter with a height of 10 m, depth of 5.80 m and width of 13.50 m. The floor of the shelter is relatively free of rock fall, even near the shelter wall. No bedrock appears at the surface near the back wall as in Lua Manggetek, suggesting that the inner zone has quite a deep deposit (see figure 5. 1 above for the position of excavated squares).

Initially, a 1X1 metre test pit (TP) was excavated down to spit 11, when archaeological materials became rarer than above. The location of the test pit was chosen because it was well away from the erosion area in the front of the shelter that seems to have produced some of the disturbance in Lua Manggetek. This test pit was then extended for another square metre and both the joined excavation areas were excavated together below spit 11. The two excavated squares are thus referred to as TP and EX below.

Stratigraphy

The deposits consist of five stratigraphic layers (fig 5.11):

Layer 1 is a dark brown sand (10 YR 3/3) with dried leaves and goat dung. This layer is only 3 cm thick and was present only in the northeast side of the trench. Micro-analysis of this layer shows there is limestone debris, hematite, and micro-debitage of chert.

Layer 2 is a dark yellowish brown (10 YR 4/4) sand layer with goat dung. The thickness varies from 3 cm on the north side to 8 cm on the southwest side. This layer contains limestone fragments, micro-debitage of chert, tiny shell fragments and dried roots.

Layer 3 is an ash layer. The colour is grayish brown (10 YR 5/2) with thickness varying from 5 cm to 10 cm. This layer also contains hematite, micro-debitage of chert, dried leaves and roots, and tiny shell fragments.

Layer 4 is a brown sandy loam layer (7.5 YR 5/4) with a thickness varying from 8 to 20 cm. Larger pieces of limestone occur than in the layers above. Micro-materials are the same as in the layers above.

Layer 5 is a brown sandy loam layer (7.5 YR 4/4), more pale in colour than those above. This layer is the thickest in the profile, generally between 30 and 35 cm. Toward the bottom of this layer, the sediment become very hard. This hard sediment is relatively sterile in the main test pit, but a small number of stone artefacts and small extremity bones were found in the extension. Below this hard sand occurred bedrock.

Archaeological Finds

Plotting the vertical distributions by layer of all cultural remains and human bones, it is apparent that pottery was found to the bottom part of layer 3 in EX. Also in EX, shell beads were found from layer 2 down to the upper part of layer 5. Other shell artefacts were found down to layer 4. In TP, shell beads were found in layer 2, but other shell artefacts were found down to layer 4. Other cultural remains, especially stone artefacts and shells, were found in all layers.

Figure 5.14: Lua Meko B Shelter
Arrow: position of excavation trench

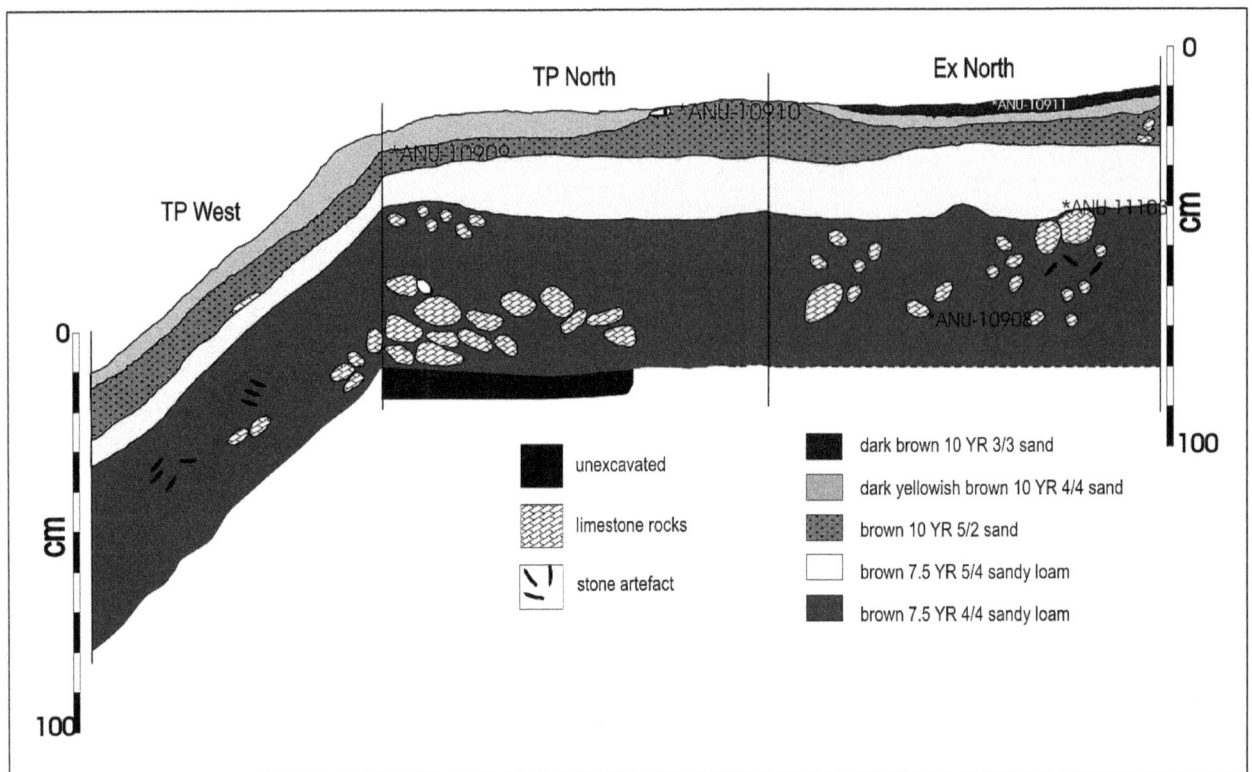

Figure 5.15: Section of Trench TP-Ex Lua Meko, Tonggobatu rockshelter

Human bones occur from layer 3 down to the upper part of layer 5 in TP, whereas in EX they occur in layer 4 and near the bottom of layer 5.

Generally, the distribution of stone artefacts shows a sharp increase above spit 9, and reaches a peak in spit 7, above which the distribution shows a gradual decrease up to spit 2. The distribution of shells is different, showing a steady low occurrence up to spit 7 (35 cm below the surface), above which it increases sharply to reach a peak in spit 3 (see table 5.9 and 5.10).

Carbon dating results for Lua Meko

Five samples for carbon dating were submitted to the ANU radiocarbon laboratory. Those from spits 1, 2, 3, and 7 are all *Turbo* opercula. The sample from spit 12 was of *Strombus* shells (table 5.11). Insufficient shells were obtained from the basal spit 14 for a date. Spit 12 to 14 do not contain as many artefacts as spit 11, and seems to belong to a separate assemblage that lacks any small flaked stone.

As can be seen from table 5.11, Lua Meko was occupied from the Late Pleistocene to at least the Middle Holocene, with three episodes of occupation possibly represented, all pre-Neolithic. The most intensive phase of occupation is represented by ANU-11103, c.10,500 BP. It is very likely that the first Lua Meko occupation occurred before the date of ANU-10908, as this sample was taken 10 cm above the basal spit, in which two rather isolated big flakes of silicified sandstone were found. The basal deposit is a very hard sand layer, at which excavation stopped prior to reaching absolute bedrock.

Apart from ANU-10911, the other four samples form a relatively regular age-depth distribution that suggests a purely average (and possibly not realistic) rate of accumulation of sediment of about 600 years per centimetre. This could imply a basal date of about 30,000 BP,

comparable with that obtained for the basal occupation in Lene Hara cave in East Timor (O'Connor 2002) and Golo Cave in Maluku Utara (Bellwood *et al.* 1998). The major question with a sequence such as this is whether the occupation was continuous but very light, or whether it occurred intermittently under conditions of continuous vertical perturbation and episodic sediment loss due to erosion.

In terms of the possibility of stratigraphic disturbance in Lua Meko, the only two sherds found (in EX) are likely from the same pot, but both come from spit 4 so the refitting does not say anything about the vertical movement of archaeological finds. Probably these sherds have penetrated down together from the shelter surface since no other sherds were found in Lua Meko at all. Spriggs (1999) is in agreement with Bellwood (1997) that pottery manufacture in Island Southeast Asia dates after 4000 BP, so the Lua Meko C14 dates are unlikely to be relevant for dating these two sherds and it appears that use of the shelter had essentially ceased before this date.

The upper three radiocarbon dates are not in sequence, suggesting that the upper part of the deposit could have been disturbed, although during the excavation there was no trace of any stratigraphic feature relating to disturbance. David Bulbeck in Appendix 1 discusses the spread of sets of human bones believed to belong to single individuals through several spits, thus throwing some doubt on the stratigraphic integrity of the site. It would appear that burial activities might have caused some disturbance between spits 3 and 9.

For the purpose of analysis, the Lua Meko deposit is divided into lower, middle and upper analytical levels. The lower analytical level (layer 5) corresponds with the Late Pleistocene radiocarbon age and the isolated presence of two large flaked stone artefacts. The middle analytical level

Table 5.10 — square TP, Lua Meko, Tonggobatu rockshelter complex

Material	0 no	0 gr	1 no	1 gr	2 no	2 gr	3 no	3 gr	4 no	4 gr	5 no	5 gr	6 no	6 gr	7 no	7 gr	8 no	8 gr	9 no	9 gr	10 no	10 gr	11 no	11 gr
stone artefacts:																								
hammer stone													1											
cores		8	5	100	3	65	1	30	12	540	5	170	3	150			1	85	4	165			2	180
all debitage @ tools			51	115	116	997	82	205	212	765	196	680	355	905	265	325	215	335	159	215	139	175	79	59
shells:																								
shell bead					3	2	1	0,5																
perforated oliva shells					1	0,5	2	0,9																
other ornament							1	4					2	10	1	0,5								
shell tool									1	5														
dentalium																	1	3						
non-artefactual shells*			110	677	186	797	191	910	12	267	8	22	27	52	14	230	3	10	5	60	5	41	3	8
crab remains							1	5	3	0,5			1	0,2									5	30
human remains:																								
bone							24	125	8	40	3	10	5	65	10	112	2	15	21	140			1	7
animal bone									2		1	0,5	3	5										

Table 5.10 Distribution of arcaheological finds in square TP, Lua Meko, Tonggobatu rockshelter complex

Table 5.11 — square EX, Lua Meko, Tonggobatu rockshelter complex

Material	0 no	0 gr	1 no	1 gr	2 no	2 gr	3 no	3 gr	4 no	4 gr	5 no	5 gr	6 no	6 gr	7 no	7 gr	8 no	8 gr	9 no	9 gr	10 no	10 gr	11 no	11 gr	12 no	12 gr	13 no	13 gr	14 no	14 gr
pottery									2	25																				
stone artefacts:																														
hammer stone	1																													
cores	1	25	2	40	2	20			3	85	3	35	2	40	4	85			3	125							1	55		
all debitage & tools			230	490	190	360	170	340			335	650	125	410	400	745	112	440	62	325	110	520	261	360					2	1435
shells:																														
shell bead			4	3	5	5	13	10	1	1	6	3	1	1							1									
perforated oliva shell					5	7					1	2																		
other shell ornament																														
shell tool									2	10											1		3							
dentalium					1	15	1	5											1											
non artefactual shells*			258	880	733	2800	355	1095	133	416	39	240	400	485	2	10	32	93	18	95	16	100			27	35	8	15	9	20
crab carapace			1	0,5																										
human remains:																														
bone			2	10			1	1	2	9	3	18	4	30									1	20			1	19		
animal bone	1	0,5	1	0,5							4	3	8	17											3	7	1	4		
turtle carapace																														

Table 5.11 Distribution of arcaheological finds in square EX, Lua Meko, Tonggobatu rockshelter complex

51

Lab no	spit	depth	layer	square	sample	uncalib 14C age (years BP)	Cal BP
ANU-10911	1	5 cm	1	EX	*Turbo opercula*	5590±110	6,602 (6,440) 6,311
ANU-10910	2	10 cm	2	TP	*Turbo opercula*	4720±100	5623 (5550) 5429
ANU-10909	3	15 cm	3	TP	*Turbo opercula*	5420±60	6,333 (6280) 6,209
ANU-11103	7	35 cm	4	TP	*Turbo opercula*	10,030±120	12,005 (11,680) 11,407
ANU-10908	12	60 cm	5	EX	*Strombus sp*	24,420±250	beyond Calib range

Table 5.12: Radiocarbon dates from Lua Meko

Level of analysis	spits	Natural layers	C14 date (approx.)
Lower	11-14	5	24 k-30K
Middle	7-10	4	12 k
Upper	1-6	1-3	6.5-5.5 k

Table 5.13: The correlations between analytical levels, spits, stratigraphic layers and radiocarbon dates for Lua Meko, Rote.

spit	square	Taxon	B/U	N	weight	remarks
3	EX	*Pteropodid*	U	1	1	proximal radius
5	TP	*Pteropodid*	U	1	0.1	phalanx shaft fragment
6	EX	Fish	?	1	1	vertebra of large fish, encrusted with calcium carbonate
6	EX	*Murid*	U	1	1	
4	TP	Uncertain	U	3	7	heavily encrusted long bone shaft fragments of turtle, pig, or dog-sized animals
5	EX	uncertain	U	2	1	As above
6	EX	uncertain	?	3	5	As above
12	EX	uncertain	U	3	7	As above
13	EX	uncertain	?	1	4	As above

Table 5.14: Distribution of animal bones in Lua Meko, Tonggobatu
B: burn; U:unburn

(layer 4) is of end-Pleistocene date, and the upper analytical level (layers 1-3) is of mid-Holocene date (table 3.4). Apart from the two sherds noted above, the whole sequence can be regarded essentially as preceramic.

4. Analysis of archaeological finds in Lua Meko

Human remains

Human remains in Lua Meko occurred from spit 3 down to spit 13, near the bottom of the excavation. The total of 54 identified secimens are discussed in David Bulbeck's appendix. Bulbeck believes that there are at least 5 individuals represented: one female sub-adult (individual 1) from spits 3 to 6; one male adult (individual 2) from spits 4 to 7; one unsexed adult (individual 3) from spits 4 to 9, one sub-adult (individual 4) from spits 4 to 9, one male adult (individual 5) from spits 6 to 9), and another male adult from spits 11 to 13. One bone comes from spit 13, thus below the date of 24,000. The precise date of deposition of these human remains and their taphonomic history remain completely unknown, and it is possible that all have been disturbed downwards from quite recent burial activities.

52

Square	Shell artefacts	provenance	Description, information
square TP	2 shell beads	spit 1	round, flat, with one hole
	3 shell beads	spit2	as above
	1 shell bead	spit3	as above
	1 perforated olive shell	spit 2	unmodified
	2 perforated olive shell	spit 3	Unmodified (figure 5.18:g,h)
	1 perforated olive shell	spit 7	Unmodivied
	1 dentalium shell	spit 8	Unmodified
	1 dentalium shell	spit 11	unmodified,
	2 shell scrapers	spit 3	unmofified veneridae shell (figure 5.16)
square EX	4 shell beads	spit 1	Round, flat with one hole
	5 shell beads	spit 2	as above
	12 shell beads	spit3	one with pointed form (figure 5.18: f), one is brown (Figure 5.18: l), all with one hole (figure 5.18: others)
	1 shell bead preform	spit 3	(figure 5.18: J)
	1 shell beads	spit 4	Round, flat with one hole
	6 shell beads	spit 5	as above
	1 shell beads	spit 6	as above
	1 shell bead	spit 11	as above
	5 perforated olive shell	spit 2	Small similar sizes
	1 perforated olive shell	spit 5	Unmodified
	1 shell tool	spit 2	scraper
	1 shell scraper	spit 3	unmodified *Geloina coaxans*
	2 shell scrapers	spit 4	1 unmodified *Geloina coaxans*, 1 (figure 5.16; retouched *Tridacna* (figure 5.17)
	1 dentalium shell	spit 9	Unmodified (figure 5.18:g)
	1 dentalium shell	spit 10	as above (figure 5.18: h)
	3 dentalium shells	spit 11	as above

Table 5.15:. Shell artefact distributions in the Lua Meko sites, by spit.

Animal bones

Only a small number of animal bones occurred in Lua Meko (table 7.9). Some are identified as Pteropodids (from subsurface down to spit 5), also fruit bats as in Pia Hudale (*Pteropus* or *Acerodon*). A large marine fish is also present, and a single rat bone possibly of *Rattus tanezumi*.

Several *Macaca* bones occurred in spit 1 in square EX (see the appendix by David Bulbeck). They could belong to a large male crab-eating macaque (*Macaca fascicularis*). This species does not live on Rote nowadays (Monk 1998), but Dr Bulbeck is certain of the identification. This animal was translocated by humans to Rote, but at an unknown date.

All other fragments could only be identified as turtle, pig or dog-sized animals by Aplin, due to their calcium carbonate encrusted conditions. Two bones from spit 5 could be *suid*, but they could also be turtle.

Shell analysis
Shell artefacts in Lua Meko

In Lua Meko, shell artefacts consist of bivalve shell tools and shell ornaments. The bivalve tools are Veneridae scrapers with concave chipping on their middle edges (figure 5.16), found from spits 2 and 3. One simple retouched shell tool of *Tridacna* sp. was found in EX spit 4 (figure 5. 17).

The shell ornaments consist of shell beads recovered from spits 1 to 3 in square TP and from spits 1 to 10 in EX. Apart from the usual round and flat type of shell bead, there is also a somewhat different type of shell bead from square EX, spit 3, that has a pointed shape (figure 5.18), perhaps function as a necklace spacer. In total, 12 shell beads were recovered from the Lua Meko assemblage. Some preforms for shell beads (without holes) were also recovered in spit 3 in squares TP and EX. Other types of ornaments (figure 5.19) were found in spits 3 and 6, made of crab carapace.

In Lua Meko, perforated olive shells occur down to spit 7. *Dentalium* shells, most likely brought to the sites other than for food purposes, were recovered from spit 8 in square TP and from spits 8 down to 10 in square EX. *Dentalium* shells were strung together to make head-dresses in the Natufian of the southern Levant (Fagan 1992), although the examples reported here were all found individually rather than in groups.

Most of the shell ornaments and scrapers found in Lua Meko are evidently preceramic in context, although some of the shell beads are very small and could have moved down the profile. Yet this seems to be an unlikely explanation for all. These shell beads were prepared by cutting, grinding, and drilling from one direction.

Figure 5.16: Bivalve shell scraper from Lua Meko

Figure 5.17: One simple retouched shell tool of Tridacna sp., from Lua Meko

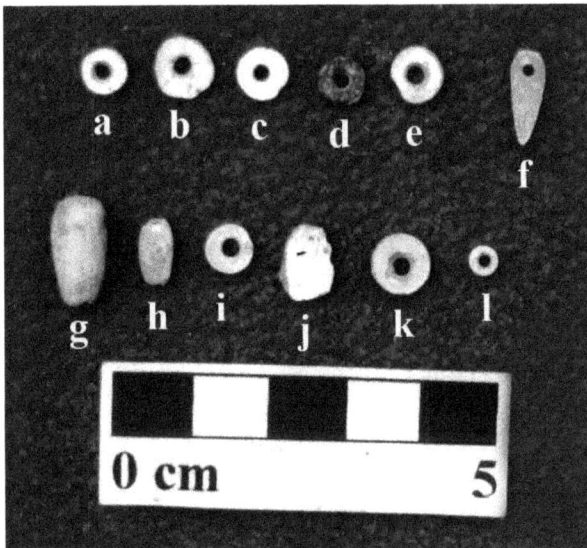

Figure 5.18: Round shell beads (a–e; i, k,l); Pointed shell bead (f), perforated Oliva shell (g,h) and shell bead preform (j), Lua Meko

Figure 5.19: Ornaments made of carapace (left) & crab carapace (right), Lua Meko

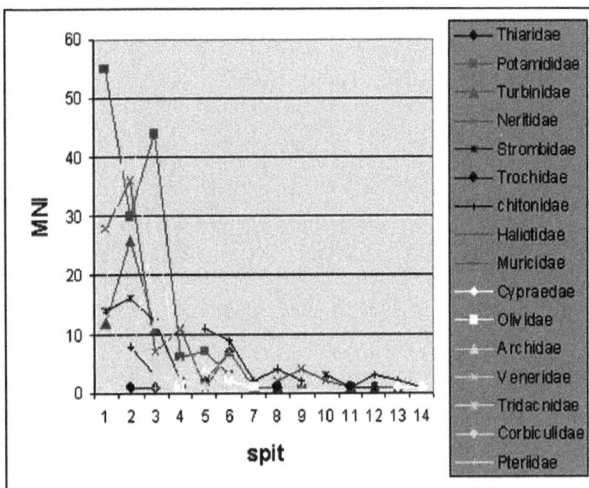

Figure 5.20: Absolute abundance of shell families, Lua Meko.

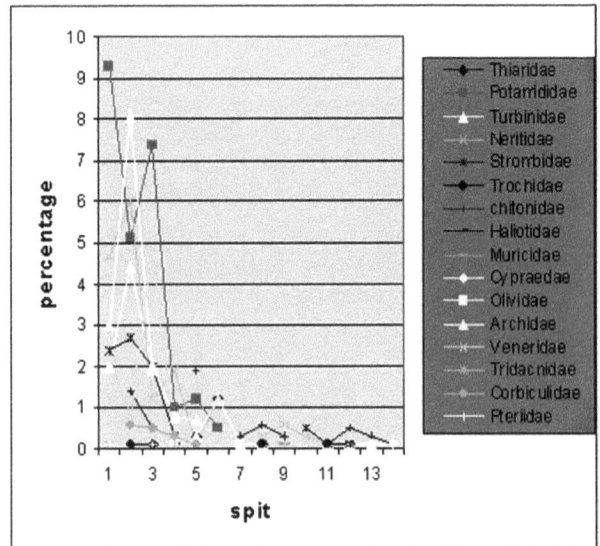

Figure 5.21: Relative abundance of shell families, Lua Meko

Non-artefactual shell in Lua Meko

Figs 5.20 and 5.21 above indicates that there are two very distinct phases in the occupation of Lua Meko as evidenced by shellfish distributions. The early phase has only intertidal reef species, whereas the later one has a much wider range of shellfish from varied habitats including muddy and sandy shores. In terms of the C14 dates from this very significant site, it is likely that these two phases correspond with glacial and interglacial sea level situations respectively.

Throughout the site occupancy, 12 shell families consisting of 29 different species were brought back to the shelter. These shellfish were exploited from six different habitats, that is freshwater, tidal mudflat, sandy intertidal, river edge, intertidal reef and upper reef.

In the lower part of the lower analytical level, shells of only three families were recovered - Chitonidae, Turbinidae, and Cypraedae - all of which come from intertidal reef habitats. Such shells occurred in spits 14, 13, and 12, and were thus exploited from the earliest occupancy. From spit 11 to spit 9 some new shell families occurred in the deposit for the first time in low numbers - Neritidae, Trochidae, Potamididae, Thiaridae and Strombidae. These come from freshwater, tidal mudflat, sandy intertidal, and upper reef habitats. This was the first time these new habitats were exploited.

The freshwater Thiaridae family occurs continuously from its first occurrence in spit 12 to the top, but never in significant numbers. Neritidae species that lived on tidal mudflats or in upper reef habitats appear first in spit 11. However, these are also rare, with only 1 or 2 individuals per spit. The same goes for Potamididae, Neritidae and Trochidae. Bivalve shells do not occur in these lower layers, but only start to occur in the upper part of the lower analytical level (spit 9), just before 10,000 BP. Veneridae (*Tapes hiantina*) continue to occur into the top layers of the middle level. Muricidae (*Drupa rubusideus*) only occur in spit 9, indicating that this shell family was not exploited for consumption.

After 10,000 years ago, new bivalve classes occur for the first time. These include Corbiculidae (*Batissa violacea*) and Arcidae (*Anadara granosa* and *A. alinea*), both from tidal mudflat habitats. While *Tapes hiantina* starts to occur in the lower level, it continues to occur in the middle analytical level. Two other new species of Veneridae (*Dosinia juvenilis* and *Gafrarium pectinatum*) start to occur at this time as well. Apart from bivalves, gastropods also increase in the upper layers of the middle analytical level. Strombidae increase with the addition of *Lambis lambis*, *Strombus urceus* and *Strombus canarium*, all of which become important and reach considerable numbers of individuals in the upper layers. New species of *Tridacna* and *Haliotis* also appear, but

very rarely. Olividae start to occur in spit 7 and continue in low numbers. All shells of this family (*Oliva oliva*) were found with holes.

In general, shellfish habitats were exploited more intensively in the middle analytical level, and the species are more varied than in the lower analytical level. Shells exploited from reef edges and upper reefs become more diversified in the middle analytical level, with the addition of two and one new species respectively. Towards the later period of occupancy, tidal mudflat habitats were exploited more intensively. In the lower analytical level, tidal mudflat species belonged to only 3 families, comprising 5 different species, with a total of 9 individuals. But in the middle analytical level there were 5 mudflat families comprising 10 different species, with a total of 428 individuals. This total represents 62 % of all shells in the middle layer. This phenomenon suggests that tidal mudflat habitats were coming within easy access to Lua Meko after 10,000 years ago.

Flaked stone artefacts analysis

A total of 4221 flaked stone artefacts made of chert, consisting of cores and core fragments, retouched flakes/blades, unretouched complete flakes, broken flakes, flake fragments and spalls was recovered from Lua Meko. Among them, a total of 1086 complete and proximal flakes and 54 cores and core fragments were measured. The high number of stone artefacts recovered from the 2x1 metre excavated trench indicate that stone tool manufacturing was very intensive in Lua Meko. To see when the most intense activity occurred, the rate of stone artefact discard during cave occupation is plotted in figures 5.22 below.

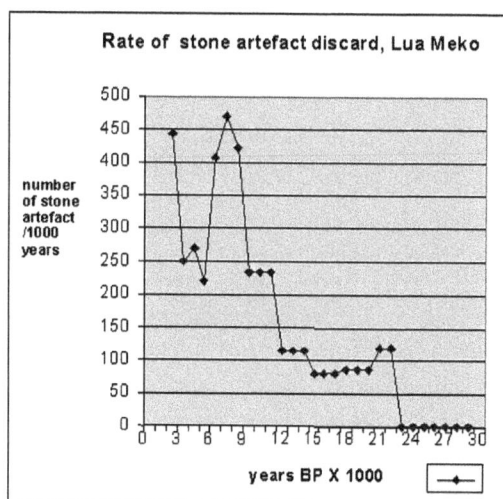

Figure 5.22: Rates of stone artefact discard for Lua Meko

Level of analysis	spit	retouched flake	unmodified gloss flake	unmodified used flake	waste flake	core	all stone artefacts
1 & 2 (lower)	11,12,13,14	2	_	_	340	3	345
3 (middle)	7,8,9,10	14	1	17	1430	14	1476
4 (upper)	1,2,3,4,5,6	14	3	31	2303	50	2401
Totals		30	4	48	4073	67	4222

Table 5.16: Distribution of stone artefact variety by level of analysis, Lua Meko

The graph shows that the highest discard rate took place around 7000 to 8000 years ago. There was a continuous increase in the discard rate after 15,000 years ago, followed by a sudden drop around 5,000 years ago, and increase again before site abandonment, aproximately around 3,000 years ago. The latter age are estimated based on the average deposition per 1,000 years.

Raw material

Most flaked stone artefacts are of chert in a variety of colours: greenish grey, yellowish brown, reddish brown and white. Yellowish brown and reddish brown are the two most common colours. It is likely that the chert brought from several river beds in the Aiutu Formation area.

Only five non-chert stone artefacts were found. These include two cores of dacite, and two big flakes of silicified sandstone with thick patinas. All the non-chert artefacts were found below spit 7 (35 cm below the surface), down to thesterile concreted sand deposit at the base of the sequence. The two big flakes made of siliceous sandstone were found right on the basement itself. The source of this non-chert material is on Rote Island, since it has a varied geology with sedimentary, igneous, and metamorphic rocks (Geological Map of the Kupang-Atambua Quadrangle, Timor, 1976).

Utilised flakes with signs of use-wear

The utilised flakes from Lua Meko consist of a small number of gloss-bearing flakes, flakes with edge striations, and flakes with edge damage (see table 5.17 above).

Glossed flakes

Seven flakes (one from the middle layer and six from the upper) have a vitreous polish (gloss) on their edge. Four have signs of use in transverse motion, having microfracturing and polish on either the ventral or dorsal side. Two have signs of use in longitudinal motion, since striations and micro-fractures are clustered on both the ventral and dorsal edges. One retouched tool with a tang has gloss on its worn edge (not on the retouched tang), suggesting that it was used on silica-rich material such as bamboo or palm leaves. Six of the gloss-bearing flakes are drawn in figure 5.23 below.

Other signs of use-wear

Both blade proportioned and normal flakes were chosen directly for use as tools. 48 flakes had more than one type of use-wear (striation, edge damage or edge dulling). Unmodified but utilised chert flakes are absent in the lower level, but occur in the middle level.

Thirty six non-retouched flakes were recognised that also have signs of utilisation in the form of striation and polish (gloss and matte polish). Only 3 worn flakes were found in the lower layers , although this low number might not reflect the actual level of flake usage since short term use might not leave any traces.

Traces of micro-fractures that do not exceed 1 mm in length on glossed flakes indicate that they were used on medium hard materials. Such flakes also have striations that go beyond the micro-fractures, across the flake surfaces.

Fifteen flakes can be identified as tools used with transverse motion, but it is difficult to identify them precisely in terms of scraping or whittling actions. Examination of edge damage, all unifacial, suggests that all were used with a scraping mode of action. Some of these fifteen flakes were used for working soft material, as indicated by the occurrence of 1 mm micro-fractures, and striations that are only visible inside the micro-fractures.

Two flakes were identified as tools used with longitudinal motion, either as a saw or as a knife.

Stone manufacturing technology
Retouched flakes

Two big flaked stone artefacts from near the bedrock are very interesting. Both are made of silicified sandstone (figure 5. 24) . One of the these large flakes does not have any sign of secondary retouch, but the other, made by splitting a big pebble, was further retouched along its margin unifacially from its ventral side. The dorsal side is not worked or retouched at all. On the middle of the dorsal surface there is an indentation which indicates use as an anvil. There are two split pebbles that are flaked monofacially from the dorsal side. Technologically, one of the big tools from Lua Meko shows a clear Hoabinhian character, although the size is bigger than commonly found in true Hoabinhian sites. The large flake is retouched monofacially along its margin and the dorsal part is not worked or modified at all. The pitting on the dorsal part represents post-manufacturing use.

There are 29 retouched pieces from Lua Meko. These retouched flakes only form a small percentage of the total artifacts in both the middle and the upper level. Seven were found clustered between 30 and 35 cm from the surface, while the rest were found spread out from the surface down to spit 13 (65 cm below the surface).

Based on the location of the retouch, these tools can be classified into four types. The first type is retouched on the margin near the proximal end and on the platform to form a tang to facilitate hafting (Figure 5.25: a). The second type has retouch along the flake or blade margin. The third type is a flake from which the proximal and distal ends have been snapped off, leaving only the middle portion. One side of this middle portion (the thinner one) is then retouched. The end result is a rectangular piece with a wedge form (figure 5. 25 : l). It is not clear whether such pieces were made intentionally, or just result from blade breakage. The fourth type has retouch on the ridge of the flake (figure 5. 25 :e).

The types of retouch on Lua Meko flaked stone artefacts can be classified into delicate retouch and hard hammer percussion retouch with negative bulbs of percussion.

The retouched pieces were probably used with transverse motions, recognisable from the directions of striation at more than 45 degrees from the working edge. One retouched piece (figure 5.25:e) probably was used as a drill. Most retouched pieces are unifacial, retouched on either the dorsal or ventral surfaces. In three cases only, retouch was applied bifacially (figure 5. 25:d, j and k). These belong to the upper layer.

56

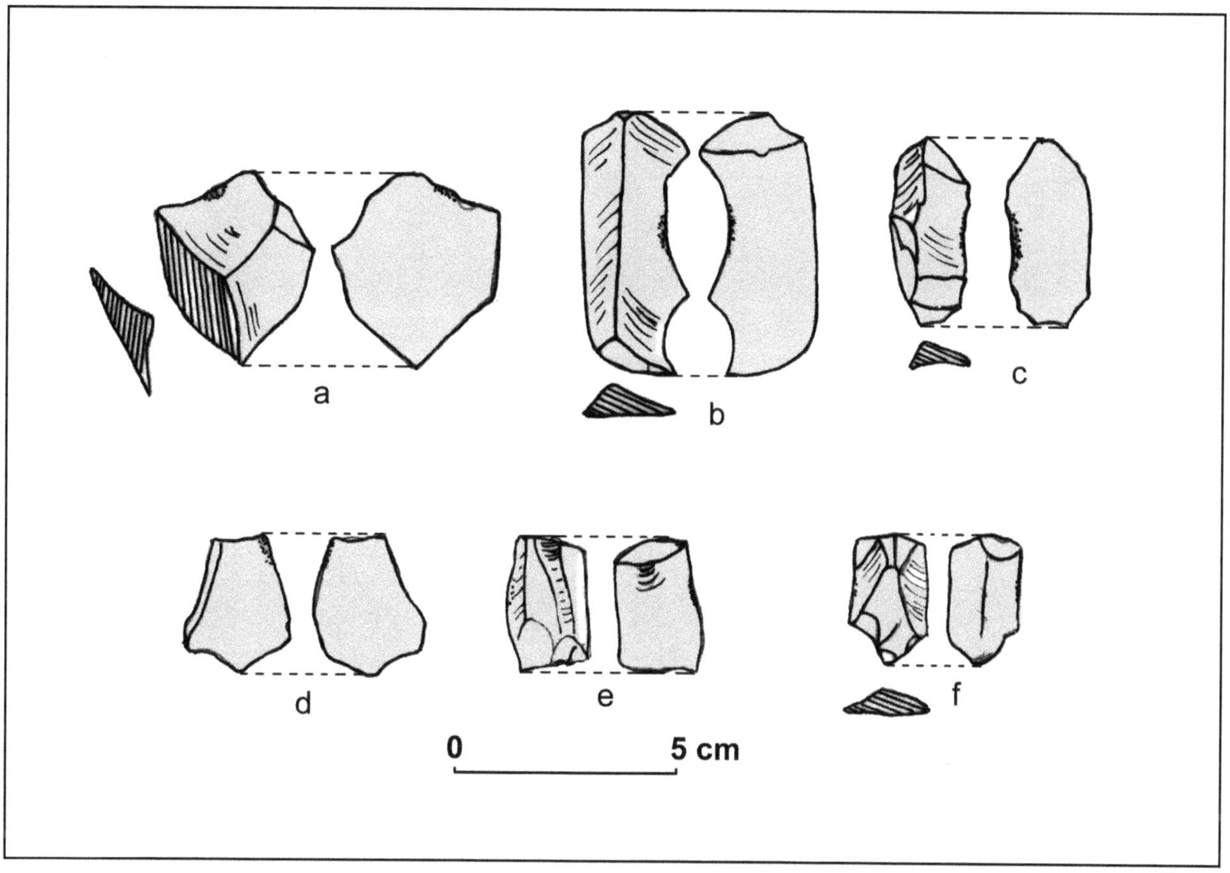

Figure 5.23: Gloss-bearing flakes, Lua Meko
a. from spit 4 , b. from spit 4, c from spit 5, d. from spit 3.e. from spit 6, f.from surface.
Stipples shows the glossed areas

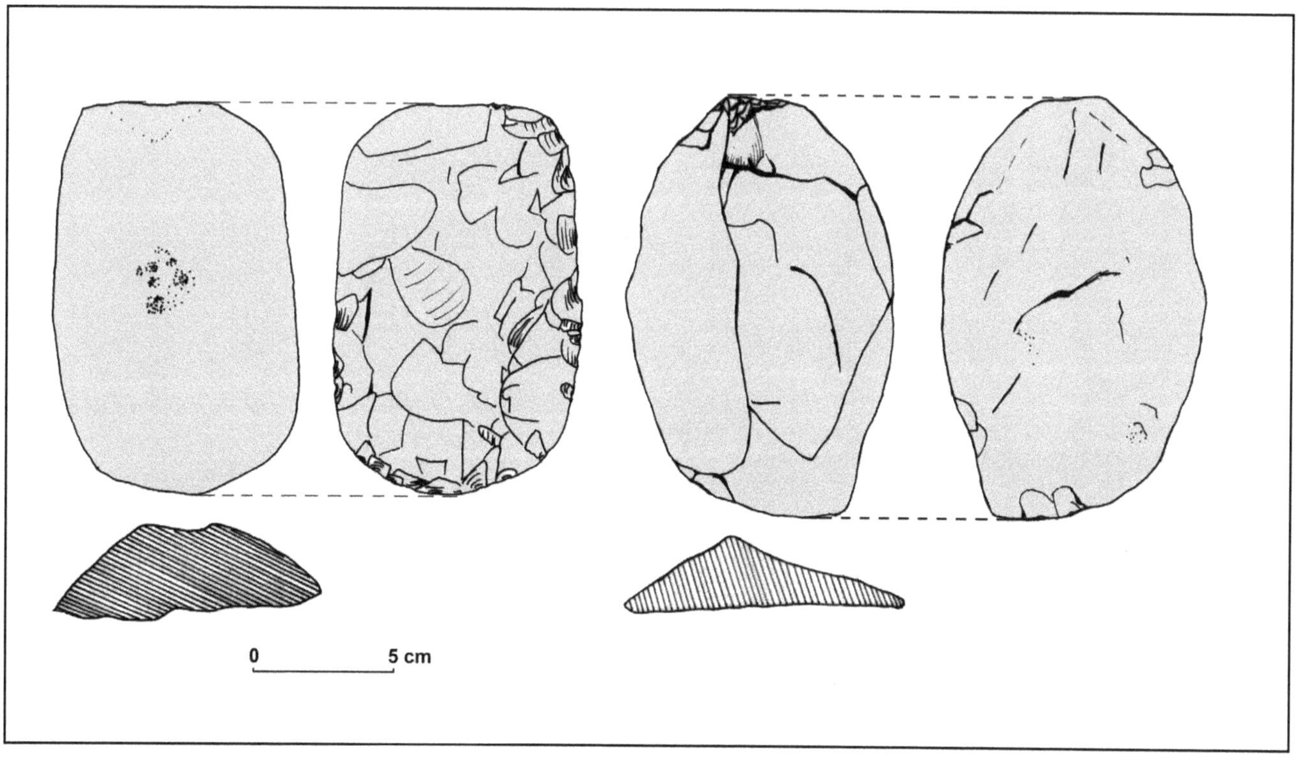

Figure 5.24: Two flaked artefacts of siliceous sandstone from the base of Lua Meko (spit 14)

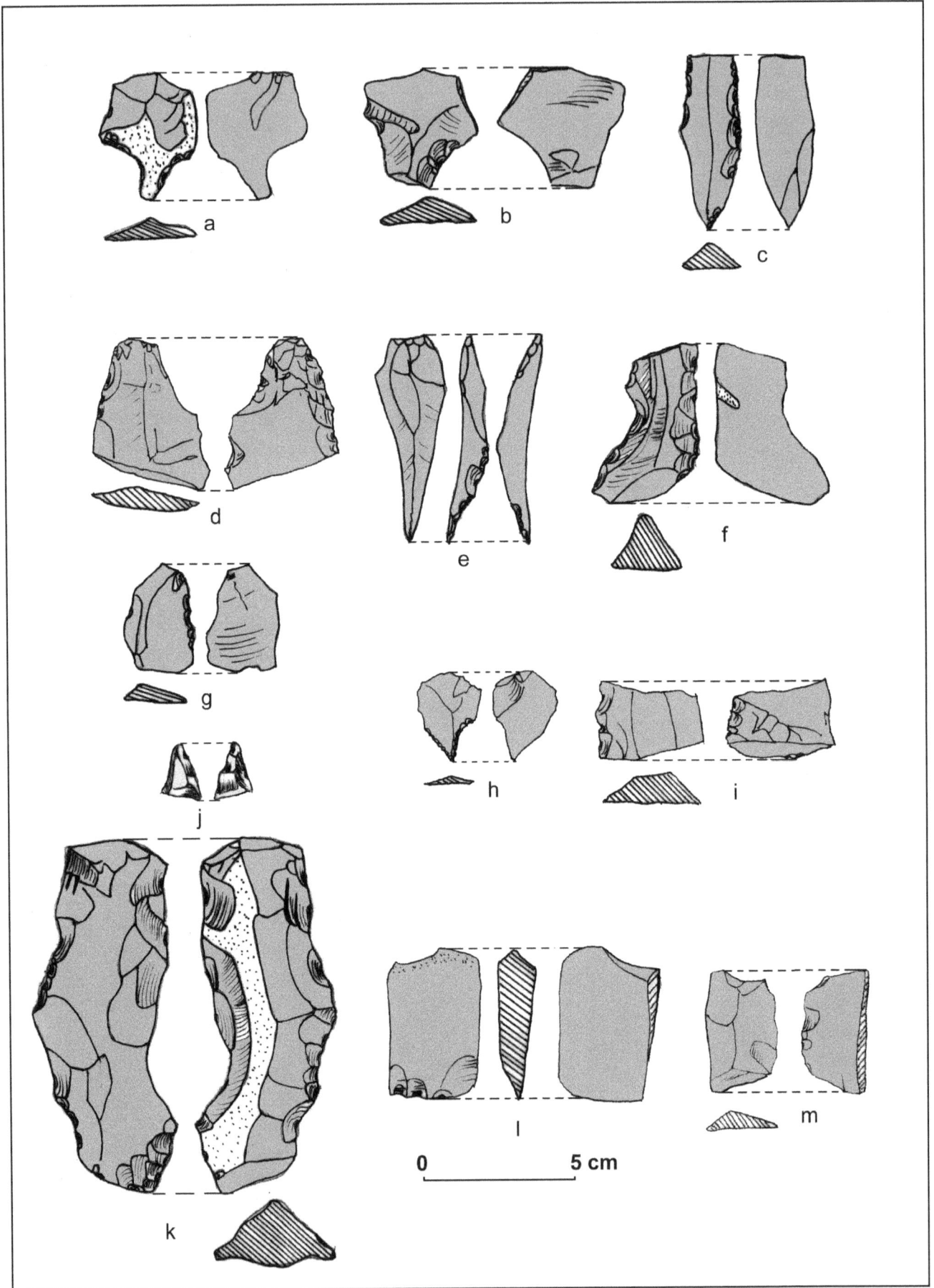

Figure 5.25: Retouched Flakes from Terminal Pleistocene to Mid-Holocene layer, Lua Meko, Rote. a. with gloss on its edge, from spit 2, b. from spit 1, c. from spit 10, d. from surface, e from spit 10, f. from spit 9, g. from spit 1, h. from spit 10, i. from spit 7, j. from spit 1, k. from surface, l. from spit 10, m from spit 7.

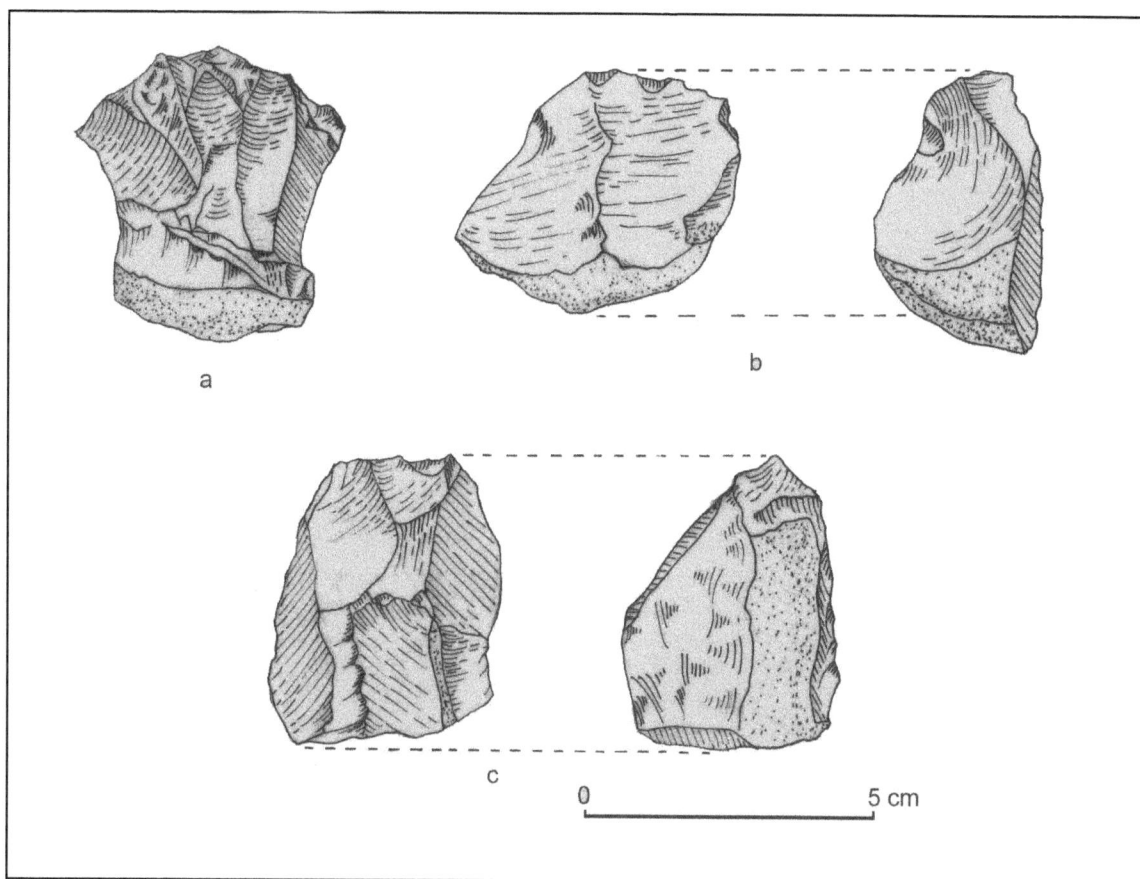

Figure 5.26: Lua Meko cores (drawn by Agus Tri Hascaryo)
a. from square Ex spit 2;b. from square TP spit 1;c. from square TP spit 8; d.from square EX spit 7

As with the other sites described, retouched pieces form only a small proportion compared with the total number of flaked stone artefacts as can be seen in table 5.18.

The table shows that the ratio of debitage to retouched flakes is lower in the middle analytical level than in the lower or upper analytical levels, suggesting more efficiency in chert usage at this time.

Analytical level	spits	Ratio of waste flakes to retouched tools
Lower	11-14	170
Middle	7-10	102
Upper	1-6	164.5

Table 5.17: Ratios of waste material to retouched items by analytical level at Lua Meko

Modes of core reduction

A total of 67 cores was recovered from Lua Meko. Two are of igneous material, recovered from spit 11. Of all the cores recovered, only one had a single platform with parallel negative scars, and this came from spit 5. This core was not completely worked and still has a 40% surface cover of cortex. This low number of blade cores need not reflect the

actual level of blade making activity in the site, because previous blade scars can easily be eradicated if core reduction continues. Other cores are of multiplatform type, with three or more striking platforms. 32 cores still retain some cortex on less than 25 % of their surfaces.

Test Statistics[a]

	LENGTH	WIDTH	PLATWIDT	PLATHICK
Mann-Whitney U	523.500	659.000	669.500	661.500
Wilcoxon W	6964.500	7100.000	6234.500	766.500
Z	-2.059	-1.396	-.540	-.658
Asymp. Sig. (2-tailed)	.039	.163	.589	.510

a. Grouping Variable: UNIT

Table 5.18: The resulst of Mann-Whitney U Test for flakes recovered from level analysis lower and middle.

Test Statistics[a]

	LENGTH	WIDTH	PLATWIDT	PLATHICK
Mann-Whitney U	15893.000	17039.000	16715.000	17009.500
Wilcoxon W	68219.000	67442.000	22280.000	70965.500
Z	-2.044	-.768	-.126	-.334
Asymp. Sig. (2-tailed)	.041	.442	.900	.739

a. Grouping Variable: UNIT

Table 5.19: The results of Mann-Whitney U Test for flakes recovered from Middle layer (unit 3) and upper layer (unit 4)

There are no definite bipolar cores. This is quite surprising, as many cores are small in size and would have been difficult to work without using an anvil. Cores with traces of crushing could have been struck in bipolar fashion. From examination of the debitage it is likely that some bipolar reduction was applied, and the indentation on the dorsal part of one of the large tools described above (figure 5.20, left) found above the sterile basement layer suggests use as an anvil. My own experiment in bipolar reduction, using an iron hammer and stone anvil, resulted in compression flakes and angular shatter of types seen in the Lua Meko assemblage.

The flakes with blade proportion (length:breadth >2:1) is only 33 out of 231 complete flakes measured in the Holocene to mid Holocene level middle and upper analytical level) of Lua Meko (14.28%). Some of them fall in the bladelet category.

However, not all of these blade proportion flakes have parallel margins. The true blades/bladelets with an index of parallelism between 0.90-1.10 are only 24 pieces of the total complete flakes measured, indicating that actual blade production was rare, a suggestion also supported by the rare occurrence of blade cores in the deposit.

A comparison of mean measurements using Mann-Whitney Test, equivalent to independent t-test analysis, between the chert flakes from the lower, middle and upper analytical levels indicates that flake sizes in the lower analytical level are the biggest. There is significant differences in flake length between the middle and upper analytical levels and between lower and middle levels but for other flakes variables, the differences are not significant (table 5.19 and 5.20).

Reconstruction of the sizes of the original raw material nodules, from cores that still retain significant amounts of cortex, indicate that average nodule size was between 40 cm and 90 cm in largest dimension. This matches the maximum lengths of flakes, these being 74.94 mm in the middle level and 63.47 mm in the lower level. An examination of the lengths of the last flakes detached from indicates that cores were discarded when the last flake that could be detached was on average 17.26 mm long. The smallest flake that has a worn edge is 19.98 mm long.

Pottery form and decoration

Only two non red-slipped body sherds were found in Lua Meko. Both are small, each about 6 cm by 6 cm, and the vessel forms can be guessed to have been globular.

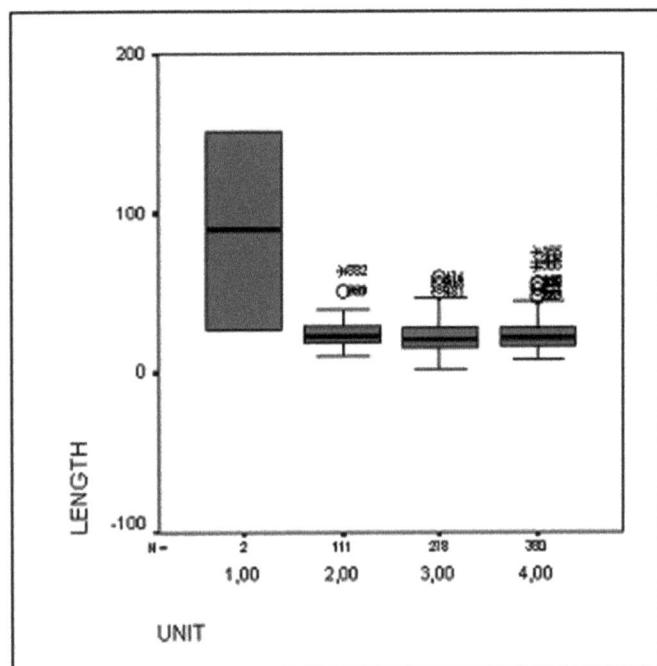

Figure 5.27: Box plot showing the spread of flake length recovered from each level of analysis, Lua Meko

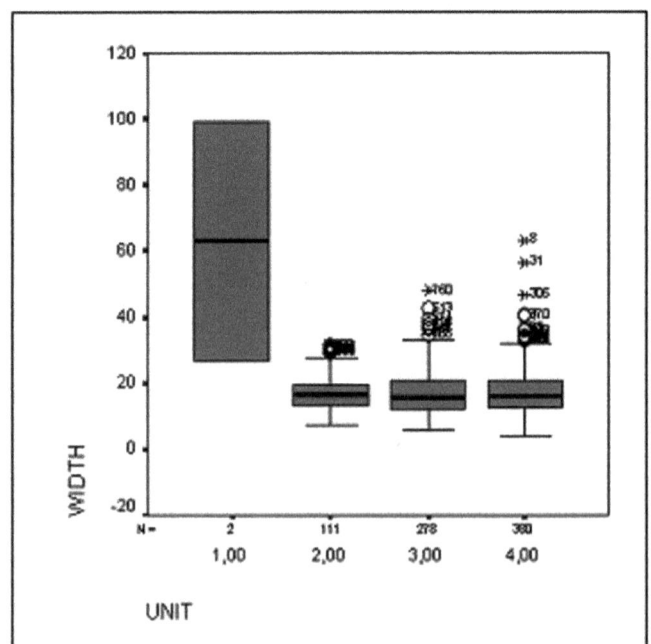

Figure 5.28: Box plot showing the spread of flake width recovered from each level of analysis, Lua Meko

5. Summary

Lua Meko reveals that Rote has been occupied since the Late Pleistocene, at least 24,000 years ago. The lithic technology of this period is quite different from that of the Holocene, and the two large silicified sandstone artifacts from the base of Lua Meko are unique in the Rote sequence. Lua Manggetek only began to be occupied in the Terminal Pleistocene.

During their later phase of usage, both shelters in Tonggobatu complex were used as loci for human burial, an activity that could have caused some disturbance. By the time pottery was introduced, both sites had virtually gone out of regular frequentation (unless the burial activity is also very young).

The rock shelter occupants used mostly chert for simple flaked lithic tools, and retouching technology was only recognised in the later period of occupancy.

There is increase intensity of site use in the later period of occupancy, as reflected by an increase in the numbers of stone artefacts (especially retouched flakes, unmodified glossed flakes, unmodified used flakes, waste flakes and cores). An increase intensity of site use with time, particularly in the early and middle Holocene, is also reflected in the MNI of each shell species.

The humans who occupied the site in the earlier period exploited freshwater shellfish, bats and rats. During the Holocene, they shifted to exploit a greater variety of resources, particularly soft shore shellfish. From the Timor evidence recovered by Ian Glover (1986), it seems likely that pottery and macaques (*Macaca fasicularis*) were introduced late in time into this region of eastern Nusa Tenggara, and perhaps together.

The major question over the sequence in Lua Meko and Lua Manggetek is whether the occupation was continuous but very light, or whether it occurred intermittently under conditions of continuous vertical perturbation and episodic sediment loss due to erosion.

6

THE LIE MADIRA CAVE

1. Lie Madira excavation

On Sawu island, an excavation was carried out in Lie Madira (figure 6.1) in Desa Daieko. Inside the cave there is a trace of a former excavation (approximately 2 by 2 m) dug in 1981 (confirmed by Dept. of Education and Culture sources), which is now refilled with stones. No other disturbance was noted. Some stone flakes and many shells were found on the surface, mostly in the front area of the cave.

A test pit measuring 1 m x 1 m was laid out about 4 m east of the previous trench (see plan of the site in figure 6.2). Although a lamp was used during excavation, it was difficult to identify some of the archaeological finds inside the cave, especially when the excavation reached the deeper spits. All finds could only be identified clearly outside the cave, during sieving. The excavation was carried out in 5 cm spits, measured below the cave floor, down to spit 28 at 140 cm below the surface. This is 25 cm below the first sterile spit, but only half the square was dug to this depth, in the eastern half of the square, since the western side was blocked by a big stone.

Stratigraphy

The excavation uncovered several stratigraphic layers, as follows (figure 6.3):

Layer 1 is a very dark brown (10 YR 2/2) humic soil containing roots, small fragments of coral and hematite. This layer is about 2.5 – 10 cm thick.

Layer 2 is also a humic layer, but mixed with ash so that the colour is only dark brown (10 YR 3/2). This layer contains small roots, quartz fragments, limestone fragments up to 0.5 cm in diameter, charcoal, coral debris, shell fragments and small fragments of bone.

Layer 3 is a thin dark brown sandy loam (7.5 YR 3/2), about 2 cm-5 cm thick. It contains limestone, quartz, green and orange-brown chert micro-debitage and shell fragments.

Layer 4 is a dark brown sandy loam (7.5 YR 4/2), about 2.5 cm –12 cm thick. It also contains quartz, orange-brown chert micro-debitage, limestone and charcoal.

Layer 5 is a dark brown sandy loam but the colour is a bit darker (7.5 YR 3/4) It contains limestone pieces up to 2 cm in diameter, dense shell fragments, charcoal, roots, and

Figure 6.1: Excavation in Lie Madira, Desa Daieko, Sawu

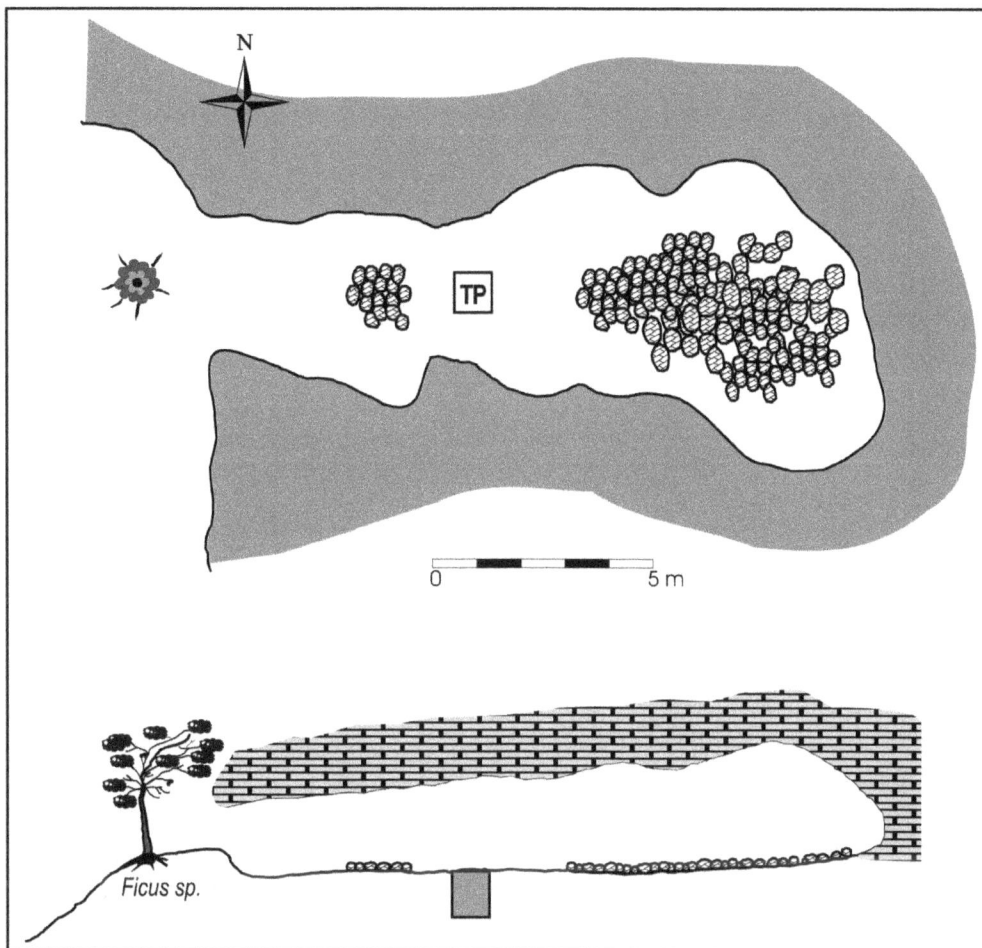

Figure 6.2: Plan and section of Lie Madira cave, showing the position of test pit

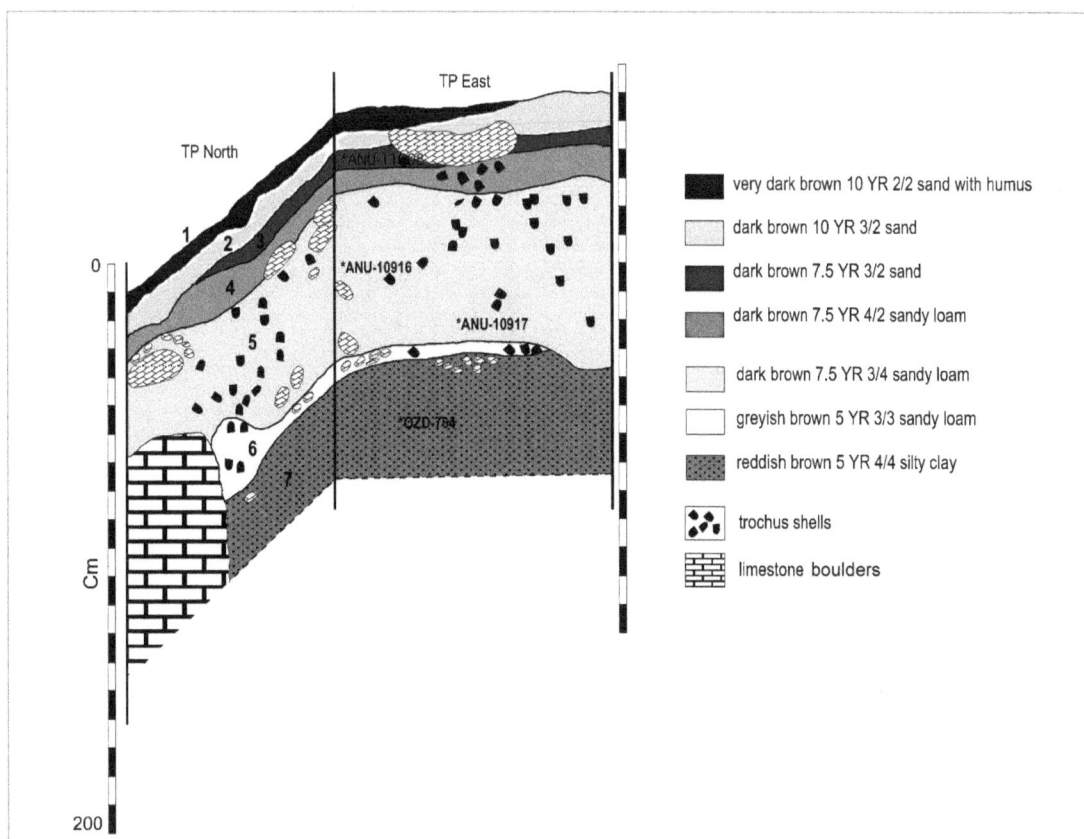

Figure 6.3: Section of tespit, Lie Madira, Sawu Island

spit	0		1		2		3		4		5		6		7		8		9		10		11	
Material	no	gr	no	gr	no	gr	no	gr	no	gr	no	gr	no	gr	no	gr	no	gr	no	gr	no	gr	no	gr
pottery	6	50	5	65	5	20			6	10														
stone artefacts:																								
hammer stone																	1							
cores											3	175	6	130	17	900	14	440	11	285	4	235		
retouched & debitage	1	15	1	20			13	100	60	290	78	460	128	535	1051	1940	76	840	132	1075	141	1159	44	550
shells:																								
shell artefact									1	5														
non-artefactual shells	18	529			11	65	28	376	51	670	71	650	85	5125	92	17025	98	9750	121	11375	115	10520	87	8250
animal bones					6	15	5	40	7	12	8	15	23	95	7	10							9	50
teeth					1				2															

spit	12		13		14		15		16		17		18		19		20		21		22		23-28	
Material	no	gr	no	gr	no	gr	no	gr	no	gr	no	gr	no	gr	no	gr	no	gr	no	gr	no	gr	no	gr
pottery																								
stone artefacts:																								
hammer																								
cores	2	50	2	45			7	85																
retouched & debitage	66	675	77	845	58	525	41	420	28	325	8	119	12	150			4	5						
shells:																								
shell bead																								
non artefacts	74	5000	59	4650	42	3900		3000	23	1500	5	150	5	500	4	15			3	15				
animal bones	6	45			18	130	1	15	10	50	10	35	6	13	1	3								
charcoal																					★			

Note: charcoal present in small quantity has sent for AMS dating

Table 6.1 Distribution of archaeological finds in the test pit (TP), Lie Madira

yellow, green and red chert micro-debitage. This layer is up to 70 cm thick.

Layer 6 is a sandy loam, slightly pale and greyish (5 YR 3/3), that contains quartz fragments, much charcoal, hematite, shell fragments, much red chert micro-debitage, and limestone pieces. This layer varied from 5 cm up to 30 cm thick in the northern corner and spread as a long lens to the east side of the square. This layer has an abundance of *Trochus* shells.

Layer 7 is clay (5 YR 4/4) and contains quartz, charcoal, shell fragments, hematite, but no chert micro-debitage, although a small number of large chert pieces were found down to 100 cm below the surface. Shells continued until spit 22, 110 cm below the surface.

Archaeological finds

There is no human remains found from Lie Madira excavation. The archaeological finds from Lie Madira are characterized by an abundance of *Trochus* shells and a fairly large average size of lithic material. Small flakes measuring under 2 cm are rare, suggesting that intensive stone working probably was not carried out in the cave, which presumably was too dark inside.

The most abundant *Trochus* shells occurred from spit 6 to spit 16. Below spit 16, cultural remains become very sporadic and a sterile layer was reached at 125 cm below the surface. Sherds occurred from the surface down to 20 cm. The distribution of the archaeological finds by spit can be seen in table 6.1 above.

Plotting the vertical distributions of archaeological finds, *Trochus* shells and stone flakes are common from layer 2 down to layer 5. Pottery was only found down to layer 2.

Radiocarbon dating results.

Three shell samples for carbon dating were submitted to the ANU Radiocarbon Laboratory, from spit 4 (*Trochus niloticus*), spit 11 (*Trochus niloticus*), and from spit 15 (*Terebra maculatus*). One sample from spit 23 (charcoal) was submitted to ANSTO in Sydney for AMS dating, using

an AINSE research grant provided to Dr. Peter Bellwood at ANU. The results and the calibration dates are presented in table 6.2.

As can be seen from archaeological finds table 6.2 above, the site was occupied intensively during the Middle Holocene period, at about 5000 years ago. Perhaps most of the recovered materials belong to this phase. The AMS date, almost modern, could be from charcoal that fell into the excavation square without being observed in the dark conditions. The sample had to be collected during sieving.

The other dates are in good order by depth and suggest a relatively undisturbed sequence of deposits. This is supported by a few interesting consistencies: sandy beach and tidal mudflat bivalves, together with shell artefacts, never occur below 30 cm; pottery and domesticated animal bones occur in the goat dung layer and on the surface only (based on positive identification). This suggests that the bulk of the deposit, and most of the finds, belong to the pre-Neolithic phase.

The Lie Madira deposit is divided into a lower analytical level, which corresponds with sporadic archaeological remains, a middle analytical level which corresponds with a dense presence of *Trochus* shells, and an upper analytical level which contains pottery and positive identification of humanly-introduced fauna. (table 6.3 beow).

2. Analyses of archaeological finds
Animal bones

In this site, animal bones occurred in all spits except the lowest. They include marine turtles, marine fish (the majority), bovid or equid, and deer (see table 6.4 to table 6.6)

Marine turtle bones occurred from spit 2 down to spit 17 (85 cm below surface), which dates between 4000 and 8000 years ago. They are quite common in the deposit compared with other animal remains.

A tooth fragment of cow or horse occurred in spit 5, just 5 cm below the first occurrence of pottery. Deer occurred from spit 2 down to spit 6, again to just before the first occurrence

Lab no.	spit	depth	layer	square	sample	uncalib 14C age (years BP)	Cal BP
ANU-11008	4	20 cm	3	TP	*Angaria sp.*	4750±90	5643 (5570) 5456
ANU-10916	11	55 cm	5	TP	*Trochus*	5800±90	6791 (6700) 6596
ANU-10917	15	75 cm	5	TP	*Terebra*	5960±70	6561 (6870) 6774
OZD-764	22	110 cm	7	TP	Charcoal (AMS)	680±40	666 (656) 564

Table 6.2 Radiocarbon dates from Lie Madira

Analytical level	spits	natural layer
Lower	17-28	lower 5, 6, 7
Middle	7-16	upper 5
Upper	1-6	1-4

Table 6.3 The correlations between analytical levels, spits and natural stratigraphic layers in Lie Madira.

spit	B/U	N	weight	remarks
2	B	1	1	carapace fragment
5	U	5	15	carapace fragment
6	U	8	49	carapace fragment and phalanges
8	U	3	12	carapace fragments and phalanx
10	U	2	17	carapace fragments
11	U	2	12	1 neck vertebra, one long bone
12	U	4	32	carapace fragments, long bone fragments
13	U	1	4	carapace fragments
14	U	10	15	carapace fragments and phalanges
16	U	5	11	carapace fragments and phalanges
17	U	4	20	carapace fragments

Table 6.4: Distribution of turtle remains, test pit square, Lie Madirta
B/U = burn/unburn

spit	B/U	No	Weight	remarks
2	U	1	0.1	spine of medium-large sized fish
3	U	1	0.2	spine of medium-large sized fish
4	U	1	0.2	cranial elements of medium-large sized fish
11	U	1	0.2	vertebra of medium-large sized fish

Table 6.5: Distribution of fish remains, test pit square, Lie Madira
B/U = burn/unburn

spit	B/U	N	weight	remarks
2	U	1	1	phalanx of adult deer
2	U	1	1	shaft fragment, possibly of deer
2	U	1	3	molar of immature deer
3	U	4	2	shaft fragments, possibly of deer, one with cut mark
4	U	3	2	two phalanx and one premolar of immature deer
5	U	1	0.5	deer molar
5	U	1	0.5	tooth fragment of horse or cow
6	U	6	4	ribs and shaft fragments
6	B	1	2	shaft fragments, possibly of deer
8	U	2	1	shaft fragments, possibly of deer or turtle
18	U	3	1	shaft fragments, possibly of deer or turtle
19	U	2	3	shaft fragments, possibly of deer or turtle

Table 6.6: Distribution of animal bones, test pit square, Lie Madira
B/U = burn/unburn

of pottery. But there is also a tentative identification of deer in spit 19 at 90 cm below surface, which dates about 7000 to 8000 years ago. It is possible that the deposit has been disturbed since there are no other indications of deer translocation at this early date, and the condition of the material did not permit an absolutely positive identification.

Fish remains occurred from spit 2 down to spit 11. All are of medium to large-sized fish, estimated by Ken Aplin to be more than 1-2 kg in weight. Sea mammals remains (dugong ?) occurred from spit 5 down to spit 19. It is not clear whether dugong were scavenged after death, or hunted. Sawu and Rote islands are also presently major nesting localities for *Chelonia mydas* marine turtles (Kitchener, 1996), so this species was probably exploited as source of food by the prehistoric inhabitants.

Shell analysis

Only one shell artefact was found during excavation, i.e. round cut Conus shell (figure 6.4).

The majority of the food shells from Lie Madira are marine gastropods from the coral reefs and sandy intertidal zones. Only rare specimens are from tidal mudflat or mangrove habitats (table 4, in appendix). From the table of MNI calculations for the site, it can be seen that the number of shells tends to increase dramatically from spit 15 (5960 ± 70 BP), before decreasing again in spit 4 (4750 ± 90 BP). Since the radiocarbon dates from the site are in relatively good order, except for that from near the base of the site, approximate rates of shell discard per 100 years can be calculated as indicators of the intensity of site use (see figure 6.6 and 6.7). Although the species of shells in Lie Madira are quite numerous, belonging to 15 families, only 3 families were commonly brought to the cave - Trochidae, Neritidae and Chitonidae. Other shell families were represented by fewer than 4 shells per spit.

Figure 6.4: Round cut Conus Shell, Lie Madira

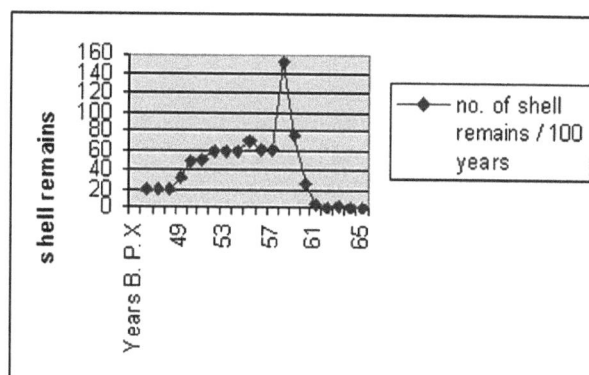

Figure 6.5: Changing rates of shell discard per century in Lie Madira,

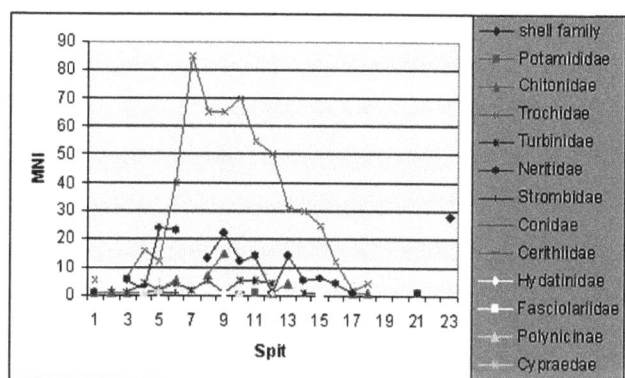

Figure 6.6: Absolute abundances of shell families, Lie Madira

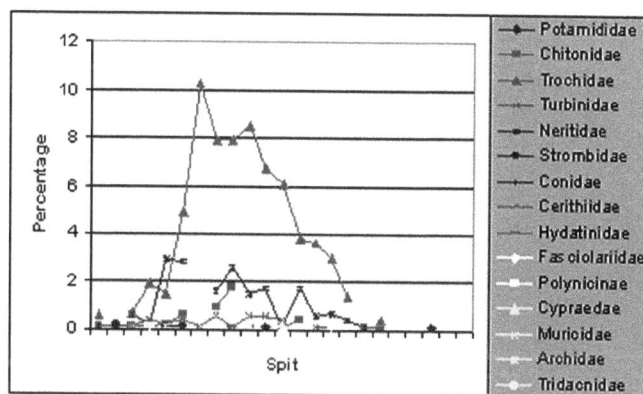

Figure 6.7: Relative abundances of shell families, Lie Madira

These above figures show that the numbers of Trochidae predominate over other shell families. The number increases continually since first appearance in spit 18, before starting to decrease in spit 6. The relative frequency graph also presents the same trend. The percentage of Trochidae in the total shell assemblage is higher than other shell families, especially between spits 6 and 15. If we look more closely, this increasing number of Trochidae is what causes the total number of shells per spit to increase. By comparison, numbers of Neritidae and Chitonidae are much steadier through time.

At the time of first occupation more than 6200 years ago, only Neritidae and Chitonidae were brought into the cave. Trochidae start to appear when spit 18 was deposited. In the most intensive phase of deposition between spits 17 and 5, dating to between 5900 BP and 4700 BP (before pottery appeared), a greater variety of shell families was brought into the cave. This may be a result of stabilisation of mid-Holocene sea level, which brought a greater range of shellfish into easier access and allowed people to live more sedentarily than before, and to use the cave more intensively. Indeed, the profile of shell discard through time, presented in figures 6.5, makes it very likely that the cave was only occupied for a relatively short period of time in the mid-Holocene, about 6000 years ago as suggested by the three marine shell C14 dates, and that most of the lowermost and uppermost material found in the deposit simply represents the results of incidental disturbance.

Intensive exploitation could have reduced both the numbers and size ranges of molluscs over time. Betty Meehan's studies among Aborigines in Northern Australia

confirm that people tend to collect mature rather than young immature shells, saving the latter for future exploitation (Meehan, 1981). The increase in taking of *Trochus* during

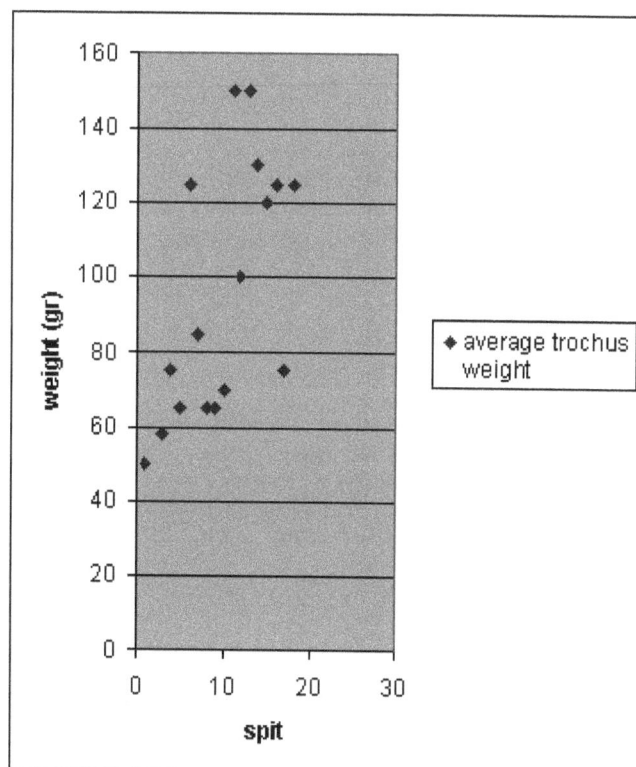

Figure 6.8: Average weights of Trochus shells by spit in Lie Madira

the period of occupation, as a result of an increasing intensity of site use, may eventually have led to over exploitation of this shell species. There is a tendency for average *Trochus* weights to decrease steadily over the period of occupation (figure 6.8 above). This phenomenon may signify over exploitation of this shell species.

Flaked stone artefacts

There are a total of 1296 flaked stone artefacts) from the Lie Madira deposit, comprising cores, secondarily worked or retouched flakes, gloss-bearing flakes, other types of utilised flakes and debitage. Included in the category of debitage are unutilised flakes, flake shatter, and non-flake shatter or spalls. The last three categories are grouped together as waste flakes and are not measured in terms of size variables in the debitage analysis below.

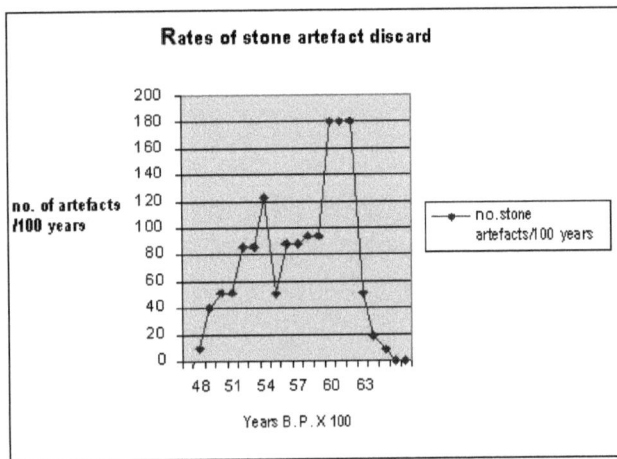

Figure 6.9: Rate of stone artefact discard per 100 year interval, Lie Madira

The rate of stone artefact discard over time during the cave occupation is set out in figure 6. 9. The figure shows that the highest rate of stone artefact discard took place around 6000-5800 years ago. This signifies that more stone working took place during the deposition of the first half of the middle level in the site sequence. In the following period, the quantity of stone working activity reduced sharply, with a slight increase about 5200 years ago. When pottery first appeared in the deposit, stone working activity ceased. Yet, pottery never appeared in large quantities, suggesting that the site was not intensively occupied in the late phase.

Raw Material

The raw material of the flaked stone artefacts from Lie Madira is exclusively chert, with a variety of colours - mostly reddish brown with minor amounts of yellow and green. From the geological map sheet Kupang-Atambua (Geological Research and Development Centre, Bandung, 1979), it can be inferred that the source of the chert could have been the Ofu Formation in the southern part of Sawu Island, and also the Bobonaro Formation in the interior, or as exotic blocks from other formations. From the mountains of interior Sawu, chert nodules are carried down by rivers to the lowlands. So, precise sources remain uncertain, and whether people collected the chert directly from outcrops or from the river beds on the northern side of Sawu can only be confirmed by further research. Although the first stage of core reduction occasionally took place in the cave, there is indication that more often this first stage was carried out at the source, since very few flakes were found with 75% - 100% dorsal cortex. Other interpretation is that the chert raw material are available in boulder size so that people broke the material into smaller pieces at the source and brought several smaller pieces to the cave.

The identification of utilised flakes

Utilised flakes recognised in the Lie Madira assemblage include gloss-bearing flakes, flakes with striations on their edges, and flakes with patterned edge damage in the form of flake scars. To be certain that unmodified flakes were actually used as tools, at least two of these forms of use wear must be present.

Gloss-bearing flakes

Throughout all units, only 8 flakes with glossed edges were found. One came from the lower analytical level, six from the middle, and one from the upper (Table 6.7). The gloss traces are small spots that occur both on retouched and on unmodified flakes/blades (figure 6.10:e-h). These gloss traces tend to be more developed on one side of each tool and do not develop symmetrically on the dorsal and ventral edges. Silica-rich plant material is presumably responsible for these patches of gloss. Since the use-wear on these pieces exists as striations perpendicular to the flake edge, it shows that these tools were used in scraping modes of activity. The gloss was recognised on some flakes that have blade proportions. Gloss was also recognised on the potential hafting area of a stone blade (figure 6.11a) that

Level of analysis	spits	retouched flakes	unmodified glossed flakes	unmodified used flakes	waste flakes	cores	all stone artefacts
Lower	17-28	1	1	_	28	_	30
Middle	6,-16	24	6	39	977	63	1109
Upper	1,-5	1	1	_	151	3	156
Subtotal		26	8	39	1156	66	1295

Table 6.7 Distribution of stone artefact variety by lebel of analysis, Lie Madira

might have been used as a knife. There are no edge striations, but these could have been erased by subsequent retouching. In this case the gloss seems to have resulted from contact with binding to facilitate hafting.

Other forms of use wear

Flakes with both blade proportions and the more usual flake proportions were chosen as instant tools by the Lie Madira occupants. Blade-proportioned flakes, not necessarily true blades, appear to have been chosen most frequently. 39 blades and flakes with patterned edge damage and striations occurred in the middle analytical level (spits 6 - 16), but none were found in the lower and upper levels. The maximum lengths of used edge on these tool is 5 mm to 25 mm. A short used edge suggests that the tool was used in a scraper mode of activity, and only used once and then discarded. Repeated and continued usage as a scraper can result in a long used edge, or several used edges on a single stone tool.Based on the direction of the striations, type of flake scar, and the edge angle, the functions of the flakes from Lie Madira assemblage can be classified into scraper modes of activity, knife modes, and possibly drill modes (borers).

Stone manufacturing technology

A total of **900** pieces flakes consisting of complete flakes and broken flakes with platform intact (proximal flakes) were measured for length, mid-point width and platform variables (striking platform width and thickness). Using these measurements, the flake tools with secondary modification and the unmodified but utilised flakes can be compared. To maximize available data, broken proximal flakes were also measured for size variables when they were present.

Secondarily worked flakes

Secondarily worked flakes in the Lie Madira assemblage consist of flakes modified after detachment from cores, either by edge retouch (figure 6.10) to sharpen the edge or to shape an attachment area or other feature (see figure 6.11). Lie Madira did not produce any of the tanged blades reported from East Timor assemblages.

From the retouched pieces recovered, three types of edge retouch can be recognised. The first is delicate edge retouch (figure 6.10: except b and c), the second is percussion edge retouch (figure 6.10 :b and c) with distinct and deep scar beds separated by spurs, and the third type is edge trimming retouch produced by a hammerstone or hardwood tool to remove the spurs and provide an even sharp edge (figure 6.10: b). Traces of holes, cracks, and scratches on the platform as suggested by Semenov (1964) to indicate the practice of pressure flaking cannot be detected.

Careful examination can show that some retouch was produced after some degree of use of the tool had already occurred. This situation is indicated by traces of use wear (striations, gloss and polish) that occur outside the borders of the retouch, and their absence within the retouch scars themselves (figure 6.11:a). Sometimes the striations can be denser on the unretouched than on the retouched surface.

The type of retouch used to blunt the edge (backing retouch) is not found in the Lie Madira assemblage.

Although there are some flakes which have blunted edges opposite to the sharp edge, such blunting was not produced after the flakes were detached. Rather, this kind of blunted edge is a result of re-directing flakes struck from core platforms.

Throughout all units, a more economical use of the chert raw material occurs with increasing depth. This can be inferred from the decreasing ratio of waste flakes to retouched tools plotted by depth (table 6. 8).

During the deposition of the middle level more stone manufacturing activity took place, as reflected by the 1109 flaked stone artefacts recovered. The higher proportion of non-retouched tools (39 unmodified used flakes) compared with retouched tools (26 specimens) indicates that people were more accustomed to chose flakes expediently rather than to manufacture special tools to suit special tasks. In fact, some of the gloss-bearing flakes were retouched after being used and so are classified as curated expedient tools. Curating retouch can prolong the use-life of tools and can thereby slow the rates of discard rate and replacement. The abundance of chert raw material close to the site probably means that the people of Lie Madira did not need to produce tools with special shaping, and neither did they need to do frequent maintenance of stone tools.

Analytical level	spits	Ratio of waste flakes to tools
Lower	17-28	14
Middle	6-16	14.15
Upper	1-5	75.5

Table 6.8: Numbers of waste flakes per stone tool, by analytical level, Lie Madira

Mode of reduction

From all cores and flakes recovered from Lie Madira deposit, it can be inferred that three modes of reduction were applied, i.e: blade reduction mode, multiplatform reduction mode and bipolar reduction mode. A total of 66 cores was recovered from Lie Madira during excavation, amongst which 63 were recovered from the middle analytical level and the rest from the upper (table 6.7 above). Based on qualitative criteria, it can be seen that two types of core reduction techniques were applied by the Lie Madira occupants. The first gave rise to semi-prismatic cores used to produce blade-like flakes (figure 6.12: a and b). These cores have parallel negative flakes scars, but there are only 4 of this type, all from the middle level. Most of the cores (99 pieces) are of the multiplatform type (89.3%), which signifies either t expedient core reduction techniques were applied. One core with crushing on two opposite ends (figure 6.11: c) is a bipolar core.

Some large multiplatform cores, however, suggest that expedient core reduction was applied from the very beginning of the core reduction process. Australian research in southeastern Australia (Hiscock 1982), and generally throughout Australia and Tasmania (Flenniken and White 1985), suggests that prismatic cores can be reduced further to produce smaller blades (bladelet) and flakes, and eventually will become subjected to bipolar reduction.

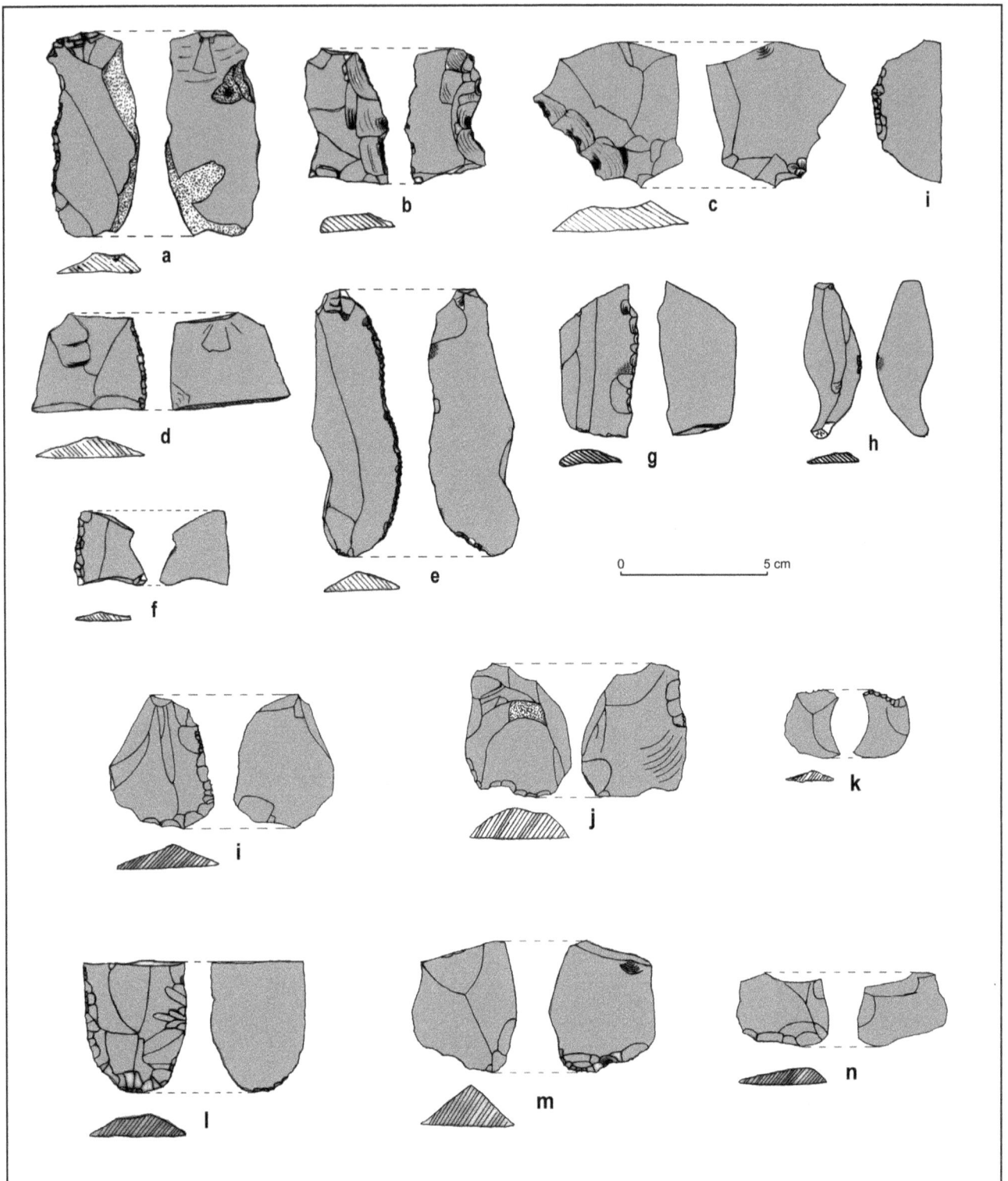

Figure 6.10: Retouched pieces from Lie Madira (except g). Stippling on the edges of e – h shows the position of gloss.
a, from spit 13; b, from spit 16; c, from spit 7; d, from spit 13; e, from spit 16; f, from spit 8; g, from spit 4;
h, from spit 9.i, from spit 14; j-m, from spit 8; n from spit 9.

The fact that most cores are multiplatform need not mean that blade reduction techniques were only rarely applied. Many blade-proportioned flakes were found in the deposit, and in qualitative terms most flakes are elongated in shape and have roughly parallel ridges and margins. There are no perimeter scars, but overhangs around striking platforms were sometimes removed.

Lie Madira stone assemblage is characterised by the abundance of blade-like flake proportion in the assemblage with the median of length/bread ratio for the total complete

flakes measured (N=348) is 1.83. In the middle level (dating from 5960±70 BP and 4750±90 BP) the mean elongation index is 2.02 mm, while the lower and upper levels are 1.58 mm and 1.59 mm respectively. Thus, more true blades occurs in the middle level. Most true blade with elongation index >2 and has parallel margin occur in this level, but again they are not many, only 26 out of 348 complete flakes measured or 0.07%). The fact that the average for retouched flakes or blades is 1.83, with a

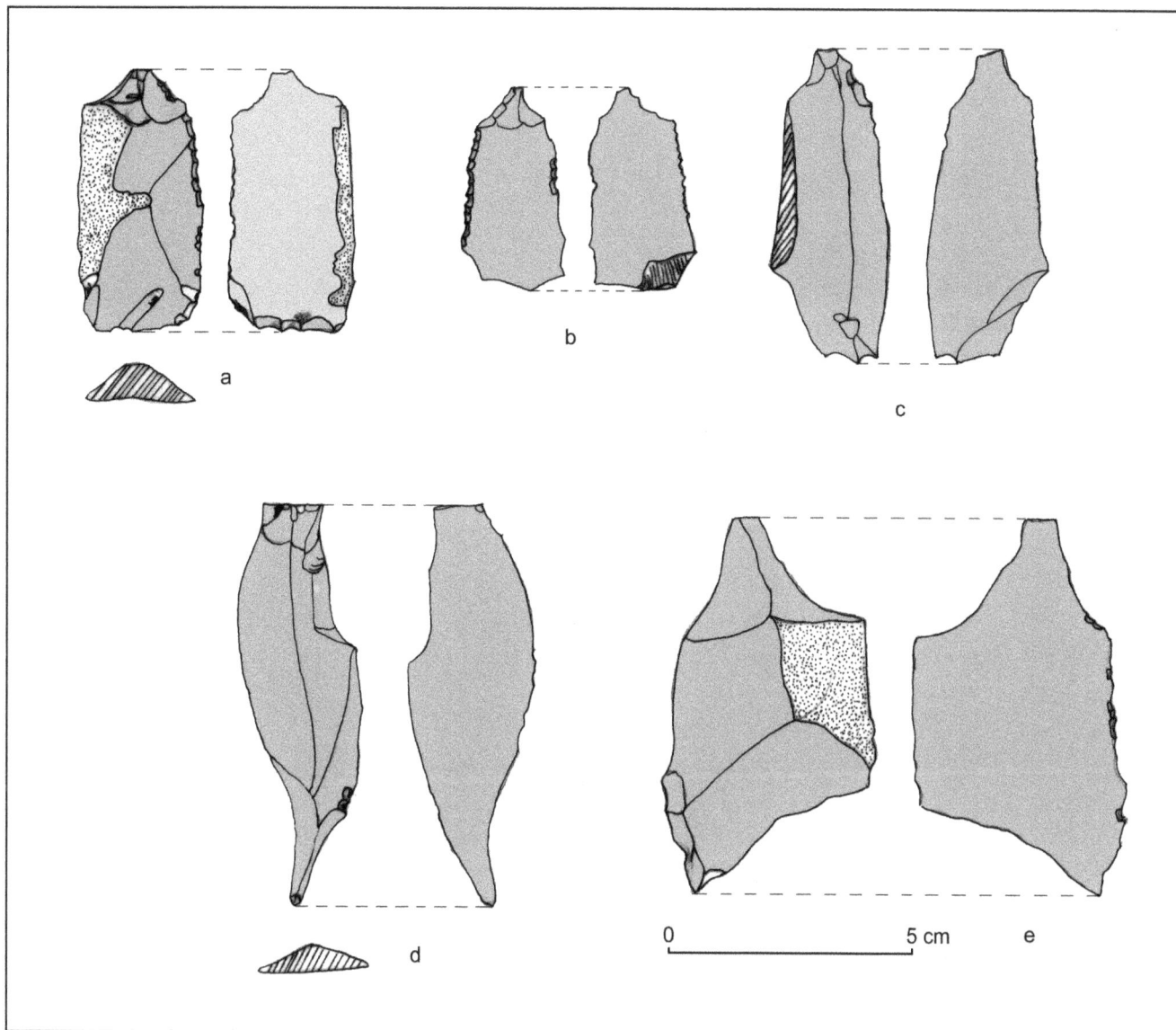

*Figure 6.11: Flakes with modification around the platform edge, presumably to facilitate hafting.
a, from spit 1; b, from spit 9; c, from spit 11; d, from spit 9; e, from spit 13.*

standard error of 0.27, indicates that all unretouched blades would have been potential tools.

Statistical analysis using Mann-whitney U test, equivalent to independent t-test indicates that there is significant difference between flakes sizes in middle and upper level, especially in flake length and platform thickness (and 6.10).

Trimming intensity

The intensity of the trimming process can be inferred from the maximum dimensions of the debitage and trimming flake characteristics (Andrefsky 1998:118). The percentages of the smaller sizes of debitage are quite low. This suggests that trimming was not frequently applied in Lie Madira.

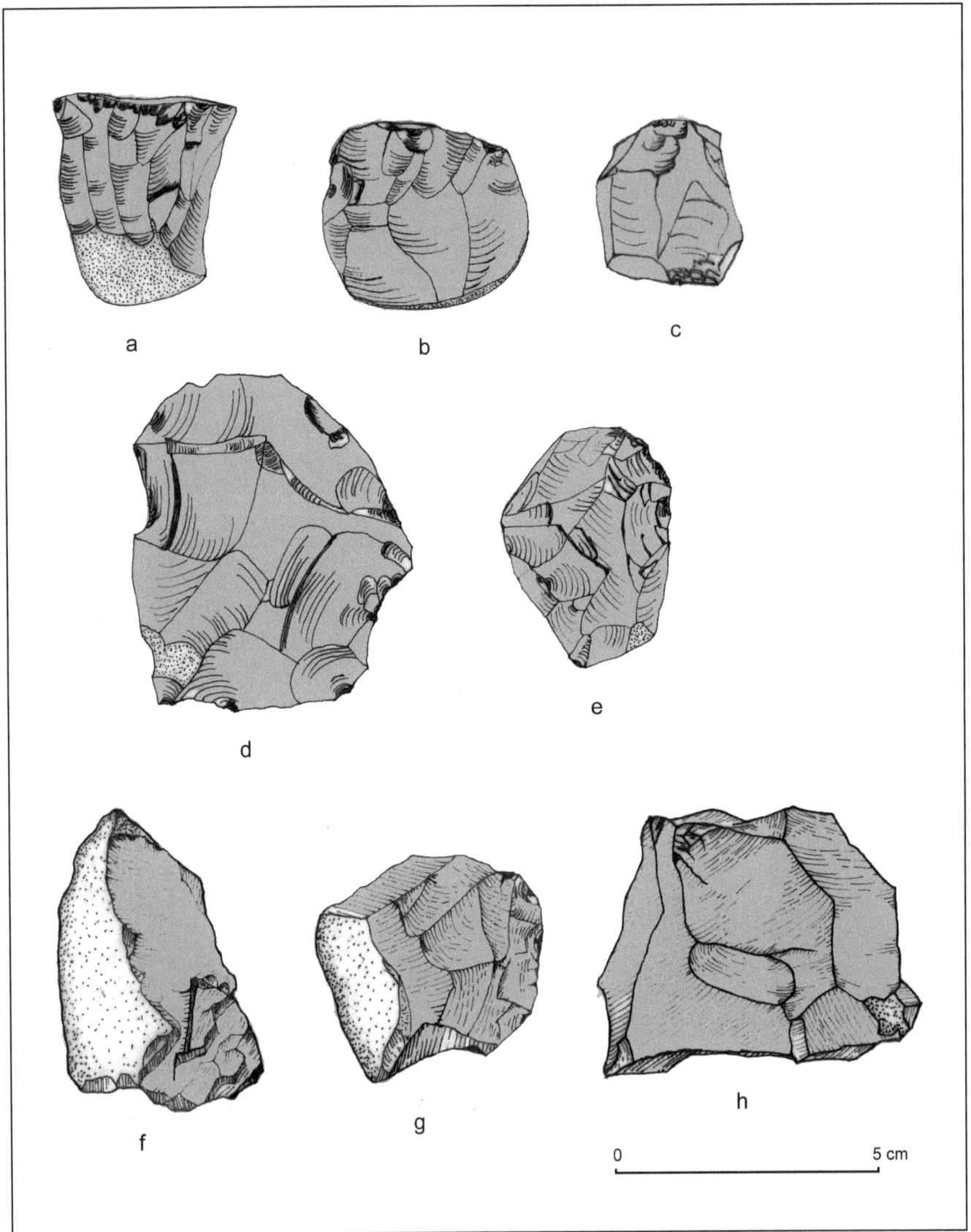

Figure 6.12: The Lie Madira cores. Those in the third row were drawn
by Agus Tri Hascaryo a, c, d, g, h, from spit 8; b and e, from spit 11; f, from spit 6.

Test Statistics[a]

	LENGTH	WIDTH	PLATWIDT	PLATTHIC
Mann-Whitney U	976.000	1429.000	2646.500	2127.000
Wilcoxon W	1031.000	1495.000	2751.500	2232.000
Z	-2.486	-1.629	-.334	-1.455
Asymp. Sig. (2-tailed)	.013	.103	.739	.146

a. Grouping Variable: UNIT

Table 6.9: The result of Mann Whitney U Test for flakes recovered in analytical level (Unit) 1 and 2.

Test Statistics[a]

	LENGTH	WIDTH	PLATWIDT	PLATTHIC
Mann-Whitney U	1881.000	2718.000	3302.000	2919.500
Wilcoxon W	2091.000	2889.000	3533.000	3129.500
Z	-3.618	-1.237	-1.637	-1.955
Asymp. Sig. (2-tailed)	.000	.216	.102	.051

a. Grouping Variable: UNIT

Table 6.10: The result of Mann Whitney U Test for flakes recovered in analytical level (unit) 2 and 3

3. Pottery form and decoration

Potsherds from Lie Madira were found down to 20 cm below the surface. Thicknesses ranged from 2 to 7 mm and most are body sherds without carinations. Only two rims were found, both from cooking pots with diameters of approximately 22 and 20 cm respectively (figure 6.13).

Both rims are classified as coming from independent restricted vessels. Since no carinations were found it is likely that the contours were inflected (see figure 2.1 C). Today, locally-produced Sawu pottery has no carinations, as can be seen from the pottery on sale in Seba market. Vessels with complex contours, such as spouted flasks or kendi (type D in Shepard's classification), common today in Java, Bali and Lombok, are not used in Sawu. Both of the Lie Madira rims are plain, one without red slip and the other, from the surface, having red slip applied outside and inside part of the rim. Apart from this, no decoration can be recognised.

4. Summary

Lie Madira was occupied quite intensively for a short period in the mid-Holocene, then abandoned as a habitation site before the Neolithic. The sherds represent only casual and rare visitation and probably do not relate to the upper C14 date at all. During pre-neolithic phase of occupation the cave occupants used chert material to produce blade-proportioned flakes, but not necessarily true blades.

The test pit has not yet reached the bedrock, thus it is still possible that older assemblages lie below the limits of my excavation. We need further research to examine this possibility.

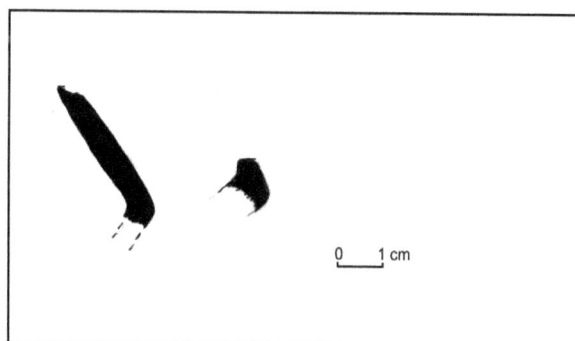

Figure 6.13: Two rim profiles from Lie Madira

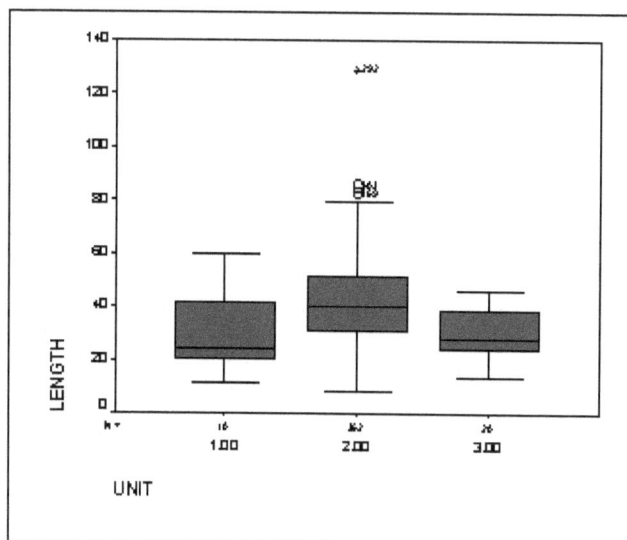

Figure 6.14: Box plot showing the spread of flake length recovered from analytical level (unit 1, 2 and 3) Lie Madira

73

7

THE ANALYSES OF POTTERY FROM SAWU, ROTE AND EAST TIMOR

1. Sherd samples from Sawu and Rote

As mentioned in chapter III, the pottery analyses presented in this chapter are mainly directed to identify the pottery-making centres. Important variables are characteristics of the pottery paste (clay) chemical compositions and specific mineral inclusions. Combinations of these variables can be used to identify pottery groups or at least pottery samples from different islands.

The chemical compositions obtained from SEM of the inclusions were compared to the known compositions of minerals (Deer, Howie and Zussman 1994), following the methodology applied by Summerhayes (1996, 2000), while the result of clay chemical composition was analysed statistically.

According to Deer et al. (1992), Rutile, ilmenite, hematite and iron chlorite are all common mineral accessories that occur in clay. Rutile is the most common form of titanium oxide in nature. It is widely distributed as minute grains in many igneous, chiefly plutonic rocks, but is also an accessory mineral in metamorphic rocks (Deer et al., 1992:550). Hematite is rare in igneous rock and occurs mainly in sedimentary and metamorphic circumstances. A large proportion of hematite is secondary, being found in soils and as a weathering product of iron-bearing minerals (Deer, et al. 1992:542). The members of the feldspar group of minerals are the most abundant constituents of igneous rocks.

All microprobe analyses under Scanning Electron Microscope for clay and inclusions, were carried out by myself, supervised by Dr Glenn Summerhayes. There were 9 chemical elements measured on 66 pottery samples from Sawu (8 samples), Rote (24 samples), and East Timor (34 samples). The oxides measured were those of Na, Mg, Al, S1, K, Ca, Ti, Mn and Fe. These pottery samples are selected based on surface decoration (red-slipped, incised, paddle impressed) or absence thereof (plain), and the variety of inclusion (coral sand temper, grog and minerals as inclusions seen under 20 X magnification. Sherd samples

Sample code	Provenance	characteristics
A	Roalie inhabitant's belonging	non red-slipped pottery
B	LM/TP/0	red slipped pottery
C	Ln/TP/1	non red-slipped pottery
D	LM/TP/1	non red-slipped pottery
E	LM/TP/1	non red-slipped pottery
F	LM/TP/2	non red-slipped pottery
H	LM/TP/4	non red slipped pottery
I	LM/Tp/4	non red-slipped pottery

Table 7.1 The analysed Sawu sherd samples
(Lie Madira pottery and modern Mesara pottery).

Sample code	Provenance	Characteristics
K	PHLD/F4/0	red-slipped pottery
L	PHLD/F4/0	red-slipped pottery
M	PHLD surface finds	red-slipped and shell impressed
N	PHLD surface finds	non red-slipped pottery
O	PHLD surface finds	non red-slipped pottery
AE	PHLD/F4/2	red-slipped pottery
AF	PHLD/F4/2	red-slipped pottery
V	Mokdale inhabitant's belonging	non red-slipped pottery
AL	Mokdale inhabitant's belonging	red-slipped pottery

Table 7.2 The analysed sherd samples from Pia Hudale, Mokdale and Oenitas, Oenale.

Sample code	Provenance	Characteristics
Q	MGT/F3/9	red-slipped pottery
R	MGT/F3/2	red-slipped pottery
S	MGT/F3/2	red-slipped pottery
T	MGT/C3D3//1	red-slipped pottery
U	MGT/C3D3//1	red-slipped pottery
AG	MGT surface find	red-slipped pottery
AH	MGT surface find	red-slipped pottery
AI	MGT surface find	non red-slipped pottery
AB	MGT/D3/1	red-slipped pottery
AC	MGT/D3/1	non red-slipped pottery
AD	MGT/D3/1	non red-slipped pottery
Z	MGT/C3D3//2	non red-slipped pottery
AA	MGT/D3/1	non red-slipped pottery
AK	MGt/F3/1	red-slipped pottery
AJ	MGT/F3/1	red-slipped pottery

Table 7.3 The analysed sherd samples from Lua Manggetek

Sample code	Provenance	Characteristics
X	MK/EX/4	red-slipped pottery
Y	MK/EX/4	red-slipped pottery

Table 7.4 The analyses sherd samples from Lua Meko

from Sawu Island consisting of seven excavated sherds from Lie Madira, both red-slipped and plain sherds) and a modern sherd sample made in the present pottery making village in Mesara. Thus, together there were 8 prepared samples for microprobe analysis from Sawu (see table 7.1).

Sherd samples from Rote Island consisting of 7 samples from Pia Hudale, 3 from present inhabitant's belonging in Desa Mokdale, 15 from Manggetek and 2 from Lua Meko (see table 7.2 – 7.4 for details).

2. Sherd samples from East Timor

Lie Siri

Lie Siri has dense sherdage in the deposit, mostly found at 30-40 cm below the surface (Horizons Vc-VII), with the densent being in Horizon VIb. Most potsherds found are plain. Some burnished body sherds occurred for the first time in Horizon Vc (5500-3700 years ago according to Glover's dating), but a large number of burnished sherds occurred in Horizon VIb. Incised, impressed and relief decoration first occurred in horizon VIa, becoming the most common in Horizon VIb. Paddle stamped potsherds only occurred in Horizons VIb and VII. A small number of angular shoulders (carinations) occurred in Horizons VIa and VIb. Thus, in Lie Siri, the plain pottery is the oldest pottery style, followed by incision and impression. The youngest pottery style is paddle impressed.

From Glover's reconstructions (1986), most vessel shapes in Lie Siri consisted of independent restricted vessels with inflected contours, although some carinated body parts were found as well (type C, see figure 3.1 in chapter III). Other pottery shapes found include simple unrestricted vessels, and a flask form (type D figure 3.1) with incised decoration found in Horizon VIb (Glover 1986, plate 19). Thirty four sherd samples were selected for both clay chemical analysis and inclusion identification, consisting of 10 from Uai Bobo 1, 11 from Uai Bobo2, 10 from Lie Siri and 4 from Bui Ceri Uato. (table 7.5 to table 7.8).

Uai Bobo 1

In Uai Bobo I, pottery first appeared in Horizon IIIa, dated 3470 ± 90 BP. As Lie Siri, Uai Bobo 1 had dense sherdage, especially in Horizon VIII. Most sherds found were plain. Some burnished body sherds occurred for the first time in Horizon IIIa, and became more common in Horizon IIIc (2190 ± 90 BP). Incised, impressed and relief decoration only occurred in horizons IVb and V, while paddle stamped pottery was absent in the deposit. Painted pottery, similar to recent pottery sold in Manatuto market (Glover 1986:plate 7) occurred in Horizon VIII. Carinations occur more frequently in Uai Bobo 1 than in Lie Siri, from Horizon IIIa onwards (Glover, 1986).

Uai Bobo 2

In Uai Bobo 2, pottery first appeared in Horizon VIII at dates of 5520 ± 60 BP (ANU-187) and 3760 ± 90 BP (ANU-239). The pottery found was similar to that from Uai Bobo 1 and included unrestricted and independent restricted vessels. Most potsherds found were plain. Some burnished body sherds occurred in Horizons IX - XI, Incised pottery occurs later, in the younger Horizons X and XI. Both burnished and incised pottery were absent in the upper levels, in constrast with Lie Siri and Bui Ceri Uato (Glover, 1986: 180-186).

Bui Ceri Uato

A large quantity of pottery was found in all horizons from V to X. As in the other sites, burnished pottery is the earliest and continues from Horizon V up to Horizon X, while incised, impressed and paddle stamped pottery occurred first in Horizon VI. Carinations occur, although rarely in Horizons VI and VII, while footrings were found in Horizons IX and X.

Four measurements were made on clay paste points to measure clay chemical composition and five other measurements to specific inclusions. All were made on each pottery thick section. The most abundant oxides measured in all samples was Si dioxide which ranged from just under 50% to nearly 75% of the clay content.

Sample code	Provenance	characteristics
tim V	LS/1	incised decoration
tim W	LS/2	incised decoration
tim X	LS/5259	plain non red-slipped pottery
tim Y	LS/6024	plain non red-slipped pottery
tim Z	LS/6809	incised decoration
tim AA	LS/6230	incised decoration
tim AB	LS/6034	incised decoration
tim AC	LS/6147	incised decoration
tim AD	LS/6240	plain non red-slipped pottery
tim AE	LS/1116	incised decoration

Table 7.5: The analysed sherd samples from Lie Siri , Timor

Sample code	Provenance	characteristics
tim A	UB1/IIIB	red-slipped pottery
tim B	UB1/IIIB/2	plain non red-slipped pottery
tim C	UB1/IIIB/3	plain non red-slipped pottery
tim D	UB1/IIIB/4	plain non red-slipped pottery
tim E	UB1/IIIA/1	plain non red-slipped pottery
tim F	UB1/IIIA/2	plain non red-slipped pottery
tim G	UB1/IIIA/3	pain non red-slipped pottery
tim H	UB1/IIIC/1	red-slipped pottery
tim I	UB1/IIIC/2	red-slipped pottery
tim J	UB1/IIIC/3	red-slipped pottery

Table 7.6: The analysed sherd samples from Uai Bobo 1 , Timor

Sample code	Provenance	characteristics
tim K	UB2/1271	plain non-red-slipped pottery
tim L	UB2/2401	plain non-red-slipped pottery
tim M	UB2/651	plain non-red-slipped pottery
tim N	UB2/1251	plain non-red-slipped pottery
tim O	UB2/3131	plain non-red-slipped pottery
tim P	UB2/VIII	plain non-red-slipped pottery
tim Q	UB2/2502	plain non-red-slipped pottery
tim R	UB2/660	plain non-red-slipped pottery
tim S	UB2	incised decoration
tim T	UB2/X904	non red-slipped pottery
tim U	UB2/X/?	plain non-red-slipped pottery

Table 7.7: The analysed sherd samples from Uai Bobo 2, Timor

Sample code	Provenance	Characteristics
tim AF	BCU/5689	plain red-slipped and burnished pottery
tim AG	BCU5334	paddle stamp decoration
tim AH	BCU/5330	paddle stamp decoration
tim AJ	BCU/6140	Plain red-slipped and burnished pottery

Table 7.8: The analysed sherd samples from Bui Ceri Uato, Timor

3. Statistical Analysis

The readings for Na, Mg, Al, Si, K, Ca, Ti, Mn and Fe as oxides in the clays were then processed statistically. The average of four chemical measurements for the clay under Scanning Electron Microscope was further analysed by Canonical Variate Analysis (CVA) and 95% confidence regions were constructed on the fist two canonical variates (CVA1 and CVA2). The analysis was kindly carried out by Mr. Bob Forrester, M.Sc. of the ANU Statistical Consultation Unit. All computations were carried out with GenStat program. Since the data are percentages and the silicon dioxide dominates all samples, this variate was not included in the analyses. The Canonical Variate Analysis was directed to see whether or not sherd samples collected from different island have different chemical compositions. Combined with mineral identification, this analysis can identify the pottery-making centres.

The usefulness of canonical variate analysis arises from the fact that it was mathematically designed and summarize variation among populations defined *a priori* while taking into account variation within populations' (Kzanowski, 2000). In a CVA the new canonical variates are obtained, as a linear combination of the original variates, in such a way that the between group variance is maximized relative to the within group variance (Forrester, pers. comm. 2007). The other benefit of CVA is that by examining the loadings, it is possible to determine which variable contributes to each canonical variate.

	Latent vector 1	Latent vector 2
Al2O3	0.0565	0.2524
CaO	0.0925	-0.0076
Fe2O3	-0.028	-0.34
K2O	0.0224	-0.3575
MgO	1.6587	0.4714
MnO2	-1.1396	4.3163
Na2O	1.2364	-0.7609
TiO2	0.0458	-0.0499

Table 7.9: The loading (latent vector) for CVA

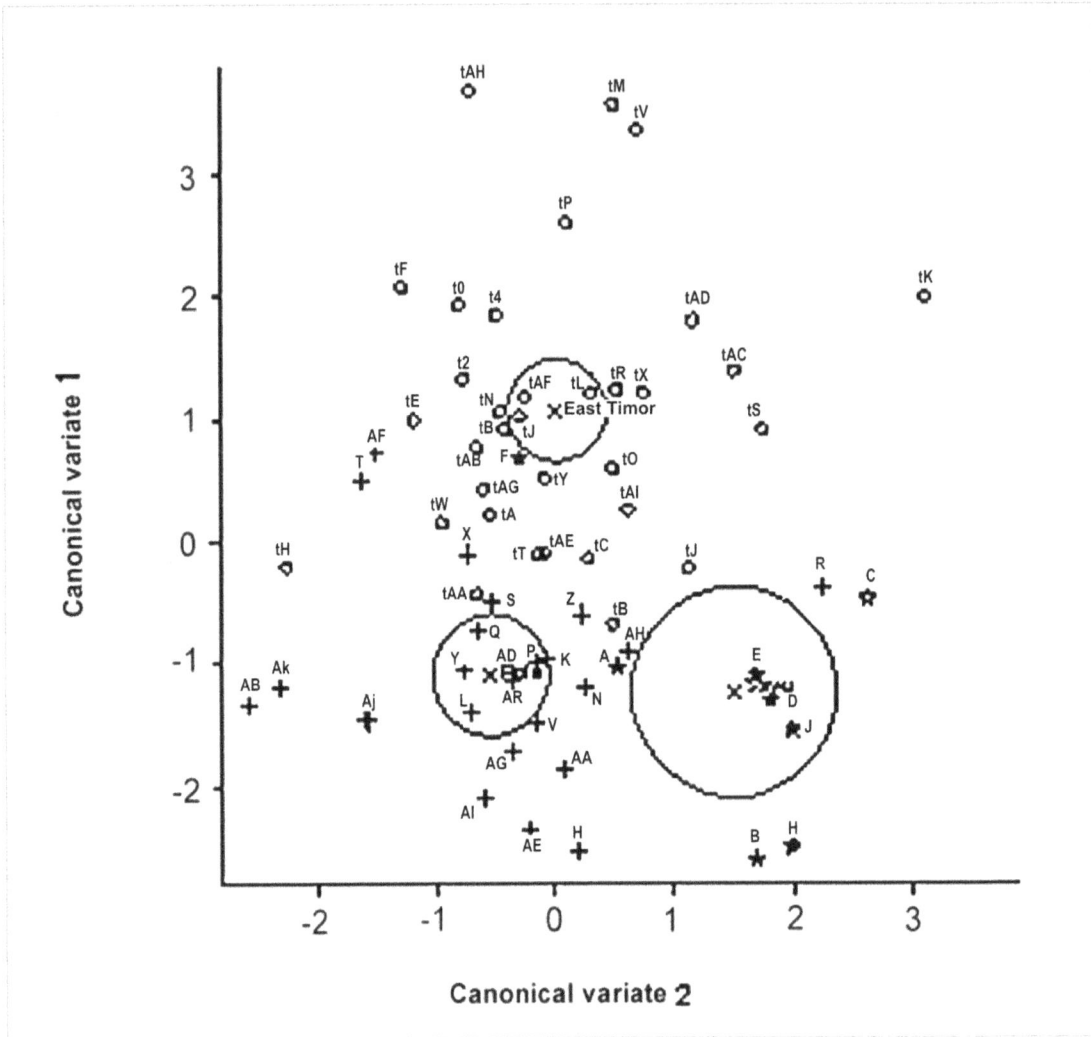

Figure 7.1: The plot of canonical variate 1 versus canonical variate 2.
Circles represent 95% confidence interval for samples collected from Sawu, Rote and East Timor

The loadings (table 7.9) indicates that the first canonical variate is predominately the effect of the percentage of manganese dioxide versus the percentages of magnesium oxide and sodium oxide. The second canonical variate is mainly the effect of overall percentage of manganese dioxide. The results can be viewed graphically in the plot (figure 7.1) where the group means for the three sites are surrounded by approximate 95% confidence intervals. The first canonical variate explained 76.3% of the variation while the second canonical variate explained 23.7% of the variation.

Figure 7.1 shows that most Sawu samples (★symbols) have high score on canonical variate 2 axis (between 0.52 and 2.62) and low scores on canonical variate 1 axis (between -2.61 and – 0.47). Sawu samples are characterized by a lower percentages of sodium dioxide compared with those of East Timor samples. Most Rote samples (+ symbols) have low scores on canonical variate 1 axis (between -2.607 an 0.710) and low scores on canonical variate 2 axis (between -2.59 and 0.63). Rote samples are characterized by very low percentage of manganese dioxides. East Timor samples (O symbols) are more spreaded than Rote and Sawu samples in the canonical variate 2 axis and have high scores on canonical variate 1 axis (between -0.678 and 3.564). Most East Timor samples

are characterized by higher percentages of magnesium dioxide and sodium dioxide compared with those of Rote and Sawu samples.

The first canonical variate in fugre 7.1 separates most of East Timor from Sawu and Rote samples. Some overlaps occur i.e: T, R, AF (Rote samples) and Sawu samples i.e: F and C overlaps on the first canonical variate with east Timor samples: sample tB, tAA, tW, tH, tJ, tC, tT and tAE. Having examined the loadings and raw data, it is known that the similarity of the percentage of sodium dioxides that cause these samples lie closer to East Timor samples.

Generally the second canonical variate separate Sawu and Rote samples with the exception of sample F (Lie Madira non red-slipped pottery) and R (Lua Manggetek red-slipped pottery). The loadings and raw data indicate that R sample (from Manggetek site, Rote Island) and pottery samples from Sawu Island has similar percentage of manganese dioxide.

The result of the first CVA indicates that some samples collected from Rote sites and 1 sample from Lie Madira have similar characteristics with pottery samples from Timor sites in term of its chemical composition. This may be a result of people brought the pottery from Timor to Rote and Sawu in the past or because the formations of these two islands are similar. To refine the analysis, mineral identification was carried out afterwards. Since sample A, made of clay from the known source in Mesara Village on Sawu, lies closer to samples B, C, D, E, H and I in the first CVA plot, it is inferred that sample A, B, C, D, E, H and I were made of the clay from Mesara.

Most inclusions in the pottery samples from Sawu, except for B, consist of coral sand and quartz, with other minerals present being rutile, ilmenite, hematite and iron chlorite (see table 7.10).

Sample	A	B	C	D	E	F	H	I
Mineral								
Carbonate	X	X	X	X	X	X	X	X
Quartz	X		X	X	X	X	X	X
Rutile				X				
Ilmenite							X	
Oxide:hematite					X	X		X
Chlorite						X		

Table 7.10: Variety Inclusions in the pottery from Sawu

Most Sawu samples do not have igneous minerals, except perhaps sample D which has rutiles. CVA of clay composition and mineral analyses indicate that the pottery samples collected from Sawu form three groups:

1. A group of pottery with clay paste composition similar to those of East Timor pottery. Characteristic inclusions consisting of coral sand, quartz and some hematites as accessory minerals : sample F.

2. A group of pottery with local clay source from Mesara and coral sand inclusions: sample B

3. A group of pottery with local clay source from Mesara and inclusions consisting of coral sand and some more accessory of sedimentary minerals : samples A, C, D, E, H, I.

Since minerals in samples F consisting of coral sands, quartz, hematite, and chlorite (non igneous minerals), while several samples from East Timor that have hematite accessory do have igneous minerals, it is inferred that F sample was not made in Timor.

The compositions of the inclusions in the Rote samples (table 7. 11) form four groups, each with certain accessory.

Minerals found in Rote samples consist of two categories: igneous and sedimentary minerals. CVA of clay composition and mineral identification indicate that the pottery samples collected from Rote form three groups:

1. A group with clay paste composition similar to those of East Timor pottery and inclusions consisting of quartz and igneous minerals but without coral sand: samples T, R, AF.

2. A group of pottery with local clay source (Oenale) with a combination of inclusions of coral sand, quartz and igneous rocks. The latter include plagioclase, pyroxene and amphiboles: samples M, N, V, AB, AC AD, AI and AL.

3. A group of pottery with local clay source and inclusions of non igneous minerals : P, Q, S, AA, AC, AE, AK, X, Y and AH.

4. A group of pottery with local clay source and grog inclusions: samples L and N.

It is known that the second group of pottery samples from Rote use clay source in Dusun Oenale since two member of this group are samples V and Al that were collected from the present local inhabitants and they bought the pottery from Oenale.

Some Rote samples that lie overlapping with East Timor samples in CVA figure 7.1 can be classified as group 1 (T, R, AF). This Group has similar mineral characteristics with East Timor samples (tB, tAA, tW, tT and tAE), in having igneous minerals. It is possible that samples T, R, and AF that were recovered from excavation on Rote Island were brought by prehistoric peoples in the past from Timor Island, since both clay paste composition and mineral inclusion in the pottery are very similar. Interestingly T, R and AF are red-slipped pottery from Rote while none of the East Timor samples with similar minerals and clay paste characteristic are incised or plain.

Mineral analyses indicate that the pottery samples from East Timor form three different mineral groups (see table 7.12): The inclusions indicate that at least three pottery making centres that collect their pottery temper from different sources. t AA, TW, tAE.

Taking into account both clay paste composition and variety of inclusions, there are actually five groups of pottery from East Timor.

1. A group of pottery with clay composition similar to Rote samples. The timor samples are tB and tT This group have quartz and some igneous minerals, but without coral sand inclusions.

2. A group of pottery that use similar clay composition with Rote samples This group has both coral sand and igneous minerals as temper: t AA, TW, tAE.

3. A group of pottery with local clay source and inclusions of coral sand and quartz, but with no igneous minerals: tA, tC, tD, tE, tL, tN, tQ, tV

4. A group of pottery with local clay from timor source with inclusions of igneous minerals and no coral sand temper, tJ, tM, tO, tR, tY,tX, tZ, tAC, tAE and tAG

5. A group of pottery with local clay source and both coral sands and some accessory igneous minerals: tAF and tAH.

4. Summary

The results of the analysis carried out on Sawu, Rote and East Timor pottery samples indicate that similar chemical compositions of clay minerals can appear in pottery samples from different islands. This is understandable, since geologically, the formations of these three islands are similar.

But, the similar clay compositions do not always mean that pottery exchange occurred in the past, since the inclusions are very different, based on mineral identification. Relative percentages of the inclusion added to the clay also vary. However, there are also some indications that prehistoric people brought some pots from Timor to Rote.

Sample	L	M	N	P	Q	R	S	T	V	X	Y	Z	AA	AB	AC	AD	AE	AF	AG	AH	AI	AJ	AK	AL
Mineral																								
Carbonate	X	X	X	X	X	X	X	X	X	X	X	X	X	X	X	X	X		X	X	X	X	X	X
Quartz	X	X		X	X	X	X	X	X	X	X	X	X		X	X		X		X	X	X	X	X
Clay	X		X																					
Rutile										X	X					X	X	X						
Ilmenite											X				X					X				X
Plagioclase feldspar		X							X															
Alkali feldspar																								
Quartz feldspar								X																
Chlorite		X																			X			
Oxide:hematite		X	X		X		X						X										X	
Pyroxene			X					X								X								
Amphibole						X			X					X				X					X	X

Table 7.11 Types of inclusion in the Rote pottery samples

sample	tA	tB	tC	tD	tE	tF	tH	tI	tJ	tK	tL	tM	tN	tO	tP	tQ	tR	tS	tT	tU	tV	tW	tX	tY	tZ	tAA	tAB	tAC	tAD	tAE	tAF	tAG	tAH	tAI
Mineral																																		
Carbonate	X	X	X	X	X	X	X	X	X	X	X	X	X	X	X	X	X	X	X	X	X	X						X			X	X	X	X
Quartz	X	X	X	X	X	X	X	X	X	X	X	X	X	X	X	X	X	X	X	X	X	X						X			X	X		X
hematite				X			X	X		X		X		X								X						X		X		X		
alkali feldspar					X	X		X	X			X			X	X	X	X	X	X		X	X					X	X		X	X		
plagioclase feldspar																	X	X				X	X					X						
ilmenite		X			X							X	X		X	X			X		X			X				X						
pyroxene		X		X						X	X			X	X	X	X				X	X												
epidote																	X				X					X	X							
prehnite							X																X							X	X			
mica								X											X	X														
rutile									X		X									X														
amphibole														X																		X	X	X

Table 7.12 Types of inclusion in the East Timor pottery samples

Figure 7.2: Section of sherd sample from Lie Madira (non red- slipped pottery)

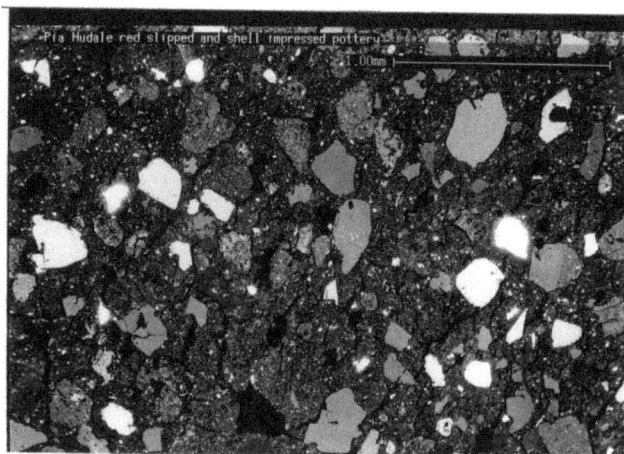

Figure 7.3: Section of sherd sample from Pia Hudale (red- slipped pottery)

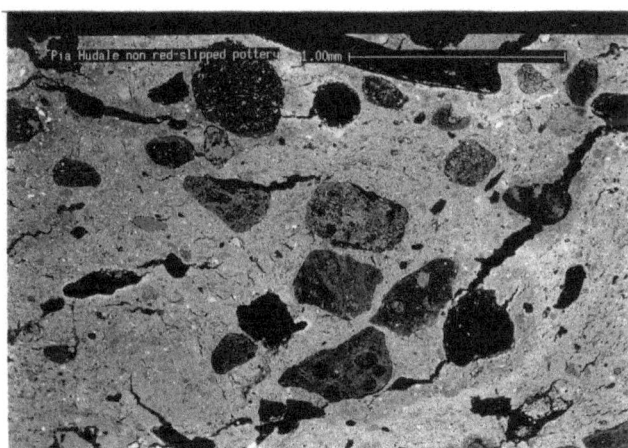

Figure 7.4: Section of sherd sample from Pia Hudale (non red-slipped pottery)

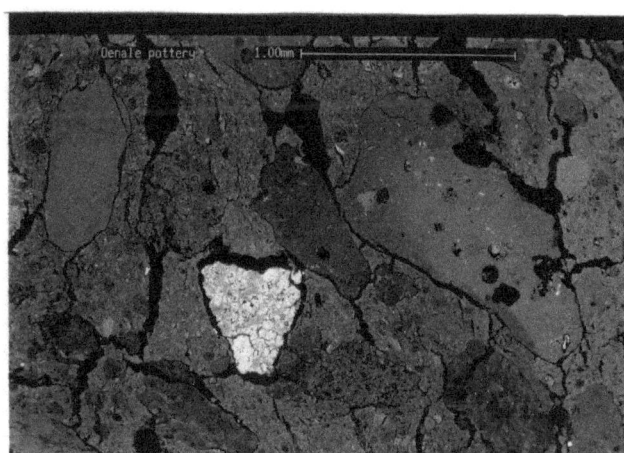

Figure 7.5: Section of sherd sample from Oenale, Rote Island (non red-slipped pottery)

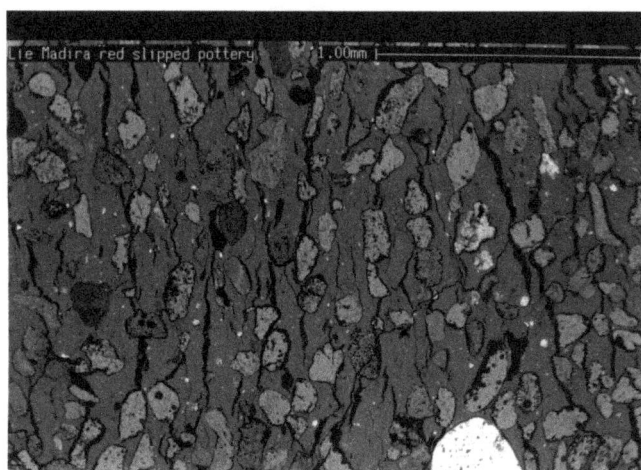

Figure 7.6: Section of sherd sample from Lie Madira (red-slipped pottery)

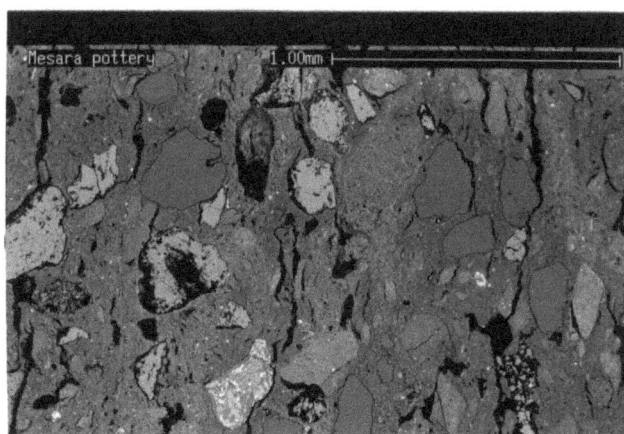

Figure 7.7: Section of sherd sample from Mesara, Sawu Island

8

HUMAN OCCUPATION
ON ROTE AND SAWU ISLANDS

1. Late Pleistocene to Holocene human occupation on Rote Island

Late Pleistocene human occupation on Rote is documented by the Lua Meko assemblage, with a basal date greater than 24,420 ± 250 bp. The absence of signs of human occupation during this period in the adjacent Lua Manggetek may reflect the sporadic nature of human occupation on Rote during this period. It may also reflect washing out of deposit, since Manggetek is lower and closer to the slope in front of the cave. However, terminal Pleistocene occupation is present in Manggetek and in Pia Hudale, dated to c.13,500 and 12,000 bp respectively. Figure 5.22 in chapter 5 shows a tendency for the rate of deposition in Lua Meko to slow down into the middle and late Holocene, suggesting that the most intensive occupation phases in the shelter were pre-Neolithic.

When occupied during the Late Pleistocene, about 30,000 years ago, the distance from Tonggobatu to the coast was about 4 km farther than at present, based on the present-day minus 50 metre sea bed contour. It was some 7 km farther than the present distance during the Last Glacial Maximum, based on the present-day minus 100 m sea bed contour. At 6000 years ago, according to Chappell's (1993) reconstruction of sea level change, those rock-shelters were slightly closer to the coast than at present.

No terrestrial animals were exploited during the early period of occupation. This is not surprising since no medium terrestrial animals are native to Rote island. Despite the distance to the coast at this time, some sandy intertidal and intertidal reef shellfish were exploited and brought to the shelters, although only in low numbers.

One interesting archaeological discovery from the Late Pleistocene in Lua Meko is the presence of human remains. Apparently, Lua Meko was used for burial during this period. David Bulbeck (appendix 1) comments on the morphological and size characteristics of these human remains, which could turn out to be amongst the oldest dated *Homo sapiens* in this region of Indonesia. However, these suggestions of early date cannot be confirmed, given the fragmentary nature of the bone survival, without direct dating of the bones themselves.

Intensities of site-use

Intensities of site-use through time can be inferred from the changing rates of shell and stone discard. The rate of stone artefact discard (figure 5. 17 in chapter 5) indicates that clear signs of human occupation in Lua Meko occur around 25,000 years BP, although there are some archaeological finds below this dated layer. This suggests that human occupied Lua Meko earlier. My recent research on Lua Meko in collaboration with Etty Indriati produced a tentative OSL dating around 29,000 years ago (Mahirta and Indriati 2006). At this time the site was only occupied, in the basal spits, by a very small number of people, with frequent mobility.

After the early initial occupation, the stone artefact discard rate reduced through the Last Glacial maximum, before rising sharply during the Terminal Pleistocene. The low number of stone artefacts discarded during the last Glacial maximum suggests that people moved to other sites, probably closer to the coast for economic reasons such as easier access to marine resources. After the Terminal Pleistocene the site was used more intensively.

The rate of shell discard reached a significant level firstly in the early Holocene, and reached a peak around 8000 years ago. This may correlate with the decrease of coastline distance from the site, allowing people to use the site more intensively. After a brief drop about 6000 years ago, the rate rose again briefly at about 3000 years ago, after which the shelter ceased to be occupied.

It can be inferred that the trend of human use of Lua Manggetek was similar to that of Lua Meko. The top 30 cm of the deposit was disturbed, and there are indications of trampling. But the deposits from approximately 7000 years ago and downwards contain dense shells and flaked stone artefacts. More stone working was carried out during the later period of occupancy, as inferred from the number of cores. The quantity of waste flake debitage, however, was greater in the lower level.

The intensity of site-use in Pia Hudale is somewhat difficult to interpret. The bedrock level of this site is dated to 11,160±220 BP, and the subsurface level to 10,440±500 BP. As mentioned before, the upper half of the deposit has been disturbed by burial and trampling. These process certainly caused some objects to move upwards and some others to move downwards. However, it is still clear that the upper deposit has denser flaked stone artefacts and shells (see table 5.9 and 5.10 in chapter V), which indicates that the site was used more intensively at this time. But just when the site was used most intensively is difficult to determine because of the lack of spread in the dates.

At Lua Meko, the rate of shell deposition increased significantly at approximately 6000 years ago, whereas the rate of stone artefact discard reached the highest level at approximately 10,000 years ago. Hence, it is likely that deposition of the lower parts of the upper horizons in Pia Hudale and Lua Manggetek, where shell numbers increase significantly in the deposits, was contemporary with the deposition of spit 3 in Lua Meko, around 6000 years ago.

Exploited resources

The Late Pleistocene to Holocene occupation in Lua Meko also demonstrates the continuation of a broadly-based marine diet. Marine resources exploited in the Late Pleistocene consisted of mostly shellfish from intertidal reef/rocky and freshwater habitats, with a rare occurrence of shellfish from sandy intertidal and mangrove/tidal mudflat habitats. Marine turtles might have been exploited during this period as sources of food, but the condition of the bones is too heavily encrusted for precise identification. No fish bones were found in Lua Meko, despite very careful sieving in the field.

Entering the Holocene period, the marine resources consisted of mostly shellfish from sandy intertidal zones and tidal mudflats. Large sized fish appear, although the method of catching is not known. Local terrestrial animals exploited consisted of murids and bats, which continued to be caught until Lua Meko was almost abandoned.

After pottery appeared in the deposit, non-native terrestrial animals also occur, including *Macaca* sp. Perhaps the introduction of pottery and macaques to Rote occurred at the same time. Apart from *Macaca* sp., no other non-native animals appear in the Lua Meko deposit. It is possible that the monkeys were brought to Rote as tame animals to help people harvest coconuts. *Rattus tanezumi,* not native to Rote, also appears in the upper level of the deposit..

The Terminal Pleistocene to Holocene human occupation in Lua Manggetek also demonstrates the continuation of shellfish exploitation. In the early occupation (Terminal Pleistocene period), no fish bones appeared in the deposit, suggesting that fish were not an important source of food. Shellfish at this time mostly came from intertidal reef and freshwater habitats. Native terrestrial animals consisted again of murids and bats, which interestingly only occur in the lower part of the deposit. The exploitation of these native terrestrial animal did not continue into the subsequent period. After 6000 years ago, fish were caught for the first time. Before pottery appeared frequently in the deposit (i.e. excluding the sherds in spit 9 in trench C3D3), only shellfish from river and intertidal reef habitats were present. Pig and deer bones in the subsurface layer suggest that, after the introduction of these animals to Rote, the shelter was abandoned.

The Terminal Pleistocene to Holocene occupation in Pia Hudale demonstrates a continuation of both shellfish exploitation and murid and bat exploitation. In the early period of occupancy, shellfish from intertidal reef and freshwater sources were the main marine resources. From the Middle Holocene, until the site was abandoned, more shellfish from more varied habitats were exploited. These include freshwater shellfish, which increased in number over time. Tidal mudflat/ mangrove species only appeared in significant numbers during this period. Apart from marine resources, terrestrial animals and fresh water turtle were also exploited. The exploitation of freshwater water turtle seems to have been common on Rote, as freshwater turtle remains were also found in Lua Meol, a site excavated by Buhler (Sarasin 1936).

Although no clear traces of plant exploitation were found, the glossed flakes are one source of evidence for plant utilization after the mid Holocene in Rote and Sawu.

Generally, all the non-native animals on Rote (deer, pig and cow) only appeared in the upper layers in Pia Hudale and the Tonggobatu shelters. Unfortunately, all the dates for layers bearing bones of these animal are imprecise. In Lua Manggetek, the layer with the first non-native animal bones dates to 7,050±80 BP, and pottery was found down into the layer dating between 7,050±80 and 13,390±430. In Pia Hudale, the surface layer bearing the bones of these animals is dated to 10,440±500 BP. But these dates cannot be taken as definite for their introduction without further research.

From a shelter near Danau Anak, excavated by Buhler in 1933, animal bones were also found in the upper layer, but they were not identified. From Lua Meol (Southwest Rote), no terrestrial animal remains were mentioned.

The Characteristics of the Rote Flaked Stone artefacts

As in the case of Lie Madira, the flaked stone artefacts are the dominant evidence of past human occupation in the Rote sites. It is apparent that people applied greater selectivity to raw materials with time over the period of occupancy.

Chert was the dominant material used throughout in all sites, but during the early sporadic period of occupation during the Late Pleistocene some other materials were used for flaked stone artefacts, including dacite, silcrete and silicified sandstone. These non-chert flaked stone artefacts were found mainly in the early sporadic period of site use, although non-chert hammerstones were used until the sites were about to be abandoned. At Lua Manggetek, the non-chert flaked stone artefacts were mainly found during the Terminal Pleistocene, except in the case of a bifacially retouched pebble in the Holocene deposit. As in Lua Meko, igneous rock hammerstones were used until the end of occupancy. At Pia Hudale, chert was the only material used for flaked stone tools throughout the deposit.

There are some clear changes in flaked stone artefact characteristics from the early sporadic phase through to the end of shelter occupancy. The early sporadic phase is represented by the flaked stone artefacts from Lua Meko only. These include a large silicified sandstone flake, a thick flake or split pebble of silicified sandstone which was retouched unifacially along its edge from the ventral side, a split pebble which was retouched unifacially from the dorsal side, and some non-chert core tools. Both percussion and bipolar techniques were applied during this sporadic phase. Pits and indentations on the surfaces of the split pebble tools suggest the application of bipolar reduction.

Generally, the Terminal Pleistocene through to Middle Holocene use of the Rote shelters (the most intensive phase of site use) was characterised by increasing stone working activity. This phase can be divided into two subphases - Terminal Pleistocene to early Holocene (until about 8000 years ago), and Early to mid-Holocene.

The first phase is characterised by rare retouching of small chert flakes, increase in stone working activity, and increase in numbers of cores. At this time, the shelters were used for burial as well as habitation. The second phase is characterised by more retouching activity, especially percussion retouch and sometimes delicate retouch. The detached chert flake debitage is bigger than in the early phase of sporadic use. The use of the shelters for burial continued.

The Middle Holocene, until near abandonment, is characterized by an occasional occurrence of bifacial technology. These bifacial tools include a bifacial pebble tool from Lua Manggetek, and a bifacial retouched flake tool, retouched point, and "handle" from Lua Meko. Buhler also identifies that partly bifacial tools occurred in Lua Meol near Danau Tua. There is also a continuation of unifacial retouched flakes from the earlier phase of occupation.

Pottery and shell ornaments

The occurrence of pottery in the upper spits signifies new connections with external sources from other islands. In the Rote sites, the occurrence of pottery is contemporary with pigs and shell beads. Some shell ornaments seem to occur earlier than pottery, but generally all shell artefacts with more complicated modification become more common in the pottery levels.

2. Holocene occupation in Lie Madira

Intensities of site-use

The bottom of the Lie Madira test pit reached sterile layers in spits 24-28. The oldest radiocarbon date from the site is 5960±70 BP (ANU 10917), but this is not from the bottom. An attempt to date the lowest layer of occupation by AMS radiocarbon dating produced a very young date, hence an ambiguous result. If the accumulation of sediment below the 5960 BP level occurred at the same rate as in the upper layer, which was actually slower than the rate for the middle level sediments, then the time span of occupation can be stretched back to about 6500 years ago.

It seems that Lie Madira was used only sporadically before 6000 years ago, as reflected by the very rare stone artefacts and shells in the deposit. The site was then used intensively around 6000 years ago. The sudden increase in the rate of shell discard around 5800 years ago may reflect more frequent use or environmental change. Surprisingly, mangrove and tidal mudflat shells only occur rarely in the deposit, and sandy intertidal shells are fewer than intertidal reef shells such as *Trochus*. This is surprising, since the mid-Holocene high sea level was usually a time of formation of more tidal mudflats. Probably, people preferred to consume *Trochus* rather than other shell species.

The intensity of site use was lower during the subsequent period, as reflected in the reduced discard rates. There was a slight increase at about 5100 BP in stone discard, but this was not reflected in the shell discard.

The Holocene record for Lie Madira also demonstrates the continuation of a broad-based marine diet, from at least 6000 years until well near abandonment. This is because of the site's location within the rich maritime zone, at only 264 m from the coast line. Before non-native animals were brought to Sawu, signified by the first appearance of deer and cow in the upper analytical level, no terrestrial animal bones were discarded in the cave. Although the Post-Pleistocene faunas of Nusa Tenggara were dominated by bat and murid species, these animals did not occur in Lie Madira.

Analysis of all vertebrate remains by Ken Aplin demonstrates that the Lie Madira occupants exploited marine turtle and fish. My analysis of the shells indicates that a wide variety of shell families from different habitats were also exploited, particularly from the intertidal reef.

The occurrence of sea mammals, possibly dugong, in the deposit indicates that sea hunting was also practised by the Lie Madira occupants. Signs of butchering have not been observed, but it is interesting that Binford (1978), as cited by Minnegal (1984), states that among the Nunamiut the sea mammal butchering practice can vary with context, taking into account for instance whether the meat is to be consumed immediately or kept for later use.

It is not clear how fish were caught since no hooks or net sinkers were found. Currently, fish traps are used by people who live along the northern coast of Sawu. Probably this technology was also introduced by Austronesians.

The terrestrial animal bones in Lie Madira are all non-native, and appear in the deposit before the first occurrence of pottery (spit 4: 20 cm below the cave floor), although this presumably reflects disturbance. However, Ellen (1993) suggests that pigs were introduced to Sawu and Rote by 5520 years ago, while goat was possibly introduced by 3500 years ago, according to dates obtained from Timor by Ian Glover. Unfortunately, pig and goat bones do not occur in Lie Madira, so their dates of introduction to Sawu cannot be confirmed.

The Lie Madira flaked stone artefatcs

In Lie Madira, flaked stone artefacts of chert are the dominant evidence of past human occupation, along with shells. Suitable chert raw materials are available in the river bed nearby, and from outcrops in southern Sawu.

There are some clear changes in stone artefact characteristics from the early phase of sporadic use before 6000 years ago, through the middle phase of intensive use at about 6000 years ago, and into the upper phase of virtual abandonment, as described below.

Sporadic-use phase:

Blades occur but are not very common. Some retouch starts to appear, but is still uncommon.

Intensive use phase:

Extending the use life of artefacts by retouching became more common, especially in the second half of this phase. A new type of unifacially retouched tool, possibly a point, made an appearance. Stone reduction activity was the most intensive in the history of the site, as indicated by the number of cores and the quantity of debitage. This phase also has a greater incidence of blades, although the core preparation to produce them was still minimal. A more efficient use of raw materials is reflected in the smaller sizes of cores and final detached flakes. Another new trend is the development of hafting, by detaching the dorsal part of the striking platform so that the piece became thinner and narrower, presumably to make it easier to insert into split wood or bamboo.

The final phase

In the final phase, blade production declined and flakes became shorter. Raw materials were used more efficiently, signified by reduced core dimensions. Stone working activity was not intense.

Exploited resources at Lie Madira

The Holocene record for Lie Madira demonstrates the continuation of a broad-based marine diet, from at least 6000 years until well near abandonment. This is because of the site's location within the rich maritime zone, at only 264 m from the coast line. Before non-native animals were brought to Sawu, signified by the first appearance of deer and cow in the deposit just below the first appearance of pottery, no terrestrial animal bones were discarded in the cave. Although the Post-Pleistocene faunas of Nusa Tenggara were dominated by bat and murid species, these animals did not occur in Lie Madira.

Analysis of all vertebrate remains by Ken Aplin demonstrates that the Lie Madira occupants exploited marine turtle and fish, as well as shellfish. My analysis of the shells indicates that a wide variety of shell families from different habitats were exploited, particularly from the intertidal reef.

The occurrence of sea mammals, possibly dugong, in the deposit indicates that sea hunting was also practised by the Lie Madira occupants. Signs of butchering have not yet been observed, but it is interesting that Binford (1978), as cited by Minnegal (1984), states that among the Nunamiut the sea mammal butchering practice can vary with context, taking into account for instance whether the meat is to be consumed immediately or kept for later use.

It is not clear how fish were caught since no hooks or net sinkers were found. Currently, fish traps are used by people who live along the northern coast of Sawu.

The terrestrial animal bones in Lie Madira are all non-native and appear for certain in the deposit rightly before the first occurrence of pottery (spit 4: 20 cm below the cave floor). Deer and a possible bovid appear at approximately 5000 BP. Ellen (1993) suggests that pigs were introduced to Sawu and Roti by 5520 years ago, while goat was possibly introduced by 3500 years ago, according to dates obtained from Timor by Ian Glover. Unfortunately, pig and goat bones do not occur in Lie Madira, so their dates of introduction cannot be confirmed.

Pottery and shell ornaments

Pottery and shell ornaments only occur in the final phase of Lie Madira occupation. The number is very limited that I incline to conclude that when the pottery and complicated shell ornaments were introduced to Sawu, that is round-cut *Conus* shell, Lie Madira and probably other caves were no longer used for regular habitation.

3. Summary

The evidence from the Sawu (Lie Madira) and Rote sites (Tonggobatu and Pia Hudale rock-shelter) throws new light on the prehistoric human occupation of eastern Nusa Tenggara. There was a significant impact from the sequence of postglacial palaeoenvironmental change, from the Late Pleistocene until the mid Holocene, that affected the cultural characteristics of the population. Changes can be plotted in the resources exploited and in flaked stone artefact technologies. Temperatures and sea levels increased, with consequences for the distances of sites from the sea and the formation of new coastal zones such as mangroves, tidal mudflats and sandy intertidal zones. After the mid-Holocene, cultural interaction with people from other islands in Nusa Tenggara shaped the cultual characteristics of Rote and Sawu further.

My study has uncovered that there were regional changes in the patterns of site-use, especially in caves and shelters, from the terminal Pleistocene to about 4000 years ago. This is signified by changes in artefact and shell discard rates in a number of sites. Generally, the course of cultural development on Rote and Sawu from the Middle Holocene onwards was somewhat different from the earlier phases, especially in flaked stone artefact characteristics.

For the moment, we can infer that the most significant period of arrival of new cultural traits (pottery, some shell ornaments, non-native mammals) was associated with Austronesian settlers, although the date of arrival of these new forms is still not clear from the current evidence. It is believed that early Austronesians developed sea craft technology, so they could reach Sawu and then Rote from either Java via Sumba or via Flores and Timor. Another route is from south Sulawesi via Flores, as currently used by Macassans (Morwood 1998). To determine the origin of the Sawu pottery, styles from each area should be compared. The problem is that the pottery recovered from my excavations is very minimal and probably does not represent the actual available variety in each island. The other problem is the date for the first occurrence of pottery, which is still ambiguous. In Lua Meko it is dated older than current radiocarbon dates for Neolithic occupation elsewhere in Indonesia, for instance at Kamasi and Minanga Sipakko on Sulawesi, where pottery is dated between 2500 and 3500 BP (Bulbeck 2002). In Liang Bua (Flores), Lewoleba (Lomblen) and Melolo (Sumba), the dates appear to be similar (Sumijati 1994), but the samples collected for dating the occurrences of pottery in these sites were not derived from the lowest pottery-bearing layers.

9

COMPARATIVE PERSPECTIVES AND CONCLUSIONS

This chapter will be focused on a comparison of the archaeological assemblages from Rote and Sawu with those from other sites occupied since the Late Pleistocene in Timor, especially Niki-niki, Uai Bobo 1 and 2, Lie Siri and Bui Ceri Uato. There are fairly good sequences of radiocarbon dates for the East Timor sites excavated by Glover (1986), although the upper layers of some sites have been disturbed. The collections from the East Timor sites are kept in the Australian Museum in Sydney and have thus been accessible for further study.

The collection from Niki-niki (West Timor) is currently kept in National Museum in Jakarta, where a quick look at the materials on exhibit was undertaken by me in 1997. The archaeological finds from the newly excavated site of Lene Hara in East Timor, of Late Pleistocene date (c.35,000 BP), are now under study by Dr Sue O'Connor (2002). In 1967, Almeida and Zbyszewski (1967) did some earlier excavations in this cave and the results have been published. My comparisons here are based on Almeida's descriptions only.

Data on intensities of human occupation, types of site usage, resources exploited, and stone artefact characteristics are compared between the various sites whenever published data allow.

1. Comparisons with Timor

The Late to Terminal Pleistocene c. 25,000 to 12,000 years ago

Occupation as old as that in Lua Meko was not present in the Timor sites excavated by Glover, although Uai Bobo 2 was first occupied during the Terminal Pleistocene. In 1967, Almeida and Zbyszewski did an excavation in Lene Hara cave (currently dated to c. 35,000 BP) and stated that they found marine shells and chert flakes down to 80 cm (Almeida and Zbyszewski 1967). No C14 dates are available from their excavation, but the illustrated stone artefacts are similar to those from the Rote sites of the Terminal Pleistocene. More recent work has now established a date for basal occupation about 35,000 BP (O'Connor 2002). However, large tools like those from basal Lua Meko have not been reported.

This Terminal Pleistocene is the phase during which shelters became used more intensively on Rote, as also in Timor (Uai Bobo 2, Uai Bobo 1 and Lie Siri). Both Uai Bobo 2 and Lua Manggetek were first occupied c.14,000 years BP, but intensive occupation started a little later, in the Terminal Pleistocene, as in Lua Meko, Lua Manggetek and Pia Hudale.

2. Terminal Pleistocene to Mid-Holocene (after 12,000 to c. 5000 years ago)

The Terminal Pleistocene phase also saw the first frequent evidence for human burials in caves in East Timor excavated by Glover, as in the Rote sites. Because of the absence of skulls in all excavated sites on Timor, Rote and Sawu, it is difficult to determine for certain the racial affinities of the *Homo sapiens* who occupied the islands during this period.

In Uai Bobo 2, human bones were mostly found below the pottery levels, but there were also human bones in the first two horizons with pottery. The number of individuals is unsure, but it seems there were at least two, of uncertain racial affinity (Glover 1986). In Uai Bobo 1, pottery was found from horizon III A up to horizon VIII (dating from 3470 ± 110 BP to recent), while human bone commenced one horizon lower, that is in horizon IIb (a deciduous lateral incisor), and again in the middle of the pottery horizon, that is in horizon IIIC (a lower left permanent premolar), dating to around 2000 years ago.

In Lie Siri, human bones occurred from horizons II to VC, represented by at least five individuals, while pottery was spread between horizons VC and VII. Thus, human burial is earlier than the pottery period in Lie Siri. Because of this consistency, I am certain that there was no Neolithic disturbance caused by burial activities in this site.

Cave occupation in the East Timor sites excavated by Glover seems longer than for those on Sawu and Rote, because the Timor caves continued to be used for habitation after the introduction of pottery, as suggested by a quite deep and abundant pottery deposit in each site. In contrast, the Lene Hara assemblage is a typical pre-Neolithic assemblage without a major pottery-bearing deposit (Almeida and Zbyszewski 1967:64), simialr to the situation in Lie Madira, Pia Hudale and the Tonggobatu rockshelters.

Flaked stone technology

There is a tendency towards contemporaneity of development of flaked stone artefact technology in Timor, Rote and Sawu, in which secondary modification by retouching of flakes and blades only appeared in the Holocene. In the Rote sites, retouching of non-massive flakes started to occur in the upper part of the lower cultural levels in Lua Manggetek and Pia Hudale, and from the upper part of the middle cultural level in Lua Meko. All these occurrences date after c.8000 years BP, while in Uai Bobo 2 the first appearance of retouch is from 7000-8000 years BP, and in Uai Bobo 1 and Lie Siri retouched tools first appear in

Horizon Ia and continue up to Horizon VII (c.9000 to 2000 years ago). These data suggest that retouching was one form of curation behaviour that was becoming more common during the Holocene, especially the Mid-Holocene, in eastern Nusa Tenggara.

Generally, non-chert materials were not commonly used for producing flakes on Rote during this phase of occupation. Buhler mentions several types of material used for stone artefacts in the four sites he excavated in western Rote, but all can be included in the category of chert. This applies to Lie Madira, where only chert was used for flake tools throughout.

In Uai Bobo 1 and 2, and also in Lie Siri, chert was also the most common material used. Several obsidian flakes were found in Lie Siri. Possibly, this obsidian was collected from the western edge of the Baucau Plateau. No clear use wear is present on these obsidian flakes and there are no traces of secondary working, as noted also by Glover.

The people who occupied the two West Timor sites excavated by Buhler, that is Niki-niki and a site in Baguia District, mostly if not always used chert (termed flint by Sarasin) for flake tools. Non-chert materials were not reported (Heekeren 1972, Sarasin 1936).

Toward the Mid Holocene, many flakes seem to have been used to scrape silica rich plants. The gloss-bearing flakes that result from such activities have been found commonly in the East Timor sites, in Lie Siri firstly in Horizon III dating to about 7500 years ago, and in Uai Bobo 1 in horizons I-V (c.7500 to 2000 BP), with the densest in Horizon IIIc. In Uai Bobo 2, glossed flakes/blades were found from Horizons IV to X (c.7000 - 2500 BP). Thus, in East Timor, the occurrence of gloss-bearing flakes is contemporary with the retouched flakes.

In the the Tonggobatu shelters and Pia Hudale the dating of glossed flakes is not very secure, but they certainly occur below the pottery levels. The first occurrence of gloss-bearing flakes in Lie Madira is more secure, at about 5960 ± 70 BP (ANU 10917).

Exploited resources

Depending on the distance of each site from the coast, during this period the resources exploited for subsistence were varied. Lie Madira has only evidence for marine exploitation while Uai Bobo 2, Lie Siri and the Rote sites have evidence for both terrestrial and marine resources.

Generally, marine exploitation became more intensive towards the Mid-Holocene, as reflected from my excavation sites and also Lie Siri and Liang Lemdubu (Aru). At present, all of these sites are located not far from the coast and probably were even closer during the Mid-Holocene phase of higher sea level. Thus, the dense shell middens deposited during this period may reflect both more people and a more sedentary lifestyle, resulting from easier access to the coast.

The exploitation of terrestrial animals on Rote was very limited and restricted to rat and bat species, plus occasional birds, as in the earlier period. Rote and the other islands in East Nusa Tenggara lack middle and large sized native terrestrial mammal species, and this is likely the reason why bone artefacts were not developed there.

Although shellfish were exploited as food, shell artefacts only appeared during the Mid-Holocene on Rote and in East Timor, except for unmodified *Dentalium* shells. In Lua Meko, *Dentalium* shells first occurred in spit 11, thus dating possibly from 24,000 years ago. In Pia Hudale, only one *Dentalium* shell was found, in the lower level (spit 8).

Several bivalve shells tools with prominent signs of use wear were found in the Rote sites. One utilised *Geloina* shell from Lua Meko was found 5 cm above the pottery layer, thus dating to around 4720 BP and older than the first occurrence of *Geloina* scrapers in Lie Siri (1039 ± 70 BP) and Uai Bobo 1 (2450 ± 95 BP).

The shellfish species exploited for food in the Rote sites were different from those in the three sites in East Timor and in Lie Madira, even though the geomorphology of the northern coasts of Rote and Sawu is quite similar. The first difference is in the quantities of terrestrial shells. These occur in Pia Hudale and the Tonggobatu shelters from the lower layers onwards, but amounts never exceed 10 grammes per spit and they are always in very fragmentary condition. They are more common at this time in the Timor sites and Lie Madira.

The second point of difference is the rarity of sandy intertidal shells in the upper levels of the Timor sites and Lie Madira. These include species such as *Strombus luhuanus*, *Strombus aurisdianae* and *Anadara sp*. This suggests that fringing reefs were more accessible from the East Timor sites than sandy habitats. In Lie Madira, likewise, sandy beach bivalves are almost totally absent from the deposit, with only one being found (in spit 3). However, in the Rote sites, sandy beach bivalves such as *Anadara* are very common.

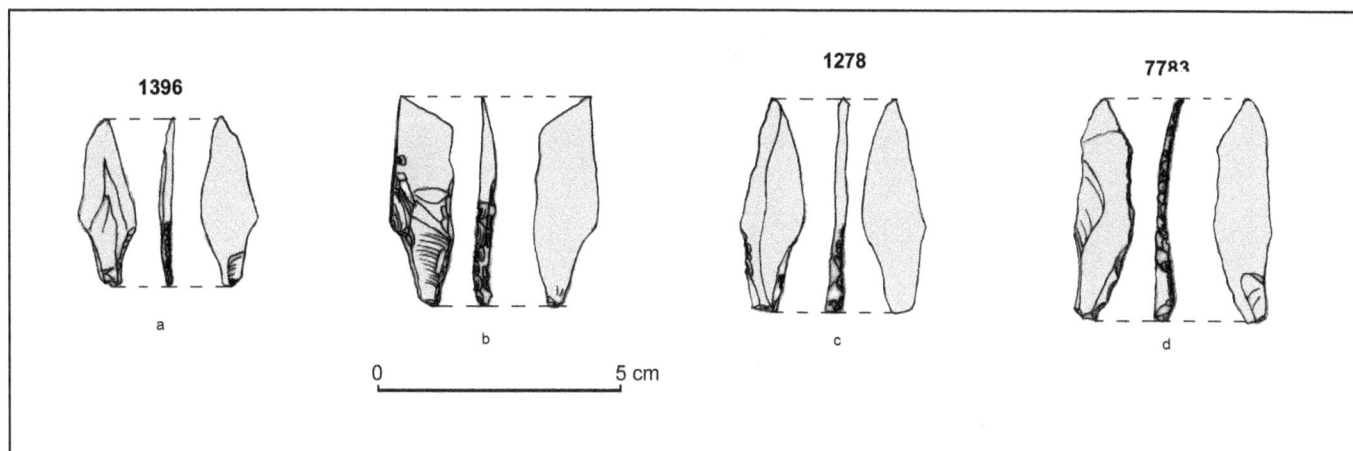

Figure 9.1: Tanged points and backed blade, Uai Bobo 1, East Timor a-c tanged points; d. backed blade.

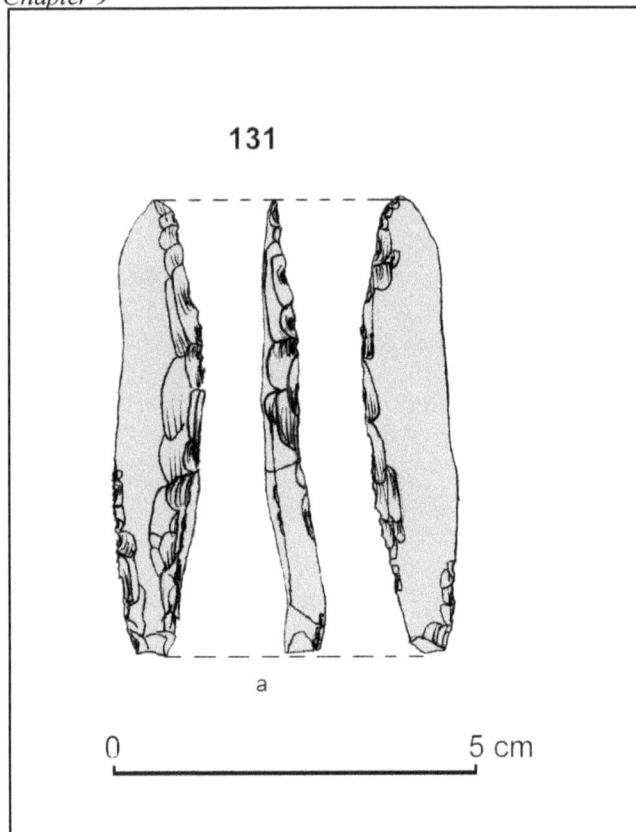

131

a

0   5 cm

Figure 9.2: Backed blade, Uai Bobo 2, East Timor

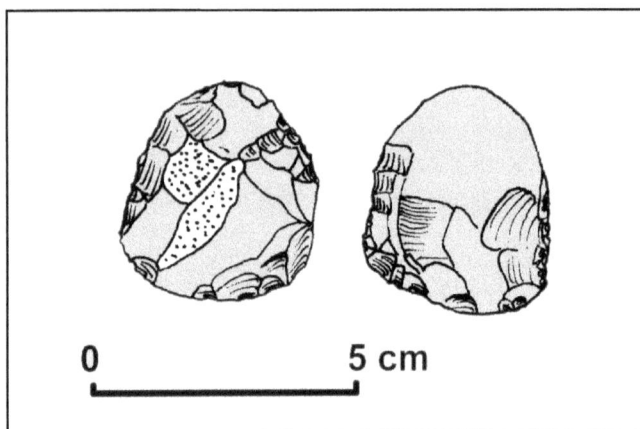

0   5 cm

Figure 9.3: Bifacial tool from Gassi Issi, surface find, East Timor

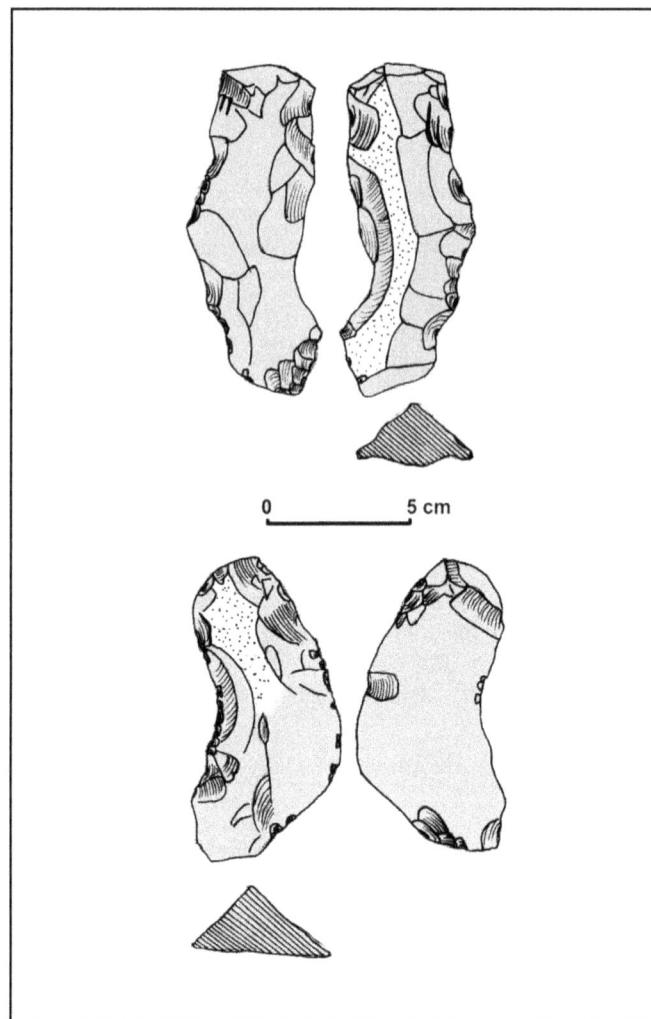

0   5 cm

Figure 9.4: Lua Meko (upper) and Uai Bobo 1 (lower) horizon III C (pottery level) retouched tools.

After the Mid Holocene

Tanged points and other retouched tools

One important characteristic during this period is the development of more advanced flaked stone technology, especially in East Timor, and the introduction of pottery. In Uai Bobo 1, hafting modification occurs above horizon IIIC (2190±80 BP), together with pottery (figure 9.1). The same occurs in Pia Hudale (figure......), where hafting modification, although not as distinctive as in Uai Bobo, occurs in the sub-surface and surface layers with pottery. In Niki-Niki in West Timor, tanged points also occur in the pottery layer, but no dating is available for this site. From the Lua Meko surface layer, there are two flakes which are retouched, bifacially and monofacially respectively, to form handles, although these are not not as distinctive as the tanged tools from Uai Bobo 1. Interestingly, although it is reported that there is are backed blades in East Timor, my

examination of the Uai Bobo assemblage revealed instances of such backing technology in Horizon III C (figure 9.1 d and 9.2). This backing technology was applied not only to produce backed blades but also the tanged points.

The backing technique applied in Uai Bobo is closer to the backing technique applied to Bondi points in Australia (Flenniken and White 1985: fig. 22; fig. 24) and Toalean. In Toalean stone industry, there are two types of flake preform used for backed artefacts, i.e: symmetrical flake and asymmetrical flake. Backed blade found from Uai Bobo 2 was applied only on asymmetrical flake.

Analysing the stone artefact assemblages from Sawu, Rote and Timor, one gets a strong indication that generally retouch was applied to resharpen flake or blade edges, and not to shape the fresh flakes detached from nodules. Some indication of this is that there are many low angle working edges on blades with signs of use wear without retouch, whereas retouch is commonly found on the steeper or high angle working edges of flakes and blades.

Pottery

The dating for the occurrence of pottery in Lua Meko is approximately the same as the pottery dates suggested by Glover for East Timor (4720 ±100 BP for Lua Meko and 4500 ± 200 BP for Uai Bobo 2). However, these date seem too old when compared with the dating for all pottery found in the islands of Southeast Asia, not so far prior to 3500 BP in the general region of eastern Indonesia. The Lua Meko date could reflect disturbance since the sherd concerned has a close chemical composition to one dated to only 900 BP from Lua Manggetek. Further comparison also suggests that the clay is the same as that used by Oenitas potters today. The fabric, however, is different, suggesting that both samples were made either in different production centres or made in the same location but by a different generation of potters.

There are three pottery surface decoration styles in East Timor - plain red-slipped, incised, and paddle impressed. The plain red-slipped pottery occurs earlier that the two other pottery styles. In his synthesis, Glover suggests that incised pottery occurred about 3500 BP, a millennium later than the first occurrence of red-slipped pottery in the East Timor deposits. No comparable incised pottery has been found yet from Rote and Sawu, where all pottery found so far is unslipped or red-slipped.

Interestingly, flask-shaped pottery was not found during my excavations, while vessels of this form were found in Metal Age contexts in Liang Bua and Lie Siri. In Melolo, on Sumba, flask-shaped vessels were decorated by incision of human face motifs on the necks. The absence of this vessel form on Rote and Sawu may strengthen the possibility that rockshelters and caves were not used any longer after pottery was introduced.

Humanly-introduced animals

The data available at present suggest that introduced animals brought purposely by humans occur earlier on Timor than on Rote and Sawu. In Uai Bobo 2, non-native animals (either domesticated or other larger animals) are not found before Horizon VII (5100-5900 BP). At about that time, the Sundaland species civet cat (right mandibular ramus) and macaque were introduced, as was the marsupial cuscus. Pig bones occur in reasonable numbers from Horizons VII-XIII (circa 5900 to 700 years ago). Dog and sheep/goat appear immediately prior to the introduction of metal (Glover, 1986: 199, 204-205, 219-222). Glover notes that all of these large introduced animals occur in association with pottery, but cuscus might have been brought to Timor before pottery was introduced. If this was the case, then there was human interaction between Timor and New Guinea immediately prior to the introduction of pottery to these areas.

In the rock shelters excavated on Rote, bones of introduced animals occur very rarely. In Lua Meko, a bone of *Macaca fascicularis* was found in spit 1 (see David Bulbeck, appendix). In Uai Bobo 1 and Liang Bua, macaque bones also occur in association with pottery (Glover 1986; Tim Puslitarkenas 1978-1986).

One pig bone was found in Lua Meko from spit 5 (25 cm below the surface), identified as probably being a disturbed layer (see explanation in Chapter IV), and one long bone between the surface and spit 3 is identified as most likely a deer long bone (Prof. Colin Groves, pers comm 1999). No pottery occurs in spit 5 where the pig bone was found, but due to disturbance it cannot be ruled out that both the introduced animals (pig and deer) are pottery associated. The date of spit 6, that is from the level below the disturbed layer, is c.7000 BP. One cow/horse bone occurs in Pia Hudale spit 1, in association with pottery. There is also a

deer ulna fragment. Unfortunately no reliable date was obtained for the upper layer of Pia Hudale.

So far, the oldest possible date for the occurrence of introduced animals with pottery in the Rote sites is around 4750 BP, from Lua Meko. Pottery and pig bones are most likely in association with pottery in Lua Manggetek, and certainly cow/horse and deer are in association with pottery in Pia Hudale. This is also the case in the East Timor sites. As discussed in Chapter VI, the dates obtained for introduced animals in Lie Madira are still uncertain.

In all excavated sites on Rote, *Rattus exulans* never occurs in the stratified deposits. This is an interesting absence, since in the East Timor sites *Rattus exulans* occurs in association with pottery or immediately before it. The presence of this rattus species is often associated with the arrival of Austronesian people. The absence of this *Rattus* species in the rockshelter sites on Rote may indicate that they were no longer used for habitation when Austronesian influence arrived on Rote.

In the Rote sites, two different robust *Rattus* species occur, that is an unnamed robust species and *Rattus tanezumi*. All the rat bones from Pia Hudale belong to the robust *Rattus*. According to Dr Ken Aplin this robust *Rattus* was most closely related to *Papagomys* and *Hooijeromys* of Flores and *Komodomys* of Komodo, Rintja and Lembata Islands. He is also certain that it is different from the *Rattus buhlerensis* identified in West Timor and different from the rat species found by Glover in East Timor (Ken Aplin, pers. comm. 2002).

Shell beads and other shell ornaments

In Lua Meko and Lua Manggetek, shell beads occurred from the surface down to spit 5. There is a 'tail', however, of one pierced *Nautilus* shell found in spit 8, most probably having penetrated down as a result of burial activity. Except for the *Dentalium* shell in spit 8, all shell ornaments occur together with *Anadara sp.* and *Gafrarium sp.*, some below the pottery, although the main concentration is in the pottery layer. Several shell beads occurred close to human skeletal fragments from spit 3 down to spit 6. Thus, the first appearance of shell beads could be the same date as for pottery in this site and the two Tonggobatu shelters.

The number of humanly-modified shell ornaments in Pia Hudale is fewer than in the Tonggobatu sites, but they are more varied. They occur only in the pottery layers, except for a shaped shell in the form of fish that was found 10 cm deeper than most other shell ornaments. In East Timor sites, generally, modified shell ornaments, including pierced shell disks, other shell bead types, and *Trochus* shell arm bands (all absent from the Rote and Sawu sites so far), occur in Neolithic association (Spriggs, 1989, Glover, 1986:117-118, 151-153, 187-190; Tim Puslitarkenas 1978-1986). This is in parallel with other sites in Nusa Tenggara: Liang Bua on Flores, Lewoleba on Lembata Island, Melolo on Sumba, and Camplong in West Timor (Sumijati 1994). Thus, in Nusa Tenggara shell scrapers can occur before pottery was introduced, but shaped and modified shell ornaments occur together with the introduction of pottery.

2. Some comparative observations on the archaeological record elsewhere in Island Southeast Asia

In the sites of Song Keplek and Gua Braholo in central Java, the Late Pleistocene phase is characterised by massive stone artefacts, including core tools. These tendencies for non-intensive occupation to be associated with massive flaked stone artefacts parallel the basal occupation in Lua Meko. There is a difference, however, in that these Javan massive stone artefacts continue to the later phase of occupation in Gua Braholo, while in Lua Meko the occurrences ceased before the Terminal Pleistocene. Unfortunately, the proportions of these limestone tools in Gua Braholo from each occupation phase are not reported, therefore it is difficult to judge whether they are more dominant in the earlier or later periods.

In new cave sites discovered in Gunung Watangan, East Java (Gua Macan and Gua Gelatik), several massive tools comparable in size with the Lua Meko basal tools were found together with stone anvils. It appears that such massive tools were found in Gua Macan as late as the level dating to 2,490 ± 90 BP (PPNY Batan Yogyakarta; Nurani and Hascaryo 2002:69). Technologically, the techniques applied to produce these stone artefacts in Gunung Watangan were similar to those used in the Pacitanian and Southern Mountain sites of Java (Hidayat 1994). Another new Javan site, Song Bentar in Gunung Kidul, was probably occupied from 40,000 years ago, according to a date obtained from an animal bone sample close to the bedrock (Yuwono 2000). But no further information is yet available.

Towards the mid-Holocene a new type of stone technology appeared in several sites in the Wallacean Islands, especially in the form of the Toalian backed blade and microlith industry in South Sulawesi. Parallels for this industry in the Rote, Sawu and Timor sites during the Holocene are recorded in the tendency towards production of blade-like flakes in Lie Madira, and in the observations given above about the presence of backing in East Timor. Also in Timor, tanged point technology developed during this period (see p.170 this chapter). These changes must reflect some degree of contact through the islands of eastern Indonesia during the mid-Holocene, mediated by the effects of locally-varying lithic resources and cultural choices.

3. Final Observations

This thesis has presented evidence for a human presence on Rote before 24,000 years ago, in apparent association initially (in Lua Meko) with an industry of very large stone tools that have possible parallels in Java. Immediately after this date, evidence appears for a small flake industry that continued through the late Pleistocene into the mid-Holocene, when the excavated rock shelters (Lie Madira on Sawu, and Pia Hudale, Lua Manggetek and Lua Meko on Rote) appear to have been abandoned as loci for regular habitation. In Lie Madira, the flake industry has a tendency towards the production of blade-like forms, parallel to but slightly different from similar tendencies in mid-Holocene South Sulawesi (Toalian) and Timor. Neolithic remains are very few in all the sites investigated, but there is some evidence for use of the caves for human burial in pre-Neolithic times. Large introduced mammals and shell artifacts appear mostly with the appearance of pottery, and although there are examples of both in earlier layers, the possibility of disturbance renders certainty in their dating elusive.

Stone tool usage and shellfish exploitation both peak during the terminal Pleistocene and early to middle Holocene, from about 13,000 to about 4000 years ago. The shell species present in Lua Meko and Lua Manggetek reveal the changing environments in the vicinity caused by the postglacial rise in sea level, leading to the formation of sandy embayments characterised by large numbers of bivalve shellfish species.

Overall, this research has illuminated an area of eastern Indonesia little researched previously, but one that was surely important in the movement of humans from Java, through Nusa Tenggara, towards Timor and Australia, during the past 45,000 years.

BIBLIOGRAPHY

Almeida and Zbyszewski. 1967. A Contribution to the study of prehistory of Portuguese Timor-lithic industries. In W. G. Solheim (ed.) *Archaeology at the 11ᵗʰ Pacific Science Congress*, p. 55-67. Honolulu: University of Hawaii, Social Science Research Institute, Asian and Pacific Archaeology Series No. 1.

Ambrose, Wal. 1992. Clays and sands in Melanesian pottery analysis. In Jean Christophe Galipaud (ed.). *Poterie Lapita et Peuplement. Noumea*, Nouvelle Caledonia: Orstom. p. 169-176.

Andrefsky,WilliamJr. 1998.*Lithics, Macroscopic approaches to analysis, Cambridge Manuals in Archaeology*, Cambridge: Cambridge University.

Anggraeni, Mahirta and Nugahani. 2000. *Eksploitasi Sumberdaya Hayati Pegunugan Seribu pada Awal Holosen and Implikasinya: studi kasus di Kecamatan Ponjong, Gunung Kidul.* Unpublisehd report. Yogyakarta: Lembaga Penelitian Universitas Gadjah Mada, Departemen Pendidikan Nasional.

Anson, D. 1983. *Lapita pottery of the Bismark Archipelago and its affinities.*Unpublished PhD thesis. Sydney: University of Sydney.

Audley-Charles 1981. *Geological history of the region of Wallace's Line.* In. T. C Whitmore. *Wallaces's Line and Plate Tectonics.* p.24-35. Oxford: Clarendon Press.

Audley-Charles 1993. Geological evidence bearing upon the Pliocene emergence of Seram, an island colonizable by land plants and animals. In *The natural history of Seram.*(eds) I. D. Edwards, A.A. Macdonald and J Proctor, UK: Intercept Ltd.

Ardika, I. W., and P.Bellwood. 1991. *Sembiran: The beginnings of Indian contact with Bali. AP* 65:221-232.

Ardika, I Wayan. 1991. *Archaeological Research in Northeastern Bali, Indonesia,* Unpublished PhD dissertation. Australian National University.

Azis, Budi Santosa 1980. Penelitian masa berburu dan mengumpulkan makanan di Nusa Tenggara Timur, tahun 1975-1981. *REHPA* I: 20-31.

Barraclough, A. 1992. Quaternary sediment analysis: a deductive approach at A-level. *Teaching Geography* 17: 15-18.

Bellwood, Peter. 1976. Archaeological research in Minahasa and the Talaud Islands, Northeastern Indonesia. *Asian Perspectives* vol XIX. No. 2: 240-288.

Bellwood, Peter. 1978. *Man's Conquest of the Pacific.* New York: Oxford University Press.

_____. 1991. *The Austronesian dispersal and the origin of languages.* Scientific American 265 (1): 88-93.

_____. 1993 Crossing The Wallcea Line in-With Style i_n Spriggs, Matthew et al. eds *A Community of Colture The People and Prehistory of the Pacific,* Canberra : RSPAS, Australian National University.

_____. 1995. Austronesian prehistory in Southeast Asia: Homeland, Expansion and transformation. In P. Bellwood, j.j. Fox. And D. tryon (eds.), *the Austronesians,* 96-111.

_____. 1996. Early agriculture and the dispersal of the Southern Mongoloids in Takeru Akazawa and Emoke J. E. Szathmary,eds. *Prehistoric Mongoloid dispersals* Oxford: Oxford University Press..

_____..1997. *Prehistory of the Indo-Malaysian Archipelago.* Revised edition. Honolulu: University of Hawaii Press.

Bellwood. Peter. A. Waluyo, Gunadi, G. Nitihaminoto and G. Irwin. 1993. Archaeological research in the Northern Maluku. *BIPPA* 13:20-33.

Bellwood. P *et. al* 1998. 35,000 years of prehistory in the northern Moluccas. In Bartstra, Gert-Jan., Jan.*Bird's Head Approaches Irian Jaya studies- a programme for interdisiplinary Research. Modern Guatenary Research in southeast Asia* . p. 233-275.

Bemmelen, R. W. van 1949. *The Geology of Indonesia.* The Hague, The Netherlands:Government Printing Office.

Begler and Keating.1979. Theoretical Goals and Methodological Realities: Problems in the Reconstruction of Prehistoric Subsistence Economies, *World Archaeology* 11: 208 – 226.

Bergh, G. van den., M. Mubroto, Fachroel Aziz., P. Sondaar and J. de Vos. 1996 Did Homo erectus reach the island of Flores. *BIPPA* 14: 27-26.

Bergh, van den. , J. de Vos, P. Sondaar, and Fachroel Azis . 1996. Pleistocene zoogeographic evolution of Java (Indonesia) and glasio-eustatic sea level fluctuations: a background for the presence of Homo. *BIPPA* 14:7-21.

Bintarti, D. D. 1986. Lewoleba sebuah situs masa prasejarah di Pulau Lembata. In *Pertemuan Ilmiah Arkeologi IV*, vol. IIa:73-91. Jakarta: Pusat Penelitian Arkeologi Nasional.

Birdsell, J. B. 1977. The recalibration of a paradigm for the first peopling of Greater Australia. In J. Allen *et. al.* (eds.) *Sunda and Sahul*.p.113-168. London: Academic Press.

Blust, Robert 1995. The prehistory of the Austronesian-speaking peoples: a view from Language. *Journal of World Prehistory, Vol. 9. No. 4* :53-510.

Bocek, Barbara. 1986. Rodent ecology and burrowing behavior: predicted effects on archaeological site formation. *American Antiquity*, 51(3): 589-603.

Bulbeck, F. David and Nasrudin 2002. Recent insights on the chronology and ceramics of the Kalumpang site complex, South Sulawesi, Indonesia, *BIPPA* 22:83-100.

Butlin 1989. N. G. (1989). The palaeoeconomic history of Aboriginal migration. *Australian Economic History Review. XXIX*:3-57.

Chappel 1991. Late Pleistocene coasts and human migrations in the Austral region. In Spriggs. e*t. al.* 1991. *A Community of Culture, the people and the prehistory of Pacific.* Canberra: RSPAS, Australian National University.

Chappell, John. 1994. Upper Quaternary sea level, coral terraces, Oxygen isotopes and deep-sea temperatures. *Journal of Geography vol. 103. No. 7(936):* 828-840.

Chappel, John. A. Omura, T. Esat, M. Mc Vulloch, J. Pandolfi, Y. Ota and B. Pillans 1996. Reconciliation of late Quaternary sea levels derived from coral terrace at Huon Peninsula with deep-sea oxygen isotope records. *Earth and Planetary Science Letters 141:* 227 – 237.

Charles., Rachanie Bannanurag, Graeme Mason and Nancy Tayles 1992. Human biology, environment and ritual at Khok Phanom Di. *World Archaeology* 24 No.1 The Humid Tropics:35-53.

Classen, Cheryl 1998. *Shells.* Cambridge Manuals in Archaeology. Cambridge: Cambridge University Press.

Dance, S Peter. 1992. *Shells.* NSW: Colin Angus & Robertson.

Flannery, T. F., P. Bellwood, J. P. White., T Ennis, G. Irwin, K. Schubert and S. Balasubramaniam. 1998. Mammals from Holocene archaeological deposits on Gebe and Morotai Islands, Northern Moluccas, Indonesia. *Journal of the Australian mammal Society.* Vol. 20 No.3:391-400.

Flenniken 1981. *Replicative Systems Analysis*: a Model applied to the vein quartz artifacts from the Hoko River Site. Washington State University, Laboratory of anthropology, Report of Investigations 59,.Pullman.

Flenniken, J. Jeffrey and White, Peter J. 1985. Australian flaked stone tools: a technological perspective. Records of the Austyralian Museum vo. 36: 131 – 151.

Freestone, I. C. 1982. Applications and potential of electron micro-analysis in technological and provenance investigations of ancient ceramics. *Archaeometry* 24:99-116.

Geologica, Research and Development Center 1979. *Geological Map sheet Kupang-Atambua*

Gillespie, 2002 . Dating the first Australians. *Radiocarbon* vol. 44 Nr 2, 2002:455-472.

Gifford-Gonzalez, Diane P., David. B. Damrosch, Debra R. Damrosch., John Pryor, and Robert L. Thunnen. 1985. The third dimension in site structure: an experiment in trampling and vertical dispersal . *American Antiquity*, 50 (4): 803-818.

Glover, I. C. and E. A. Glover. 1970. Pleistocene flaked stone tools from Timor and Flores. *Mankind*, 7: 188 – 190.

Glover, I. C. *1972 Excavations in Timor: a study of economic change and cultural continuity in prehistory.* Unpublished PhD thesis. Canberra: Australian National University.

Glover, I. C. 1972. Alfred buhler's excavations in Timor: a re-evaluation. *Art and Archaeology Research Papers2*:117-42.

Glover, I. C. 1981. Leang Burung 2: an upper palaeolithic reockshelter in South Sulawesi, Indonesi. In G-J Bartstra and W.A. Casparie (eds) *Modern Quaternary Research in Southeast Asia,* :1-35.

Glover, I. C and G. Presland 1985. Microliths in Indonesian Flaked stone industries. In V.N. Misra and P.S. Bellwood (eds.) *Recent Advances in Indo-Pacific Prehistory,* p. 185-195., New Delhi: Oxford-IBH.

Glover, I. C 1986 Archaeology in Eastern Timor, 1966-67. *Terra Australis II*, Canberra: Department of Prehistory, Research School of Pacific Studies, The Australian National University.

Groves, C. P. 1981. *Ancestors for the Pigs: taxonomy and phylogeny of the genus Sus.* Canberra: Department of Prehistory, Research School of Pacific Studies, Australian National University.

Hayden, B. 1977. Sticks and stones and edge-ground axes. In J. Allen et al. (eds.) *Sunda and Sahul* p. 73-109.

Heekeren, H. R. van. 1972. *The Stone Age of Indonesia.* 2nd edition. The Hague: Nijhoff.

Heffernan, K. 1980 *Moluscan resources and Talaud economy: ecological and cultural parameters in the study of refuse.* Unpublished BA (Hons.) thesis. Canberra: Australian National University.

Hidayat, Mohammad. 1994 LHPA *Bentuk-bentuk Pemanfaatan sumber daya Alam Tahap II di Kabupaten Wonogiri.* Unpublished report. Yogyakarta: Balai Arkeologi Yogyakarta.

Hiscock, Peter. 2002. Pattern and context in the Holocene proliferation of backed artefacts in australiaIn Robert G. Elston and Steven L. Kuhn (eds). Thinking Small: Global Perspectives on Microlithization. *Archaeological papers of the American Anthropological Association (AP3A)* 12:163-177.

Hooijer, D. A. 1957. *A Stegodon from Flores. Treubia* 24:119-29

Hunt, Terry. L. 1989. *Lapita Ceramic Exchange in the Mussau Islands, Papua New Guinea.* Unpublished PhD. Thesis, Seatle: University of Washington.

Hunt, Terry L. 1993. Ceramic provenance studies in Oceania: Methodological Issues. In Fankhauser, B. L. and Bird,. J. R. (eds.) *Archaeometry: Current Australasian Research,* p. 51-56. Occasional papers in Prehistory 22, Canberra: Department of Prehistory, Research School of Pacific Studies, Australian National University, Canberra.

Irwin, Geoffrey. 1991. *The Prehistoric Exploration and Colonisation of the Pacific.* Cambridge: Cambridge University Press.

Jacob, Teuku. 1967. *Some Problems Pertaining to the Racial History of the Indonesian Region.* Neerlandia-Utrecht: Drukkerij.

Limbrey, Susan. 1975. *Soil Science and Archaeology.* London: London Academic Press.

Liong, Lie Goan. 1965. Palaeoanthropological results of the excavation at the coast of Lewoleba (Isle of Lomblen). *Anthropos 60:* 39-623.

Mahirta 2000. The Development of Mare Pottery Traditions in the Northern Moluccas. Bulletin of the Indo-Pacific Prehistory Association 20 volume 4: 124-132.

Minnegal, Monica. 1984. A Note On Butchering Dugong At Princess Charlotte Bay, *Australian Archaeology* No 19 December 1984 p.15-20

Monk, Kathryn A. Yance de Fretes, Gayatri Reksodiharfo-Lilley. 1997. *The Ecology of Nusa Tenggara and Maluku.* Singapore: Periplus Editions (HK) Ltd.

Morwood, Mike, 1998. *Stone tools and fossil elepahnts: the archaeological of eastern Indonesia and its implication for Australia.* NSW: University of New England.

O'Connor, Sue. Spriggs M, Veth, P. 2000. *After Wallace: preliminary results of the first season's excavations of Liang Lembudu, Aru Islands, Maluku.* Unpublished report. The Australian National University, Canberra.

O'Connor, Sue. M Spriggs, P. Veth. 2002. Excavation at Lene Hara cave establishes occupation in East Timor at least 30,000-35,000 years ago. *Antiquity* 76:45-50.

O'Connor , M. Spriggs, and P. Veth ed. 2005. The Archaeology of the Aru Islands, Eastern Indonesia. *Terra Australis 22.* Canberra: Research School of Pacific and Asian Studies, Pandanus Books, The Australian National Univrsity

Odell, Hamley and Odell-Vereecken. 1980. Asking the reability of lithic use-wear assesments by blindtest: the low power approach. *Journal of Field Archaeology vol 7 :*87-120.

Heekeren, H. R. van 1992. New investigations on the Lower Palaeolithic Pacitan culture in Java. *Berita Dinas Purbakala.* No. 1:1-21

Hughes, P. J. and V. Djohadze. 1980. Radiocarbon dates from archaeological sites on the south coast of New South wales and the use of depth/age curves. *Occasional Papers in Prehistory No. 1:* 1-28.

Hunt, terry L., 1993. Ceramic provenance studies in Oceania: methological issues. In Fankhauser, Barry and J. Roger Bird. *Archaeometry* : Current Australian research. Canberra: Department of Prehistory, Research School of Pacific and Asian Studies, Australian National University.

Kaars, W. A. van der. 1991. Aspects of Late Quaternary palynology of Eastern Indonesian deep-sea cores . *Netherlands Journal of Sea Research:* 24 (4): 495-500.

Kaars, W. A. van der , 1991. Palynology of eastern Indonesia marine piston-cores: A Late Quaternary vegetation and climatic record for Australasia. *Journal of Palaeogeography,Palaeoclimatology,Palaeoecolgy* 85: 239-302.

Kamminga, J. 1982. *Over the Edge.* Occasional Papers in Anthropology No. 12. Anthropology Museum, University of Queensland.

Kealhofer, Lisa. 1996. The human environment during the Terminal Pleistocene and Holocene in Northeastern Thailand: Phytolith evidence from Lake Kumphawapi. *Asian Perspectives* vol 35. No. 2: 220-254.

Keegan, William F., and Diamond, Jared M 1987. Colonisation of island by human: a bibliographical perspective, *Advances in Archaeological Method and Theory,* No. 10: 49-92.

Kersaw, A. Peter. 1995. Environmental change in Greater Australia. Transitions. *Antiquity* vol. 69, special number 265:656-675.

Krzanowski, W. J. 2000. *Principles of Multivariate Analysis*: a user's perspective. 2nd edition. Clarendon Pres.

Kitchener and Suryanto 1996. The status of green and hawksbill turtle rookeries in Nusa Tenggara and Maluku Tenggara, Eastern Indonesia-with observations on other marine turtles in the region. *Proceedings of the first international conference on eastern Indonesian-Australian vertebrate fauna.* Spriggs Menado, Indonesia.

Mahirta. 2004. *Human Occupation on Rote and Sawu Islands, Nusa Tenggara Timur.* Unpublished PhD thesis. School of Archaeology and Anthropology, The Australian National University.

Mahirta dan Indriati 2006. *Kronologi Penghunian Manusia dan Perkembangan Budaya di Pulau Rote (Nusa Tenggara Timur) pada Masa Prasejarah.* Laporan Hasil Penelitian Fundamental DIKTI, Universitas Gadjah Mada, Yogyakarta.

Maloney, B. K. 1992. Late Holocene climatic change in Southeast Asia: the palynological evidence and its implications for archaeology. *World Archaeology* 24 no. 1: 25-34.

Marhaeni, Etik. 2002. Late Pleistocene vertebrates in Gunung Sewu. In Truman Simanjuntak (ed.). *Gunung Sewu in Prehistoric Times.* Yogyakarta:Gadjah Mada University Press.

Maringer, J. and Th. Verhoeven. 1970. Note on some stone artefacts in the national Archaeological Institute of Indonesia at Djakarta, collected from the Stegodon-fossil bed at Boaleza in Flores. *Anthropos.* 65: 638-639.

Maringer, J. und Th. Verhoeven. 1972 Steingerate aus dem Waiklau-Trockenbett bei Maumere auf Flores, Indonesia. *Anthropos* 67:129-137.

Mc.Carty, F.R 1967. *Australian Aboriginal Stone Implements.* Sydney: Australian Museum.

Meehan, Betty. 1982. *Shell Bed to Shell Midden.* AIAS new Series no. 37, Australian Institute of Aboriginal Strudies, Canberra ACT.

Monk. 1997. *The Ecology of Nusa Tenggara and Maluku.* The ecology of Indonesia series vol. 5. Singapore: Periplus editions.

Mulvaney, John and Kaminga, Johan 1999. *Prehistory of Australia.* NSW: Allen and Unwin Pty Ltd.

Nies Anggraeni 1989. Pola Pangan Masyarakat Penghuni Gua Oelnaik Desa Camplong, Kabupaten Kupang, *Proceeding AHPA* II: Jakarta: Puslitarkenas.

Nurani and Agus T. Hascaryo 2002. Pola pemanfaatan lahan gua pada komunitas Gunung Watangan. *BPA* No. 15. Jogyakarta: Balai Arkeologi Yogyakarta.

Odell, Hamley and Odell-Vereecken 1980. Asking the reliability of lithic use-wear assesments by blindtest: the low power approach. *Journal of Field Archaeology* vol. 7:87-120.

Orton, Clive; Tyers, Paul and Vince, Alan. 1993. *Pottery in Archaeology.* Cambridge Manuals in Archaeology. Cambridge: Cambridge University Press.

Prasetyo, Bagyo 2002. The bone industry, in Truman Simanjuntak. (ed.) *Gunung Sewu in Prehistoric Times.* Yogyakarta: Gadjah Mada University Press.

Richardson, N 1992. Conjoin set and stratigraphic integrity in a sandstone shelter: Kenniff Cave (Queensland, Australia) *Antiquity 66:* 408-418.

Rye, O. 1981. *Pottery Technology: Principles and Reconstruction.* Washington: Taraxacum.

Sarasin, P. 1936 . Beitrage zur Prahistoria der Inseln Timor und Roti. Verh. Naturf. Ges. In *Basel* 47:1-59.

Sartono, S. 1979. The age of the vertebrate fossils and artefacts from Cabenge in South Sulawesi, Indonesia. *Mod. Quaternary Research in Southeast Asia* 65-81.

Schiffer, Michael B. 1987. *Formation Process of the Archaeological Record.* Salt Lake City: University of Utah Press.

Simanjuntak, Truman. 1992. *Nusa Tenggara Timur: Exploitasi Pada Akhir plestosen dan Pada Kala Holosen.* Unpublished report.Jakarta: Pusat Penelitian Arkeologi Nasional.

_____. 1993. Perwajahan mesolitik Indonesia. *Amerta* 13: 1-16.

_____. 1998. Budaya awal Holosen di Gunung Sewu. *Evaluasi Hasil Penelitian Arkeologi.* Unpublished proceedings. Cipayung: Puslitarkenas.

_____. 2002. Cave settlement, new trend in the Late Pleistocene. In Truman Simanjuntak (ed.) *Gunung Sewu in Prehistoric Times.*p. 89-96. Yogyakarta: Gadjah Mada University Press.

_____. 2002. Keplek Cave: Settlement in the Late Pleistocene-Holocene in Truman Simanjuntak (ed.) *Gunung Sewu in Prehistoric Times.* P. 109-118. Yogyakarta: Gadjah Mada University Press.

_____. 2002. Braholo Cave, an ideal settlement site in Western Gunung Sewu. In Truman simanjuntak (ed.). *Gunung Sewu in Prehistoric Times.* P. 119-128. Yogyakarta: Gadjah Mada University Press. .

Smith, Mike. 1993, M. Spriggs and B. Fankhauser. *Sahul in Review.* Canberra: Department of Prehistory, Research School of Pacific Studies, Occasional Paper 24.

South 1977. *Method and theory in Historical Archaeology.* New York: Academic Press.

Soejono, R.P 1980. Data baru industri Palaeolithic Indonesia . *Pertemuan Ilmiah Arkeologi* II, Jakarta

Soejono 1987. Lingkungan dan Budaya Plestosin Indonesia in *Geologi Kuarter dan Lingkungan Hidu*p: Pusat Penelitian dan Pengembangan Geolog p. 31-41

Spriggs, Mattew 1998, Aru. In the foot steps of Wallace: the first two seasons of archaeological research in the Aru Islands, Maluku. *Cakalele.* Vol. 9:63-80.

_____. 1999. Archaeological dates and linguistic subgroup in the settlement of the Island Southeast Asian-Pacific region. Bulletin of the Indo-Pacific Prehistory Association 18 Vol 2: 17 – 24.

_____. 2000. Out of Asia: the spread of Southeast Asian Pleistocene and Neolithic maritime cultures in Island Southeast Asia and the Western Pacific. *Modern quaternary Research in southeast Asia.* Vol. 16:51-70.

Stein, Julie K. 1987. Deposits for archaeologists in Michael B. Schiffer.ed. *Advances in Archaeological Method and Theory*. Vol. 11.p. 337-395. London: Academic Press, Inc.

Steed, Lyndall G. and Sheridan J. Coakes. *SPSS, analysis without anguish*. Brisbane: John Willey & Son Australia, Ltd.

Specht, Jim. 1968. Preliminary report of excavations on watom island. *In The joirnal of the Polynesian Society*. Vol. 77. No. 2: 117-133.

Stoltman, James B. 1989. A quantitative approach to the petrographic analysis of ceramic thin sections. *American Antiquity* 54: 147-160.

Stoltman, James B. 1991. Ceramic pretrography as a technique for documenting cultural interaction: An Example from the upper Mississippi Valley. *American Antiquity* vol. 56: 103-120.

Summerhayes. Glenn and Walker. 1982. Elemental analysis and taxonomy of prehistoric pottery from Western Java. *Archaeometry: an Australasian perspective*: 60 - 67

Summerhayes, Glenn. R. 1996. Interaction in Pacific Prehistory: *An approach based on the production, distribution and use of pottery*. Unpublished Phd. Thesis. Bundoora Victoria: La Trobe University.

Tringham, Cooper,G. Odell, G, Voytek 1974 ,Experimentation in the formation of edge damage: a new approach to lithic analysis, *Journal of Field Archaeology*, 1: 171-195

Shepard , Anna O. 1974. *Ceramics for the Archaeologist*. Washington D.C: Carnegie Institution Publication 609.

Sullivan, III and Rozen, Kenneth C. 1985. Debitage Analysis and Archaeological Interpretation. *American Antiquity* 50: 755 – 759.

Sumijati 1994. *Gerabah Prasejarah di Liang Bua, Melolo dan Lewoleba: tinjauan teknologi dan fungsinya*. Unpublished PhD thesis. Yogyakarta: Universitas Gadjah Mada.

Summerhayes, G. R. and Walker, M. J. 1982. Elemental analysis and taxonomy of prehistoric pottery from Western Java, in W. Ambrose, and P. Ambrose, (eds.)*Archaeometry: An Australasian Perspective*,p. 60-67.Canberra: Departement of Prehistory, Research School of Pacific Studies, Australian National University.

Summerhayes, Glenn R. 1996. Ceramics: electron microprobe analysis of pottery in Frankel, David and Jennifer M. Webb. Mazki Alonia, an early and Middle bronze Age Town in Cyprus excavation 1990-1994. *Studies in Mediteranean Archaeology* vol. CXXIII:1 p. 175-181., Jonsered: Paul Astrosus Forlag .

Thomas, K 1985. Land Snail Analysis in Archaeology: Theory and Practice, in Fieller, N., Gilbertson, D., and Ralp, N. (eds.). *Palaeobiological Investigation*. British Archaeological Reports, International Series 266 (Oxford, BAR): 131-135.

Tjia, H. D. 1983. Quaternary tectonics of Sabah and Sarawak, East Malaysia. Sains Malaysiana, v. 12 2),. P. 191-215.

Tim Peneliti Puslitarkenas. 1978-1986. *Laporan ekskavasi Liang Bua*. Unpublished report. Jakarta: Puslitarkenas.

Tite, M. 1992. The impact of electron mocroscopy on ceramic studies, in A.M. Pollard (ed*.), New Developments in Archaeological Science*, p. 111-131. Proceedings of the British Academy 77, Oxford:Oxford University Press.

Verheijen, A. J., 1990. *Dictionary of Plant Names in the Lesser Sunda Islands. Pacific Linguistics Series D no. 83*. Department of Linguistics. Research School of pacific and Asian Studies, Australian National University.

Verhoeven, Th. 1953. Eine mikrolithenkultur in mittel und west Flores (Indonesie). *Anthropos* 48: 597-612.

_____. 1964. Stegodon-fossilien auf der insel Timor. Anthropos 59

Villa, Paola. 1982. *Conjoinable pieces and site formation processes*. American Antiquity 47:276-290.

Wang, Xuan, Kaars, Sander van der, Kershaw, Peter, Bird, Michael, Jansen, Fred. 1999. *Palaeogeography, Palaeoclimatology, Palaeoecology 147 : 241 – 256*.

Widianto, Harry 2002.The Pacitanian culture:who owns it. in Truman Simanjuntak 2002. *Gunung Sewu in Prehistoric Times*. Yogyakarta: Gadjah Mada University Press.

Young , David E and Bonnichsen 1984. *Understanding Stone Tools: A Cognitive Approach*. Orono, Maine: Center for the study of early man. University of Maine at Orono.

Late Pleistocene and Holocene Human Remains from the Island of Rote, Indonesia

David Bulbeck

Department of Archaeology and Anthropology,

Faculty of Arts, Australian National University, ACT 0200

Date of Report: 25 May 2000

This report assesses the fragmentary remains provisionally identified as human by Mahirta from her excavations at three rock shelters on Rote, Nusatenggara. Mahirta, a lecturer in archaeology at Gadjah Mada University, Yogyakarta, excavated the sites for her Ph.D. dissertation research at the Australian National University. Her oldest human remains date to well before the Holocene but, unfortunately, the assemblage is very fragmentary, and contains very few of the skeletal elements of main interest to biological anthropology (i.e. cranium, jaws and teeth). In many cases it has proved difficult to certify a fragment's human as opposed to non-human status, let alone suggest the age or sex of the represented individual. This uncertainty often persisted even after the carbonate calcretions on the fragments' surface had been removed.

The present analysis had not been allowed adequate time for me to loosen the calcretions by chemical means (e.g. a dilute solution of acetic acid), so I cleaned the fragments mechanically. Notes were taken of the thickness and hardness of the calcretion, as well as the degree of apparent fossilization of the bone. These clues are crucial in terms of assessing the likely antiquity of the fragments, and hence which fragments may have come from the same individual. This line of enquiry has major repercussions on the possible levels of post-depositional disturbance to the sites' deposits. Another topic of investigation involves the behavioural activities that could account for the distribution of the fragments in the deposits. Some interesting information can also be gleaned on the health and

lifestyle of the inhabitants. Finally, this report also notes the fragments which appear not to be human, after comparison with the human and non-human skeletal specimens in the biological anthropology laboratory at my department.

Wherever possible osteological measurements were taken, given in millimetres, following Martin (1957) and identified by the appropriate number (M1, etc.) in his system.

Pia Hudale (PHD), Rote Island

The Pia Hudale site yielded a small complement of human remains in each excavated square. The available dates from the excavation fall at around 10 kya, according to Mahirta, and the fully fossilized status of some of the human fragments at the surface would be consistent with a lack of habitation throughout the Holocene. However, other human fragments would appear to be quite recent. The C3, E4 and F4 squares all have fully fossilized fragments at or on the surface, overlying remains that are merely semi-fossilized, or even unfossilized, towards the bottom (Table 1). In square E4, a tooth stained through betel-nut chewing was recovered in a lower spit. These cases of older, conceivably Pleistocene human remains underlain by younger, Holocene fragments point to substantial disturbance of the deposits.

The deposit in the B2 square may have suffered less disturbance, as it exhibits a change with depth from semi-fossilized to fully

Square/ spit	Unfossilized, no real calcretion	Semi-fossilized, no real calcretion	Semi-fossilized, light calcretion	Fully fossilized, thin hard calcretion	Fully fossilized, heavy calcretion
B2/1			X		
B2/3			X		
B2/4					X
B2/5					X
C3/1					X
C3/3					X
C3/5					X
C3/6	X				
D3/1					X
D3/2				X	
E4/0		X			
E4/1					X
E4/3					X
E4/5			X		
E4/6		X			
F4/0					X
F4/1				X	
F4/2		X			

Table 1. Bone fossilization and extent of calcretion on the Pia Hudale human remains

fossilized human remains. As a further positive sign, the small complement of human material in square D3 is all fully fossilized (notwithstanding a thinner calcareous crust with depth). Overall, however, the prospects for the Pia Hudale deposit to register an undisturbed cultural sequence appear glum, based on the condition of the incorporated human material.

The entire human complement consists of one second molar, two clavicle fragments and a scapula fragment, two rib fragments, two humerus fragments, a humerus or radius fragment, a humerus or ulna fragment, three ulna fragments, two radii represented by their fragments, another forearm fragment, a fourth metacarpal fragment, two proximal manual phalanges (first and fifth), one medial manual phalanx, two femur or humerus fragments, two femur fragments, two tibia fragments, a fibula fragment, a third metatarsal, and a fifth metatarsal. This wide representation of the human skeleton in the form of scattered fragments, none of which would need to involve duplication of the same anatomical element, does not in this case indicate the representation of a single individual. We know that at least several individuals are involved given the spatial distance between the test pits, the widely variable state of fossilization of the fragments, and the representation of at least one adult male, one adult female and one male teenager among the remains.

The human material could have entered the deposits in a variety of ways. The tooth might have been lost through trauma. There may have been some consumption of human meat, given the strong representation of the shafts of limb bones. Further, seven fragments appear burnt, in only three cases post-depositionally (as far as could be determined). Secondary burial practices would also seem to be implicated, in the cases of the larger fragments, and the barely fossilized remains that probably postdate the major period of occupation at the site. Recognition of human interments at Pia Hudale would also help to account for the evidence of substantial disturbance of the deposits.

PHD/B2 Spit 1. Burnt. Probably a **radius or ulna** fragment.

PHD/B2 Spit 3. One **right rib** fragment with a robust costal groove and associated rib. One thin shaft fragment that could have come from a **third metatarsal**.

PHD/B2 Spit 4. Bone burnt black inside. Probably **femur or humerus** shaft fragment to judge by the thick compact bone (up to 5.8 mm thick).

PHD/B2 Spit 5. One possible juvenile or small female **left fifth metatarsal** proximal shaft. **Three non-human** fragments, evidently from a small mammal.

PHD/C3 Spit 1. Left or right **ulna** fragment, comprising the ridge along the posterior border in the medio-proximal segment of the shaft.

PHD/C3 Spit 3. One **femur** shaft fragment (made from two joining fragments). One **radius** shaft fragment (made from two joining fragments). One tiny, well-calcined (burnt) fragment which could come from the shaft of a **femur or a humerus**. One fragment which is **not human** and, from the lack of a Haversian structure, appears not to be bone at all – possibly limestone which has come out of solution.

PHD/C3 Spit 5. One fragment which would appear to be from the shaft of a rugged (male?) **ulna**, with thick compact bone (3.6-6.8 mm thick). One second to fifth **medial manual phalanx** represented by its head and distal shaft; either female or sub-adult to judge from the small size of the phalanx.

PHD/C3 Spit 6. **Right fifth proximal manual phalanx. Adult** as shown by the fused base. Phalanx length (M3) would be about 30 mm, which is quite short compared to the average male lengths among Australian Aborigines (32.7 mm, Rao 1966) and North Chinese (32.5 mm, von Bonin 1931), and so may suggest a **female** status. Well burnt.

PHD/D3 Spit 1. **Right clavicle** fragment comprising the angle near the acromion. Small but very rugged with a huge conoid tubercle enclosing a single foramen, and sub-adult as the sternal epiphysis had not yet fused on. **Male teenager**.

PHD/D3 Spit 1. **Ulna** shaft fragment, probably the left distal shaft. Quite rugged with the compact bone measuring 3.4-8.8 mm thick, enclosing a very narrow medullary cavity (3.3 mm diameter). Probably **male**. A gravel-sized lump of lime that has precipitated out of solution, staunchly adhered to the fragment, indicates abandonment of the site over a long period following the deposition of the spit 1 deposits in square D1. Another smaller fragment from a long bone, found in this spit, could also be human.

PHD/D3 Spit 2. Fragment from a long bone shaft, most likely the **humerus or the radius**. Quite thick bone, 5.2 to 6.2 mm, but this would be compatible with a radius as the limb bone fragments from this site do seem to possess quite thick bone. The fragment's calcreted skin appears burnt, post-depositionally.

PHD/D3 Spit 2. A long bone shaft fragment which could possibly be from a human **humerus**, with a burnt surface (presumably post-depositionally). Another fragment, possibly from a human **long bone shaft**, has been subjected to high temperatures making the interior compact bone appear white to light grey, and to lose the clarity of its Haversian structure through melting.

PHD/D3 Spit 4. Two tiny fragments of bone, **neither** of which looks convincingly **human**. One may be a rodent's long bone shaft.

PHD/E4 Spit 0 (surface). **Right first proximal manual phalanx** to a **juvenile**, lacking only the as yet unfused base. The extant length (M3) of 25.3 mm would translate into a length (allowing for the contribution made by the base) close to the average male values of 28.9 recorded on North Chinese (von Bonin 1931) and 29.8 recorded on Australian Aborigines (Rao 1966). Hence the represented individual may have been a **male teenager**.

PHD/E4 Spit 1. **Fibula diaphysis** fragment. Side, sex and age indeterminable. A break near the middle reveals a narrow medullary cavity.

PHD/E4 Spit 3. Four original fragments cross-mend to produce two non-joining fragments from the same bone, being the medial and distal segments of a **radius shaft**. The compact bone is quite thick, 2.6 to 4.6 mm near the mid-shaft. The available measurements are the least shaft circumference (M3) of 32 mm, the transverse shaft diameter at the site of the maximum development of the interosseous border (M4) which is 13.5 mm, and the sagittal diameter of 9.0 mm at the same location (M5). These measurements all fall 3 to 5.5 mm beneath the average measurements recorded on Japanese females (Mizoguchi 1957), but within 1 to 3 mm of the recorded Australian Aboriginal female averages (Rao 1966:265). The Pia Hudale specimen is either **female and/or sub-adult** and, if a female adult, it would display the gracile morphology that otherwise tends to characterize Australian Aborigines. Post-depositional burning stains were evident on the heavy calcreted skin.

PHD/E4 Spit 5. **Right upper second molar**. The minimal wear, "a" in the system of Murphy (1964) and "1" in the system of Smith (1984), suggests the tooth had recently come into occlusion before the individual died, i.e. as a **teenager**. The lack of traces of caries or calculus would be consistent with a young age. A strong reddish brown stain covering most of the buccal and lingual surfaces would appear to reflect habitual **betel-nut chewing**. According to the standards established by the Arizona State University system, the metacone and hypocone both have "4" development, the metaconule is "3", there is a clear buccal groove corresponding to a "4" parastyle but no trace of Carabelli's cusp development, there is no enamel extension or enamel pearl, and the tooth is two-rooted. Only the last trait could be considered at all unusual by the standards of Southeast Asian and Pacific populations, and even it has been recorded at frequencies up to 50% among populations in New Guinea and Polynesia, as well as Siberia and prehistoric Japan (see Scott and Turner 1997). The tooth is large, with a mesio-distal diameter of 10.65 mm and a bucco-lingual diameter of 12.46 mm. Comparably large teeth occur among recent Southeast Asian males, e.g. the Javanese sample measured by Mijsberg (1932), but as an average tendency are found only among populations with relatively larger teeth such as New Guinea Highlander males (see Doran and Freedman 1974). Population affinity is obviously indecipherable from a single tooth, but its status would seem to be **male**. The low degree of fossilization, and the betel-nut staining, both indicate a late Holocene antiquity, and it may well be from the same individual as represented by the first proximal manual phalanx from the surface of this test pit.

PHD/E4 Spit 6. The medial angle of the **left clavicle**, from the costoclavicular ligament impression to the groove for the *subclavius* muscle. Either a **juvenile or a female**, to judge from the small size and gracile morphology. Made from two joining fragments.

PHD/E4 Spit 6. Probably the spine to the **left scapula**, in which case of adult size.

PHD/E4 Spit 6. The larger fragment comes from the shaft of a **left humerus** near its head, in the area where the quite well developed *lattisimus dorsi* and *pectoralis major* muscles would have attached. Another fragment matches the proximal epiphyseal facet of a **tibia**. Two more fragments may well represent human **limb bone** shaft. One last tiny fragment is **non-human**, possibly a rodent long bone shaft.

PHD/F4 spit 0 (surface). The proximo-medial segment of the shaft of a **right femur**, reaching proximally almost to the gluteal tuberosity. The compact bone at the mid-shaft is quite stout, varying between 5.3 and 7.8 mm thick. An **adult male** status is indicated by the rugged *linea aspera*, the midshaft diameter (M8) of approximately 87 mm, and the sagittal and transverse diameters (M6 and M7) of about 27.7 mm and 24.5 mm respectively. These values compare well with the male averages recorded on Australian Aborigines (82.5 mm, 27.6 mm, 24.7 mm) and Japanese (82.2 mm, 26.5 mm, 25.3 mm) (see Davivongs 1963; Abe 1955).

PHD/F4 spit 0 (surface). A proximo-medial fragment from the shaft of the **right tibia**. The compact bone is again stout, varying between 3.6 and 7.1 mm thick. In the general region of the mid-shaft, the circumference measures 76 mm, the sagittal diameter measures 28.7 mm (M8) and the transverse diameter 18.2 mm (M9). These values essentially lie between the averages recorded for Australian Aboriginal males (83.8 mm, 30.8 mm, 21.2 mm) and females (72.0 mm, 25.6 mm, 18.6 mm) (Rao 1966). The sagittal diameter exceeds the average recorded on Japanese males (27.6) whereas the transverse diameter is less than the Japanese female average (19.0 mm) (Inabe 1955), suggesting that the Pia Hudale specimen has a shape more resembling Australian Aboriginal than Japanese tibiae. As the specimen's sex is indeterminate on the basis of these univariate comparisons, the best guide may be the likelihood that it derives from the same individual as the femur, and hence would probably be **adult male**.

PHD/F4 spit 1. Long bone shaft fragment, probably from the **humerus or the ulna**. Also the neck/tubercle region of a **right rib** fragment, probably the sixth to ninth rib, and of average adult size. The third fragment from this spit is **shellfish**.

PHD/F4 spit 2. An adult (or possibly teenager's) **fourth right metacarpal** including the head fused to the distal half of the shaft. The size is rather small by adult standards.

Lua Manggetek (MGT), Rote Island

The Lua Manggetek human remains show increased fossilization with depth, unlike the Pia Hudale remains. Hence they admit at least some stratigraphic integrity of the deposit. Mahirta mentioned radiocarbon dates lying between approximately 7 kya and 13 kya, notwithstanding the occurrence of some potsherds as deep as spit 6. There is only one semi-fossilized human fragment excavated from Lua Mangettek, in spit 6 of the F3 square, and it may well be of broadly middle Holocene antiquity. All the other fragments, starting in spit 7, appear fully fossilized, and are probably of early Holocene or terminal Pleistocene age. These fully fossilized fragments are consistently coated in a tightly adhering but thin calcreted skin. The condition of bone would not therefore indicate a great elapse of time during the deposition of these fully fossilized fragments.

The semi-fossilized fragment from the F3 square would appear to be an adult male. The fully fossilized fragments from F3 possibly both represent a child. The fragments from the C3D3 test pit

comprise calvarium (1), ribs (6), right humerus (1), left or right humerus (2), radius (1), right ulna (1), left or right ulna (3), other arm (2), right femur (1), left or right femur (1), tibia (1), fibula (1), undiagnostic limb (4), proximal manual phalanx (1), medial manual phalanx (1), fourth and fifth distal manual phalanges (1 each), left third metatarsal (1), and proximal pedal phalanx (1). None of these remains are clearly sub-adult but sufficient variation is suggested in the size of the original bones to insinuate the representation of both male and female individuals. If so, the female would have been distributed from spit 7 to 12 and the male from spit 8 to 13. Given the lack of duplication of any of the anatomical elements, and the representation of much of the skeleton, it is possible that all the C3D3 fragments represent the one interred individual, an adult of uncertain sex and with highly variable size of its body parts. Even if the interpretation of two individuals is preferred, then they would have been buried in such a way as to churn up the deposit between spits 7 and 13. The inclusion of a tiny calvarial fragment hardly allays the impression that the mortuary practice specifically excluded the skull from the secondary burial of the other body parts.

MGT/F3 spit 6. The **fourth medial manual phalanx** from the left hand of an **adult**, as shown by the fully fused base. The phalanx length (M3) of 25.4 mm is close to the averages of 26.5 mm and 25.7 mm recorded respectively on male Australian Aborigines (Rao 1966) and North Chinese (von Bonin 1931). The rugged plantar surface of the Lua Manggetek specimen supports the inference that it may too be **male**.

MGT/F3 spit 7. One fragment from a **rib** shaft. Another fragment is a second, third or fourth **medial manual phalanx**, represented by the head and the most of the shaft. The base may be absent because it had not fused to the shaft before the death of the individual, and the small size of the phalanx certainly indicates a **child**. The third fragment (also fully fossilized) is **non-human**, and would appear to be a monkey's metatarsal shaft fragment – the shape is too slender and narrow, and the size too small, to qualify as human.

MGT/C3D3 Spit 7. Two cross-mending fragments from the distal shaft of the right humerus, extending distally as far as the olecranon fossa and the lateral epicondyle. The fused status of the distal epiphysis demonstrates it is **adult**, and probably **female** to judge from the small size and gracile morphology of the represented humerus. The maximum diameter at the mid-shaft (M5) would be approximately 19.3 mm, the least diameter at this point (M6) approximately 14.0 mm, and the circumference (M7a) about 57 mm. These values all fall within a millimetre of the averages recorded on female Japanese (Sendo 1957), while the diameter measurements lie midway between the male and female averages recorded on Australian Aborigines (van Dongen 1963:471), and so confirm the likelihood of a female status. The olecranon fossa lacks a foramen.

MGT/C3D3 Spit 7. The head of a right **ulna** articulates perfectly with the preceding specimen and clearly derives from the same individual. The small and quite gracile nature of this ulna head, and its fusion to the shaft, confirm the **adult female** status of the person.

MGT/C3D3 Spit 7. Nine original fragments which can be cross-mended to produce **six burnt** fragments. Five are probably human even if the identification is not entirely certain. One, from the shaft of a **humerus**, has stout compact bone up to 6.6 mm thick. The **two rib** fragments include one from the shaft near the vertebral end, and one from the medial section of the shaft. One derives from the medial section of a **radius or ulna**, and one comes from the shaft of the **humerus, radius or ulna**. The last fragment, with a rounded ridge of irregularly stout compact bone, is best classified as **non-human**. All these fragments have been calcined to leave a surface which is variably white, light grey or dark grey, concealing the bone underneath which is frequently burnt black.

MGT/C3D3 spit 7. 11 original fragments cross-mended to produce **eight unburnt** fragments. All could be readily human although their status is not always certain. They include a distal fragment from the ventral shaft of a **femur**, a gracile **humerus** shaft fragment, a distal shaft fragment from a gracile **right ulna**, a probable **tibia** shaft fragment, a fragment from the distal shaft of the **fibula**, another shaft fragment (**tibia, radius or ulna?**), a fragment from a floating **rib** (eleventh or twelfth), and a tiny **calvarial** fragment. This last fragment has normal diploic bone and is of normal thickness, measuring approximately 5 mm thick (cf. Brown et al. 1979).

MGT/C3 spit 8. An **adult right femur** head with a vertical head diameter (M18) of 45.7 mm. This value approximates the average recorded on Japanese males (Abe 1955) and exceeds the average recorded on Australian Aborginal males by 2.6 mm (Davivongs 1963), and so would almost certainly represent a **male**. Another **femur** fragment, in this case from the shaft, exhibits a surface damaged post-depositionally.

MGT/C3D3 spit 8. A fire-cracked splinter of burnt bone, which could be from a human long bone shaft, or might not be human at all. It would appear to relate to the burnt fragments in spit 9.

MGT/C3D3 spit 9. A fragment from the medial shaft of **one of the caudally located ribs** (eighth to tenth).

MGT/C3D3 spit 9. A fragment from the distal shaft of a **radius**. The radius would have been small, suggesting a child or a small woman. Medially the compact bone is quite stout (3-4.5 mm thick) leaving a narrow medullary cavity (3.1 by 3.7 mm in diameter).

MGT/C3D3 spit 9. Two **unburnt shaft** fragments from human limb bones. One would appear to be from the distal **ulna**, apparently from a small person such as a child or a small woman. As with the radius fragment from this spit, the compact bone is quite stout (2.6-3.6 mm thick) and the medullary cavity narrow (1.0 by 3.0 mm in diameter).

MGT/C3D3 spit 9. Eight tiny fragments of **burnt** bone. They are too small to be declared human or non-human. They are either white and crackled, or exhibit shades of black and grey.

MGT/C3D3 spit 11. An **adult right fourth proximal pedal phalanx** represented by most of its shaft and fused base. Its sex cannot be divined.

MGT/C3D3 spit 11. A fragment from a **rib** shaft, close to the sternal end. The calcreted skin has been burnt following deposition.

MGT/C3D3 spit 12. Complete examples of the **fourth and fifth distal manual phalanges** (side indeterminable). **Adult** based on their fully fused epiphyses. Their (M3) lengths of 15.2 mm and 14.3 mm are 2 to 3 mm less than the average lengths recorded on North Chinese males (von Bonin 1931), and 3 to 4 mm less than the corresponding Australian Aboriginal male averages (Rao 1966). Hence the Lua Mangettek specimens could represent a **female**.

MGT/C3D3 spit 12. The head and shaft of a **proximal manual phalanx**, possibly the third or the fourth to judge by the size of the phalanx represented. Not necessarily adult as the head is fused throughout life.

MGT/C3D3 spit 12. A **rib** shaft fragment, located towards the sternal end. **MGT/C3D3 spit 12**. A fragment from the distal portion of the **ulna**. It could belong to the same individual as represented by its radius and ulna fragments in spit 9. Morphological similarities include the gracility of the fragment combined with quite stout compact bone (1.9-3.0 mm thick) enclosing a narrow medullary cavity (2.1 by 3.2 mm in diameter).

MGT/C3D3 spit 12. Two fragments of burnt shaft bone which are completely undiagnostic as regards their **human or non-human** status.

MGT/C3D3 spit 13. An **adult left third metatarsal** represented by its base (fused) and proximal shaft. The metatarsal would have been quite large and rugged, so may be male.

MGT/C3D3 spit 13. Five small unburnt shaft fragments consisting of part of a **humerus or femur**, part of a **metacarpal or metatarsal**, a **medial manual phalanx** fragment, and two nondescript fragments (radius, ulna, fibula, metacarpal, metatarsal?).

MGT/C3D3 spit 13. Two tiny **burnt** fragments which are clearly or probably **non-human**.

The Lua Meko Test Pit (Mk/TP or Mk/Ex), Rote Island

According to radiocarbon dates mentioned by Mahirta, the upper deposit in the Lua Meko test pit between spits 2 and 5 would date to the middle Holocene, and the lower deposit from spits 7 to 12 would date from the Holocene/Pleistocene junction back to about 24 kya. All of the human fragments from the excavation are well fossilized, and most are coated with a heavily encrusted calcretion. These fossilized remains range between spit 3 at the top and spit 13 at the bottom. The deepest fragments are distinguishable from limestone only on the basis of shape, and readily appear to be in the order of 20,000 years old. The probably represent the oldest remains of *Homo sapiens* yet discovered in Indonesia.

The 54 identifiable fragments include several cases of duplication of the same anatomical region (Table 2). In addition, some of the fragments clearly came from juveniles and others from adults, and the adult fragments further show sufficient morphological and metrical variation to suggest the presence of both sexes. There is also a fair degree of variation in the extent of fossilization of the bone, and the growth and tenacity of a surface calcretion. Accordingly an attempt is made below to assign the fragments to a number of specific individuals. The topmost individual, between spits 3 and 6, is probably but not certainly distinct from Individual 4, the juvenile whose arm and hand bones are spread between spits 4 and 9. Spits 3 to 9 also contain the mingled remains of two adults, one evidently a male, and the other possibly female. The remains of a separate male adult (Individual 5) begin in spit 6 and appear concentrated in spit 9. A small assemblage of tiny human fragments in spit 11 could belong to Individual 5 but is treated as unassigned. The deepest remains, three extremity fragments in spit 13, appear to be significantly more fossilized than the fragments between spits 3 and 9, and so probably represent a different individual. But they could conceivably belong to Individual 5, with the differences in fossilization, and extent of surface calcretion, attributable to variation in preservation conditions.

The approach taken here, which recognizes six individuals (including one "unassigned"), is conservative in that it attempts to minimize the extent of the vertical distribution of any recognized individual. However, this approach correspondingly increases the number of individuals involved and, hence, the likelihood of disturbance of the deposits through repeated burial events. The remains clearly stem from interments, rather than some other activity, as shown by their quantity, the substantial size (after reconstruction) of the largest specimens, and the evidence that burning of the fragments was mainly post-depositional. It is most unlikely that spits 3 to 9 contain any remnant stratigraphic integrity, given the succession of at least four burials. Indeed, some of this mortuary-related disturbance could extend down to spit 11 or even spit 13. In all of the burials, mainly arm and leg bones (including the hands and the feet) appear to have been involved. There is minimal representation of the human trunk, and no representation whatsoever of the skull.

The first individual, represented from spits 3 to 6 (including a single femur from both spits 3 and 6), is characterized by unburnt chalky bone coated by a heavy, tightly adhering crust. Removal of the crust probably incurred some loss of the relief of the fragments' surface anatomy, but the gracile morphology is unmistakable. Only shaft fragments are represented, which militates against assessing age from the degree of epiphyseal union and, hence, determining whether a small adult (presumably female) or a teenager would be represented.

The second individual, represented by fragments between spits 4 and 7 (including a femur fragment made of bone from both spits 4 and 7), involves bone that is less chalky than is the case with Individual 1. This may reflect post-depositional heat exposure, as evidenced by sporadic and superficial traces of burning. The individual is an adult male.

The third individual is represented by fragments between spits 4 and 9, including a radius fragment reconstructed from fragments in spits 4 and 7. It is characterized by arm bones with remarkably stout compact bone and a narrow medullary cavity. This apparently

	Ind. 1 (female/ sub-adult)	Ind. 2 (male adult)	Ind. 3 (unsexed adult)	Ind. 4 (sub-dult)	Ind. 5 (male adult)	Unassigned (male adult)	Total
Left scapula					1		1
Ribs		2			4	1	7
Pelvis						1	1
Right humerus	1	1	1				3
Left humerus	1		1				2
Humerus (side?)		1	2	1			4
Right radius			1				1
Left radius				1			1
Right ulna	1				1		2
Left ulna			1				1
Right 3rd metacarpal				1			1
Right 4th metacarpal				1			1
Right 5th metacarpal				1			1
Other metacarpals	4						4
Right 3rd proximal manual phalanx				1			1
Right 4th proximal manual phalanx				1			1
Proximal manual phalanx	1			2			3
Medial manual phalanx				1	1	1	3
Right femur					1		1
Left femur					1		1
Femur (side?)	1	1			2		4
Right tibia	1						1
Tibia (side?)		1					1
Right fibula			1				1
Fibula (side?)	3						3
Right 1st metatarsal						1	1
2nd metatarsal						1	1
Metatarsal			1				1
Right 5th proximal pedal phalanx		1					1
Total	13	7	8	10	11	5	54

Table 2. Distribution of the Lua Meko human remains and their assignment to individuals

101

pathological condition could have been caused by treponematosis (yaws), an infection that may result in narrowing of the medullary cavity through poRotec expansion of the subperiosteal surface (Nancy Tayles, pers. comm.). The sex of the individual is uncertain but the bones would have been smaller and less robust than the other adult bones from the site, and so may be female. Fibula and metatarsal fragments are also assigned to this individual.

The fourth individual (spits 4 to 9) consists of juvenile arm and hand bones. Almost all of the fragments show traces of burning and some appear to have smouldered over a reasonable elapse of time. In this case, exposure to heat may have resulted as part of the mortuary procedure rather than as a post-depositional phenomenon. Condition of the bone is similar to Individual 3.

The fifth individual consists of apparently male adult fragments of a hard, chalky consistency, evidently more fossilized than the fragments assigned to Individuals 1 to 4. It includes fragments from spit 6 to spit 9. A gap in the distribution of human remains in spit 10 suggests, but does not prove, that the fragments in spit 11 belong to another individual rather than Individual 5. No traces of burning are evident.

The lowest fragments, in spit 13, which lie beneath a radiocarbon determination of 24 kya, are the most comprehensively fossilized human remains from Mahirta's excavations. Their fossilization, and the evident representation of a large robust foot, are consistent with an antiquity in excess of 20 kya. Unfortunately, the foot is not considered of particular use to the reconstruction of ancient population relationships.

Non-human

Spit 1. The fused head and distal shaft of a left fourth metacarpal, and a shaft fragment from a proximal manual phalanx. Although adult and quite rugged, the metacarpal is less than half the size to be expected of a human, but its size and morphology perfectly match a young baboon's. The manual phalanx would also have been about half human size. Both fragments can be ascribed to a fair-sized **monkey**, presumably a large male crab-eating macaque (*Macaca fascicularis*), even though Monk et al. (1997:461) do not report the presence of this species in Rote. Both fragments are well fossilized and presumably of middle Holocene age.

Spit 6. An apparently polished fragment of **marine shell**.

Spit 11. Two fragments of fully fossilized **tubular coral**. The shape of the fragments, and the thickness of the outer tube, strongly resemble the features of a human femur, but the parallel longitudinal and aslant striations disprove any such identification. The grooves on the two fragments appear to run together, so one original stalk of coral was probably involved. It would be up to the excavator to decide whether the coral had been brought into the site or whether it might have fallen out of the walls of the limestone shelter.

Individual 1

Spit 3. Two non-joining limb bone shaft fragments, apparently the left and right antimeres of the proximal to medial **humerus shaft**. This identification accounts for the ovoid cross-section, large medullary cavity and moderate external diameters, while the gracility of the surface relief could suggest a female or sub-adult status.

Spit 3. Two **non-joining** fibula shaft **fragments, gracile as with the previous specimens, possibly from the same bone or from the left and right members.**

Spit 3. Two joining fragments from the distal **shaft** of the **right tibia**. The tibia would have been small and gracile.

Spit 3. **Five extremity shaft** fragments, all probably from the hand. One is compatible with a second to fourth **manual proximal phalanx**, three are compatible with the second to fifth **metacarpals**, and one is unassignable.

Spits 3-4. Seven joining fragments of the **right ulna shaft**, extending from the point immediately distal of the proximal

tuberosity, and reaching distally almost as far as the head. The maximum length may be estimated at about 220 mm, based on the shaft's extant length of 153.5 mm, while the minimum shaft circumference (M3) measures 32.5 mm. These values are close to the averages recorded on Japanese females (Mizoguchi 1957). However, they suggest a shorter ulna with a larger circumference than is the average among female Javanese (231.0 mm, 29.0 mm; Bergman and The 1955) and female Australian Aborigines (231.4 mm, 30.3 mm; Rao 1966). The point of these comparisons is not to stress the Japanese-like metrics of the Lua Meko ulna, but to emphasize its probable female (or else sub-adult) status, as also suggested by the scant development of ridges and muscular attachments on the specimen.

Spits 3 and 6. Eight cross-mended fragments from spit 3 make an acceptable join with a relatively large fragment from spit 6 to produce part of the proximal **shaft of a femur**. The femur would have been quite slender and gracile, especially in its slight development of the *linea aspera* (present at the most medial part of the extant shaft). The same female (or possibly sub-adult) status is implied as for the previously described fragments. The side represented is unclear.

Spit 4. Two non-joining **fibula shaft** fragments, possibly from the same bone or from the left and right members. Although they appear more rugged than the two fibula fragments from spit 3, this could reflect variable morphology along the fibula shaft, and there is no reason to suspect the representation of a separate individual.

Spit 4. The fragment of the **shaft** of a second to fifth **metacarpal**, suggestive of even more slender, gracile manual extremity bones than those represented in spit 3.

Individual 2

Spits 4 and 7. **The medial and distal shaft of a right humerus**, reaching distally as far as the initiation of the lateral supracondylar ridge. The medial segment is represented by two cross-mending fragments from spit 4, and the distal segment (which joins to the medial segment) is represented by two cross-mending fragments from spit 7. The medial segment is burnt black in patches, obviously through post-depositional exposure to heat (as the distal segment is unaffected). This fragment represents a different individual compared to the humerus fragments in spit 3, as shown by its greater dimensions of the shaft, enhanced development of the deltoid tuberosity, and the possible duplication of the same section of the right humerus. An estimated mid-shaft circumference (M7a) of 65-70 mm exceeds the male average of Japanese (Sendo 1957), a population characterized by a stout humerus shaft, indicating a male status for the Lua Meko specimen.

Spit 4. Two limb bone shaft fragments, **one** from the anterior ridge of the **tibia**, with a condition of the bone, and encrustation of the surface calcretion, that are similar to the corresponding features on the previously described fragment from spit 4.

Spit 4. Two burnt rib fragments can be assigned provisionally to the same individual. One is the section that includes the tubercle from the shaft of a large rib. The second refers to a smaller rib shaft, and so could have derived from one of the lower ribs (tenth to twelfth). The surface skin has also been affected by the heat exposure which, accordingly, would appear to have occurred post-depositionally.

Spit 6. A distal shaft fragment from a humerus, probably male to judge by its robusticity. The fragment has been crushed, distorted and burnt post-depositionally. The compact bone is quite stout, varying between 4.9 and 9.4 mm thick.

Spit 7. A femur fragment with similar effects, from burning, as the previously cited fragment. The anterior and medial surfaces (but not the *linea aspera*) of the medial shaft would appear to be present. The compact bone is quite thick (4.3 to 7.3 mm).

Spit 7. A complete adult **right fifth proximal pedal phalanx**. Probably **male** as its length (M1) of 21.1 mm closely matches the male averages of 21.4 mm and 21.5 mm measured on male Europeans and north Chinese respectively (von Bonin 1932), and

21.6 mm measured on male Australian Aborigines (Rao 1966). Other measurements are its medial shaft breadth (M2) of 5.7 mm and medial shaft height (M3), also 5.7 mm. No traces of burning in evidence.

Individual 3

Spits 3 and 7. The medial and distal **shaft** of the **right radius**, with remarkably stout compact bone (3.0-6.6 mm thick) and narrow medullary cavity (5.2 by 5.6 mm in diameter medially, 1.3 by 2.3 mm distally). The medial segment comes from spit 3, and the distal segment from two cross-mending fragments in spit 7. The estimated transverse mid-shaft diameter (M4) of 13.4 mm resembles the female averages recorded among Japanese (14.6 mm) and Australian Aborigines (12.8 mm), while the estimated sagittal mid-shaft diameter (M5) of 12.3 mm resembles the male averages on Japanese (11.8 mm) and Australian Aborigines (11.7 mm) (Mizoguchi 1957; Rao 1966). Despite the lack of evidence of post-depositional burning, the thickness of the compact bone and the dimensions of the shaft invite comparison with the next fragment to be described.

Spit 6. The medio-proximal **shaft fragment from a left ulna.** The stout compact bone (3.8-7.2 mm thick) leaves a miniscule medullary cavity of about 4 mm diameter. The solid triangular cross-sectional shape stems from the strong border ridges and the rugged furrow for the *flexor digitorum profundis* attachment. Dorso-volar and transverse diameters (M11 and M12 respectively) along the upper third of the shaft are approximately 11.5 mm and 14.7 mm respectively, resembling the averages recorded on female Australian Aborigines (Rao 1966) and female Japanese (Mizoguchi 1957). Thus the shaft fragment combines masculine robusticity with feminine shaft diameters. Traces of superficial, presumably post-depositional burning.

Spit 7. A very round limb bone fragment which must be from the **medial shaft of a humerus**, despite the total lack of evidence for development of the deltoid tuberosity. The stout compact bone, 4.1 to 5.7 mm thick, encloses a narrow medullary cavity only 5.3 by 6.7 mm in diameter. The mid-shaft measurements are approximately 17.2 mm as the maximum diameter (M5), 14.9 mm as the minimum diameter (M6), and 54 mm as the circumference (M7a). These diameters compare quite well with the female averages recorded on Australian Aborigines (17.3 mm, 12.9 mm) and Japanese (19.9, 14.9 mm). The mid-shaft circumference measurement resembles the Japanese female average (57.2 mm) but, naturally enough, tends to exceed the average **minimum** shaft circumference among female Japanese (55.1 mm), Javanese (51.0 mm) and Australian Aborigines (48.5 mm). (Comparative data taken from Bergman and The 1955, Sendo 1957, and van Dongen 1963.) Hence a female status is suggested, despite the thickness of the compact bone.

Spit 7. The distal epiphysis (malleolus) and shaft of a **right fibula. Adult** as indicated by the fused status of the epiphysis, and probably **female** as reflected in its small lower epiphysis breadth (M4(2)) of about 14.6 mm, less than the average of 16.4 mm recorded on female Japanese (Inabe 1955). Lack of any medullary cavity at this point conforms to the normal morphological condition.

Spit 9. Three fragments that can be assigned to the **humerus.** One is a medial shaft fragment very similar to the spit 7 humerus mid-shaft fragment mentioned above, and almost certainly its antimere. Similarities include the lack of any observable deltoid tuberosity; the mid-shaft measurements of 18.0 mm as maximum diameter (M5), 15.4 mm as minimum diameter perpendicular to the maximum diameter (M6), and 56 mm as the circumference (M7a); the stout nature of the compact bone (5.6-6.3 mm thick); and the narrow medullary cavity (6.0 by 6.6 mm in diameter). The two other humerus fragments from spit 9 include a possible fragment from the proximal epiphysis, laterally of the head, and a possible proximal shaft fragment.

Spit 9. The distal shaft and commencement of the fused head of an **adult metatarsal.** Its assignment to Individual 3 is supported by the relatively stout condition of the compact bone, but it could represent

Individual 2 or 5. It could belong to any digit between the second and the fifth.

Individual 4

Spit 4. A virtually complete, **right-hand adolescent third proximal manual phalanx.** The base or proximal epiphysis is absent as it had not fused to the shaft prior to the time of death. The extant length (M3) of 36.8 mm is about 7 mm shorter than the male averages recorded for North Chinese (von Bonin 1931) and Australian Aborigines (Rao 1966), confirming the adolescent status of the Lua Meko specimen. Post-depositional burning has added a light grey colouration to the bone surface and the covering calcareous skin.

Spit 4. Two burnt limb-bone shaft fragments with similar preservational characteristics to those of the previous specimen. One comprises two cross-mending fragments and may represent a radius shaft. The other could represent the radius or equally the humerus, tibia or femur.

Spit 6. The **fourth right proximal manual phalanx of a juvenile**, including the plate where the unfused basal epiphysis would have articulated. This bone almost certainly derives from the same hand as the manual phalanx from spit 4. Its extant length (M3) of 36.2 mm is 2.5 to 4 mm less than the averages recorded on male North Chinese (von Bonin 1931) and Australian Aborigines (Rao 1966). Slight (post-depositional?) burning is evident.

Spit 6. A fragment from the **distal shaft of a left radius** can also be tentatively assigned to the same individual. However, in this case the bone is burnt black right through, and is covered with a dark reddish grey skin, suggesting the fragment had smouldered in a fire over a fair period. The gracile interosseous border, and probably small size of the original radius, are consistent with a sub-adult status.

Spit 6. Another limb bone shaft fragment, quite possibly from the **humerus**, resembles the previously described specimen in appearing well burnt right through, as though it had smouldered in a fire. Another fragment is the distal shaft and fractured head from a **medial manual phalanx.** Its apparent heat-fracture lines, and the reddish brown colour of the bone beneath the light brown exterior, are consistent with lengthy heat exposure.

Spit 9. Four burnt extremity fragments whose bone is consistently coloured grey to dark grey from the surface to the medullary cavity, suggesting they had smouldered in a fire over a fair period. All appear **juvenile** from their small size and lack of epiphyses. One is the complete shaft of a third or fourth **proximal manual phalanx,** including the proximal plate where the base would have fused on. One is a **fifth right metacarpal** that comprises the shaft and the distal plate where the head would have fused on. One is the virtually complete shaft of a **third right metacarpal.** The last specimen is a very partial fragment from the **fourth right metacarpal.**

Spit 9. A fragment which appears to be the proximal shaft of a **juvenile** third to fifth **proximal manual phalanx.** Despite having no traces of burning, its morphology matches that of the other proximal manual phalanx from this spit, suggesting that it derives from the same individual. Hence the heat exposure that affected the burnt specimen would appear to have oventuated following the fragments' deposition.

Individual 5

Spit 6. An unburnt, heavily fossilized (Pleistocene?) **left femur shaft** proximal fragment. A **male adult** status is indicated by the proximal extension of a massive *linea aspera*, and the rugged ridge for the attachment of the *vastus intermedius* muscle. The measurable circumference of 85 mm, as close to the mid-shaft as possible, exceeds the average mid-shaft circumference of male Japanese (Abe 1955) and Australian Aborigines (Davivongs 1963), thus confirming the evident male status of the specimen. The compact bone is also very stout towards the mid-shaft, measuring from 7.2 to 10.9 mm thick, enclosing an oval medullary cavity that measures 9.0 and 12.7 mm in its diameters.

Spit 8. Two further leg bone fragments with a similarly hard chalky consistency as the spit 6 femoral fragment. One is an inferior fragment from the greater trochanter of the **right femur** where the *gluteus minimus* muscle attaches, evidently **male** from the rugosity of this attachment. The second is a medial shaft fragment from a tibia, with thick compact bone (7.1-10.8 mm) at its robust anterior spine. Its maximum dorso-volar mid-shaft diameter (M8), in excess of 30.9 mm, and its transverse diameter at the same point (M9) of approximately 20.5 mm, closely match the corresponding male averages recorded on Australian Aborigines (30.8 and 21.2 mm) and Japanese (30.6 and 21.1 mm) (see Rao 1966; Inabe 1955).

Spit 9. **Left scapula** coracoid process, probably male to judge by its robust appearance.

Spit 9. **Two femoral shaft** fragments, made respectively from two and three cross-mending fragments, of which one represents the medio-proximal shaft and the other possibly represents the proximal shaft. The larger fragment, despite being badly worn, crushed and distorted, appears to be the right antimere of the left femoral shaft fragment from spit 6, to judge by their morphological details and the condition of the bone. This crushed fragment has remnants of a marked *linea aspera* and a diameter above the mid-shaft of at least 79 mm, not very different from the circumference measured on the spit 6 femoral fragment. The compact bone measures between 3.3 and 9.6 mm thick on the spit 9 femoral fragments, and the medullary cavity has diameters of 10.3 and 10.7 mm at the measurable point. These measurements overlap those recorded on the spit 6 femoral fragment, confirming the likelihood that they all represent the same **male** individual.

Spit 9. **Four rib fragments** very tentatively assigned to Individual 5, based on their crushed condition and chalky fossilized bone, though one or more of them could readily represent Individuals 2 to 4. One fragment is identified as the head (based on its small size) of a right upper (second to fourth) rib. A second fragment from a small shaft probably derives from the sternal end of a rib. A fragment from a medium-sized shaft may represent the sternal end of a ninth or tenth rib, while a broad-shafted fragment would be more compatible with a third to seventh rib (from near the sternal end).

Spit 9. A shaft fragment from a **medial manual phalanx** may also represent Individual 5, based on its adult-like size and the chalky unburnt nature of the bone.

Spit 9. Three fragments that appear to join to make the distal shaft of a **right ulna** and the beginning of the fused ulna head. Evidently **adult and apparently male**, as the estimated least circumference of the shaft near the distal end (M3) of about 40 mm exceeds the corresponding male average on Japanese (Mizoguchi 1957), and greatly exceeds the average minimum shaft circumference recorded on Australian Aboriginal males (Rao 1966).

Unassigned (Individual 6?)

Spit 11. A fragment from the **iliac crest of the pelvis**, probably the medial segment of this crest. The robust, stout nature of the fragment suggests an **adult** and, possibly, male status.

Spit 11. The sternal end of a smallish **rib**, either the floating rib (e.g., ninth or tenth) of a male, or a female or sub-adult rib.

Spit 11. A fragment from a **long bone shaft**, possibly the ulna, though also potentially the radius, humerus or tibia. The bone is lightly burnt a light yellow brown all the way through, possibly post-depositionally, but if so then shortly after deposition, as the calcreted mass that covered the fragment did not show signs of being burnt.

Spit 13. The shaft of a **right first metatarsal**. The extent of fossilization makes the fragment appear more massive and thick-boned than it really was, but it would have been a large metatarsal, probably from an **adult male**. The compact bone measures about 2.7-4.1 mm thick.

Spit 13. The shaft of a left or right **second metatarsal**, and the distal epiphysis (or head) and distal shaft of a third or fourth **medial manual phalanx**. Both fragments exhibit quite stout compact bone, and could have derived from the same **adult male** as the first right metatarsal did. The medial manual phalanx would have exceeded 27 mm in length (M3). Hence it would have been longer than the average male third and fourth medial manual phalanges of North Chinese (27.0 and 25.8 mm respectively; von Bonin 1931) and, probably, the same phalanges among male Australian Aborigines (which respectively average 29.9 and 26.5 mm; Rao 1966).

Summary

The assemblages of human remains excavated by Mahirta from Sawu and Rote span the period between the Late Pleistocene, as early as 24,000 years ago, and the late Holocene. Despite this enormous time depth the assemblages are remarkably consistent in their strong representation of the limbs and extremities, their modest representation of the human trunk, and the virtual absence of the skull. Throughout this period the local mortuary practices would appear to have involved prior decapitation, presumably to preserve the skull as a momento to the ancestors. The frequent inclusion of extremity bones, the occasional occurrence of small bones from the same region (e.g the right-hand metacarpals and proximal manual phalanges of Individual 4 at Lua Meko), and the substantial representation of some of the long bones, are inconsistent with the practice of secondary burial following previous defleshed of the corpse. Repeated primary burials of (headless) corpses will have the effect of disrupting the articulated status of previously buried remains, and also help to fragment the bones. Secondary burials were undoubtedly also involved, but they could not have been the only mortuary practice. The use of the excavated rock shelters for burials unfortunately spells problems for the stratigraphic interpretation of the deposited habitation debris.

Approximate age at death of the buried individuals was inferred on the basis of epiphyseal union (following the criteria in Brothwell 1981). Sex of the adult and male teenager bones was estimated by comparison with the averages recorded on recent Australian Aboriginal, Javanese, Japanese and North Chinese populations. Sub-adults were buried in all four sites. Male adults were interred in all three Rote sites. The burial of female adults was more difficult to determine but certainly occurred at Pia Hudale, and probably the other two Rote sites.

Owing to the scrappy preservation of the remains, and the virtual absence of skull, comparisons have not been made here with the skeletons excavated from Flores (Jacob 1967) or the Melolo burials from Sumba. Isolated, individual comparisons cannot accommodate the metrical and morphological variability present in all human populations and, accordingly, are unlikely to lead to useful insights or productive conclusions. Possibly, at some future point, the measurements recorded here can be combined with data from other human remains in the region, of a similar antiquity, to build up a regional sample, but such an exercise would lie beyond the scope of this report. From the standpoint of biological anthropology, the most interesting observations would be the indication of contracted treponematosis on Individual 3 at Lua Meko.

References

Abe, Hideyo. 1955. Anthropological studies on the femur of Kyushu Japanese. *Jinruigaku-Kenkyu* 2:121-141.

Bergman, R.A.M. and The Tiong Hoo. 1955. The length of the body and long bones of the Javanese. *Documenta de Medicina Geographica et Tropica* 7:197-214.

Bonin, G. von. 1931. Preliminary study of the northern Chinese hand. *Anthropologischer Anzeiger* 7:241-256.

Bonin, G. von. 1932. Preliminary study of the northern Chinese foot. *Anthropologischer Anzeiger* 9:214-227.

Brothwell, D.R. 1981. *Digging up Bones*. 3rd edn. London: British Museum (Natural History).

Appendix 1

Brown, T., S.K. Pinkerton and W. Lambert. 1979. Thickness of the cranial vault in Australian Aboriginals. *Archaeology and Physical Anthropology in Oceania* 14:54-71.

Davivongs, V. 1963. The femur of the Australian Aborigine. *American Journal of Physical Anthropology* 21:457-467.

Dongen, Robert von. 1963. The shoulder girdle and humerus of the Australian Aborigine. *American Journal of Physical Anthropology* 21:469-488.

Doran, G.A. and L. Freedman. 1974. Metrical features of the dentition and arches of populations from Goroka and Lufa, Papua New Guinea. *Human Biology* 46:583-594.

Inabe, Katsuto. 1955. Anthropological studies on the tibia and fibula of Kyushu Japanese. *Jinruigaku-Kenkyu* 2:1-39.

Jacob, Teuku. 1967. *Some Problems Pertaining to the Racial History of the Indonesian Region.* Utrecht: Netherlands Bureau for Technical Assistance.

Martin, R. 1957. *Lehrbuch der Anthropologie.* Band I. Stuttgart: Gustav Fischer Verlag.

Mijsberg, W.A. 1932. Recherches sur les restes humains trouvés dans les fouilles des abris-sous-roche de Goewa-Lawa à Sampoeng et des sites préhistoriques à Bodjonegoro (Java). *Homm. Serv. Arch. Premier Congr. Préhist. D'Extrème-Orient à Hanoi,* pp. 39-54. Batavia.

Mizoguchi, Shizou. 1957. Anthropological studies on the radius and ulna of Kyushu Japanese. *Jinruigaku-Kenkyu* 4:237-272.

Monk, K.A., Y. de Fretes and Gayatri Reksodiharjo-Lilley. 1997. *The Ecology of Nusa Tenggara and Maluku.* Sydney: Periplus.

Murphy, T. 1959. The changing pattern of dentine exposure in human tooth attrition. *American Journal of Physical Anthropology* 17:167-178.

Rao, P.D.P. 1966. *The Anatomy of the Distal Limb Segments of the Aboriginal Skeleton.* Unpublished Ph.D. thesis. Adelaide: University of Adelaide.

Scott, G.R. and C.G. Turner II. 1997. *The Anthropology of Modern Human Teeth.* Cambridge: Cambridge University Press.

Sendo, Tokiyoshi. 1957. Anthropological studies on the humerus of Kyushu Japanese. *Jinruigaku-Kenkyu* 4:273-293.

Smith, B.H. 1984. Patterns of molar wear in hunter-gatherers and agriculturalists. *American Journal of Physical Anthropology* 63:39-56.

Appendix 2

spit		1	2	3	4	5	6	7	8	9	10	11	12	13	14	15	H
shell family and species																	
Thiaridae																	
Melanoides funiculus		193	334	148	146	69	74	11	8	1	1	7	1				FW
Turbinidae																	
L!/nel!a cinerea		13	32	32	23	20	15										RU
Turbo argyrostomus		27	18	2	15	4	3	5		1							SI
Angaria delphinulus		3	1		1			4									.81
Chitonidae																	
chiton sp		63	32	29	30	10	4	2	2	2	1	2					RI
Potamididae																	
Terebralia palustris		52	9	36	23	14	11	4									TM
Strombidae																	
Strombus luhuanus		34	4	4	12	5											SI
Strombus mutabilis		8	3	1	6												51
Strombus labiatus		3	1	1		2											51
Lambis lambis		1	1		4												51
Strombus canarium			1	1													SI
Conidae																	
Conus gubemator						1											RU
Neritidae																	
Nerita undata		16	12	14	7	11	6	2				2			1	1	RU
Nerita lineata		7	2														TM
Nerita costata		3		4	10		1										RU
Nerita gigates		1	-	1													RU
Nerita albicilla		9	4	5	5	5	2	1									TM
Nerita planospira		5	7	1			1										RU
Veneridae																	
Gafrarium tumidum		49	18	56	9	4		1	1								51
Gafrarium pectinadum		30	39	3	9	2		2	-								SI
Tapes hiantina					1	1											TM
Tapes litteratus						1											TM
Olividae																	
Oliva oliva		1															51
Vasidae																	
Vasum tubiferum		1															RI
Vasum turbinellus		1															RI
Tridacnidae																	
Tridacna squamosa		1															RE
Tridacna costata		1															RE
Pteriidae																	
Pinctada radiata		1															RU
Archidae																	
Anadara alinea		13	5	1	8												51
Anadara nodifera		10															51
Anadara granosa ..,-		31	8	3		1	1										SI

Table 1 Minimum Number of Individuals of shell species in all squares, Pia Hudale. H: habitat, FW: fresh water, RU: upper river, TM: tidal mudflat, RU: upper reef, SI: sandy intertidal, RI: reef intertidal

Table 1 continued

trochidae																
Trochus maculatus	2	4	6	25	7	--	-	-	--	-	1	-	-	-	-	RI
Trochus niloticus',.	2	1	--	-	--	--	-	-	---	-	--	--	--	--	--	RI
Trochus stellatus	---	4	-	1	-	--	--	--	---	-	--	--	--	--	-	RI
Trochus hanleyanus	---	---	1		--	--	--	--	---	--	--	---	--	--	n	RI
Trochus dentatus	---	---	-	-	-	1	-	-	--	-	-	--	--	-	--	RI
Tectus fenestratus	---	-	3	-	--	--	-	-	---	-	--	-	-	-	-	RI
Tectarius grandinatus	---	--			1	--	--	---	---	-	n	---	--	-	--	
Littoridae																
Uttorina granocostata	---	-	6	-	-	-	-	-	-	-	-	-	-	-	-	RI
Nodilittorina milegrana	_n	--	2	-	-	-	--	-	---	-	-	-	--	-	--	RI
Spondilidae																
Spondylus sp	--	--	--	1	---	---	-	-	---	-	---	--	--	-	--	RE
Tridacnidae																
Tridacna squamosa	1	--	-	1	--	---	---	--	---	n	n	--	--	--	n	RI
unidentified species	6	4	-	-	--	n_	--	1	---	-	--	--	--	-	-	
other unidentified	-	1	6	-	--	-	-	-	---	-	--	n	--	-	--	
total	590	545	366	337	158	119	32	12	4	2	12	1		1	1	

Table 1 Minimum Number of Individuals of shell species in all squares, Pia Hudale
H: habitat, FW: fresh water, RU: upper river, TM: tidal mudflat, RU: upper reef, SI: sandy intertidal, RI: reef intertidal

Appendix 2

spit	1	2	3	4	5	6	7	8	9	10	11	12	13	h
shell family and species														
Thiaridae														
Melanoides funiculus	21	4					37	28					54	FW
Potamididae														
Terebralia palustris	15		29	55	50	33	5	6						TM
Archidae														
Anadara qranosa	44	70	50	36	40	25	21							81
Anadara alinea		9				8								81
Neritidae														
Nerita lineata	3						5			80	20	19	21	RU
Nerita polita	3			9			5	22			20	6		RU
Nerita undata								28				13	4	RU
Nerita plicata											20	19		RU
Nerita albicilla							5						8	RU
Trochidae														
Trochus niloticus	3											6		RI
Trochus maculatus	3													RI
Strombidae														
Strombus lentiginosus	3	4	7		6	8								RE
Strom bus sp						8								RE
Tridacnidae														
Tridacna maxima	3													81
Chitonidae														
Chiton sp			14			17	21	17		20		18	4	RI
Olividae														
Olivia maniacea		4												81
Turbinidae														
Turbo sp											40	13	8	RE
Cypraeidae														
Cypraea tiQris												6		RE
Muricidae														
Drupa rubusideus	3	4												RI
Total	101	99	100	100	96	99	99	101		100	100	100	99	

Table 2 Minimum Number of Individuals of shell species in square C3D3, Lua Manggetek
H: habitat, FW: fresh water, RU: upper river, TM: tidal mudflat, RU: upper reef, SI: sandy intertidal, RI: reef intertidal

spit	I	2	3	4	5	6	1	8	9	10	11	12	13	14	st	H
shell family and species																
Archidae																
Anadara granosa	20	55	15	6	4	5									105	51
Anadara alinea	16	43	10	5											74	51
Potamididae																
Telescopium telescopium	6	15	8			3									32	TM
Terebralia palustris	49	15	36	6	7						1				1.14	TM
Veneridae																
Calista erycina	13	5	3	1	4	1	1		1						29	51
Dosinia iuvenilis			18												18	TM
Gafrarium pectina!:.um			8												9	SI
Turbinidae																
Tutbo argyrostomus	12												1		13	51
Tutbo Sf)		9	10		2	7"									28	51
Anaaria Sf)		17	1												18	SI
Lunella cinela							1	1			1	1			4	51
Neritidae																
Nerita lineats	2	19		4	1	7			2	1					28	TM
Nerita f)/anos,,;ra	26	15		5						1					47	R
Nerita *f)O/ita*		2													2	R
Neverita didymus			7	2				2	2		1				14	TM
Strombidae																
Strombus lentiginosus	11		12	1				1		3		1			29	51
Strombus urceus L	2	1													3	SI
Lambis lambis	1-			1											2	SI
Strombus canarium L		15													15	SI
Tridacnidae																
TricJacna maxima	1														1	51
TricJacna SQuamosa				1											1	51
Corbiculidae																
Batissa violaces		4	3	2	1	3									13	TM
Trochidae																
Trochus macufatus		1													1	R
Umborium vestiarium								1			1				2	R
Chitonidae																
hiton sp		8	3		11	9	2	4	2		1	3	2	1	46	R
Haliotidae																
Haliotis asinina				1											1	R
Muricidae																
Drupa rubusideus Roding									1						1	R
Cypraedae																
Cvf)raea vitellus													1	1	2	R
Pteriidae																
Pinctsda radiata	1		1												2	R
Olividae																
Oliva oliva				1		2	1								4	51
Thiaridae																
Melanoides funiculus		1	1		2	7		1		1		1			160	FW
Total	160	225	145	36	32	44	5	11	8	6	5	6	.-	2	689	

Table 1 Minimum Number of Individuals of shell species in all squares, Lua Meko
H: habitat, FW: fresh water, RU: upper river, TM: tidal mudflat, RU: upper reef, SI: sandy intertidal, RI: reef intertidal

Appendix 2

spit	1	2	3	4	5	6	7	8	9	10	11	12	13	14	15	16	17	18	19	20	21	22	H
shell family and species																							
GASTROPODS			I										I					I					
Potamididae																							
Terebra crenulata											1										1		TM
Terebra macU/atus	.		I												1								TM
Chitonidae																							
Chiton sp.	1	1	1		2	5		7	15			1	4				1	1			-		R
Trochidae																							
Trochus niloticus	5		3	4	6	28	75	63	60	60	50	36	31	30	25	12	2	4					R
Trochus maculatus			3	12	3	12	10	2	5	10	5	14											R
Tectrus terestratus					3																		R
Turbinidae																							
Turbo argirostomus			1		1	1	1		1														SI
Angaria delpinulus																							SI
Angaria sp				4	1	3	1	5		5	5	4		1	1								SI
Neritidae																							
Nerita potita			1		24	10		13	21	6	14	1	14	5	6	2					1		R
Nerita tineata	1															2							TM
Nerita albicilla			2		13																		R
Nerita pice a			1	2																			R
Nerita undata			1						1														TM
Neritina communis										6							1						R
Strombidae																							
Lambis-/ambis		1			*I*																		SI
Strombus labiatus											1												SI
Strombus luhuanus		1			1	1																	SI
Conidae																							
Conus litteratus				1																			SI
Cerithiidae																							
Cerithium aluco					1																		SI
Cerithium nodulosum										1													SI
Hydatinidae																							
Hydatina physis									1														TM
Fasciolariidae																							
Latirus potigonus															1								R
Latirus nodatus				1																			R
Polynicinae																							
Polynices tumidus										1													SI
Polyniees flemingiana				1																			SI
Cypraedae																							
Cypraea tigris												1											R
Muricidae																							
Purpura persiea										1													R
Drupa rubusideus					5																		R
BIVALVES																							
Tridacnidae																							
Hippopus hippopus				1																			R
Archidae																							
Anadara antiquata												1											E
Barbatia foliata					1																		R
Total	7	3	13	27	48	73	87	90	104	91	75	58	49	36	34	16	4	5			2		822

Table 1 Minimum Number of Individuals of shell species in square TP, Lie Madira. H: habitat, FW: fresh water, RU: upper river, TM: tidal mudflat, RU: upper reef, SI: sandy intertidal, RI: reef intertidal

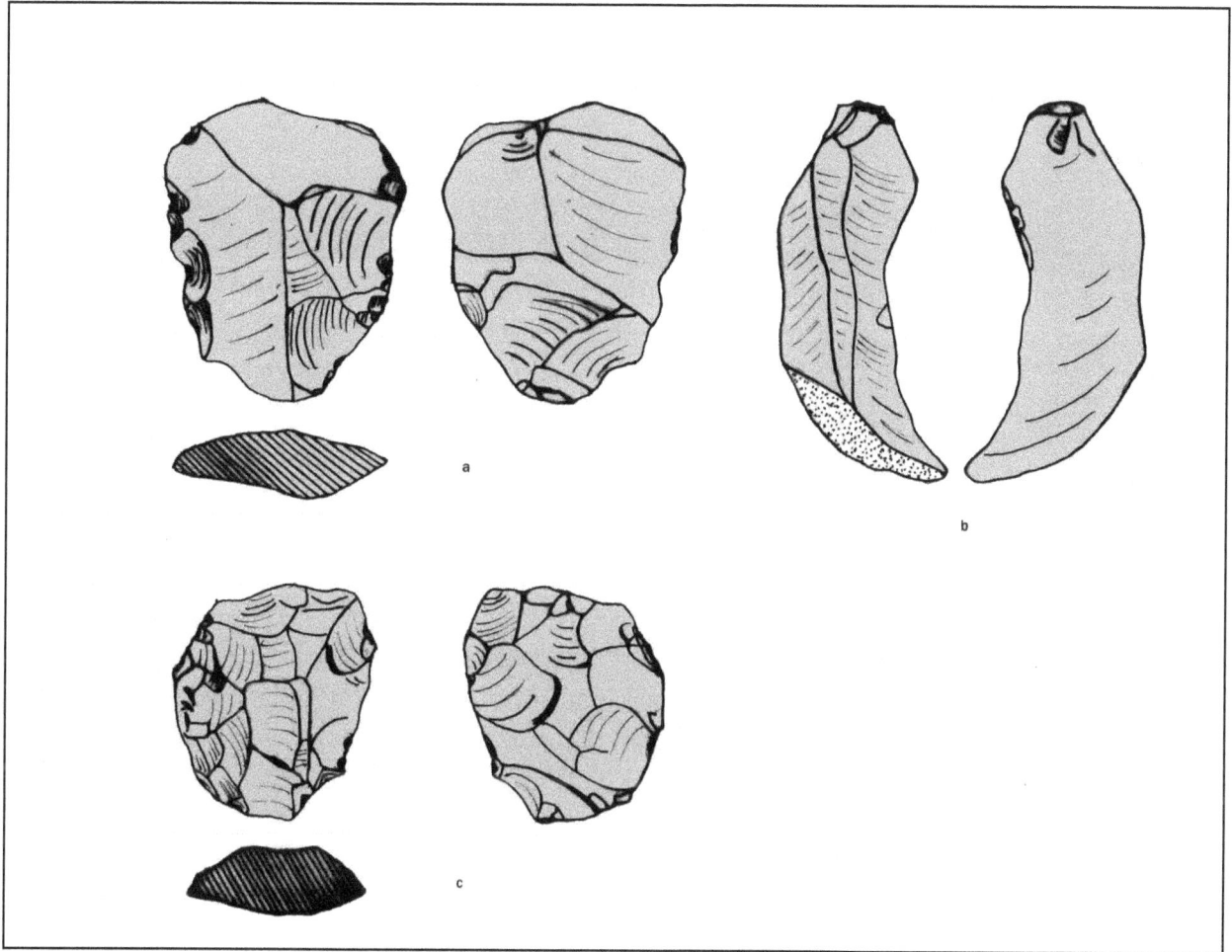

Figure 1 Stone artefacts, Lie Da, Sawu Island. All are surface finds

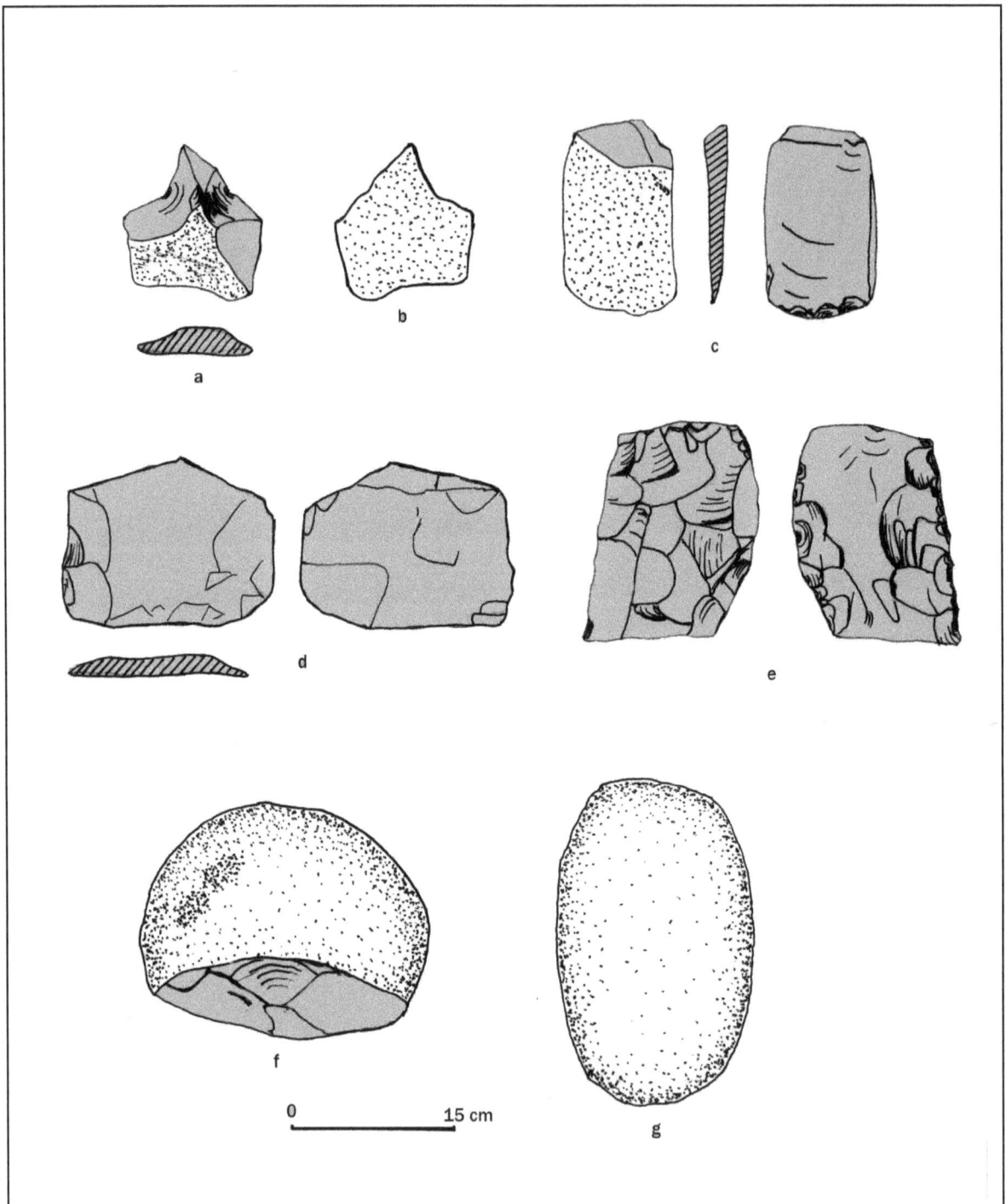

Figure 2 Stone artefacts Lie Da, Sawu Island. All are surface finds.